Called by the North

Extraordinary Adventures of the Fur Trade, Shipbuilders, Navigators and Traders in Northwestern Canada and Alaska

Following the collapse of whaling in Canadian western Arctic waters at the start of the 1900s, vessels facing the perilous voyage around the Alaskan Peninsula came in pursuit of Arctic fur trade. They came initially from the old whaling ports of California and settled locations in Alaska, but after 1914 also from Vancouver on Canada's west coast. The vessels included those owned – or in support of – large fur trading companies and also those of adventurers bent on making their fortunes in the rich trade. Arctic transportation was also provided by expansion of the existing Mackenzie River system from the interior of Canada through the Boreal Forest and Mackenzie Delta. This book provides a fascinating account of the ships, shipbuilders and navigators of these waterways, and how the Arctic fur trade, pioneered by American entrepreneurs, was finally taken over by the Hudson's Bay Company. Expanding eastward, the Company achieved many Arctic "firsts." In 1930 a relay of company vessels successfully made the first west to east transit of the Northwest Passage; and several fur trading posts developed into permanent northern settlements. These, and many other intriguing stories, are enriched through 193 photographs, maps and diagrams; appendices; a bibliography; and an index to full names, places, and subjects, all adding value to this unique work.

Called by the North

Extraordinary Adventures of the Fur Trade, Shipbuilders, Navigators and Traders in Northwestern Canada and Alaska

George H. S. Duddy

HERITAGE BOOKS
2022

HERITAGE BOOKS
AN IMPRINT OF HERITAGE BOOKS, INC.

Books, CDs, and more—Worldwide

For our listing of thousands of titles see our website
at
www.HeritageBooks.com

Published 2022 by
HERITAGE BOOKS, INC.
Publishing Division
5810 Ruatan Street
Berwyn Heights, Md. 20740

International Standard Book Number
Paperbound: 978-0-7884-2400-7

To Blair who will never be able to read the words of these pages
but because of loving outgoing cheerfulness
puts sunshine into many lives

Contents

Photos and Illustrations

Maps and Diagrams

Foreword

George Duddy and I share a common love of ships, particularly wooden vessels, so it's a great delight to dig into a book in which the first several chapters are devoted to the work of a master shipwright, George Askew. During the first-half of the 20th Century in which Askew pursued his trade, there were no electric hand tools, saws, drills, etc., to ease the building process, and one need only view a photograph of a ship under construction, to appreciate the enormity of bringing a single one to life, let alone the dozens with which Askew was involved.

Moreover, these ships were built outdoors, often in cold, damp, rainy weather for which the Canadian and U.S. Pacific Northwest is well known. These were the good conditions. When work was scarce, Askew had to go North to find employment. Not some reasonable distance; northward of Vancouver, where he spent much of his time, but NORTH to Alaska or the Yukon, where bitter winds from the slopes ringing the harbour sites where he worked met the sea, and many, if not most, days were characterized by bleak, grey skies. Of course, others did much of the work, but Askew was the architect of the resultant products, as well as wielding tools himself. As noted by Emerson in "Of History" from *Essays*:

> The true poem is the poet's mind; the true ship is the shipbuilder.

The author has a special affinity and appreciation for ships and the sea; because his family lineage stretches back several generations across the Atlantic to Britain. One of his forefathers, Midshipman Percival George Duddy, tragically lost his life after a fall from the mast of a Royal Navy ship during the age of sail; his great-great-grandfather, as Master in both sail and steam, ended his career as marine superintendent for the Leith, Hull & Hamburg Steam Packet Co.; and his great-grandfather was a pioneering Leith steamship owner. His father, as a schoolboy, took photographs of surrendered German battleships in the Firth of Forth near the end of World War I, and later emigrated to Canada.

In addition to being a retired professional engineer, George Duddy is also a former keen yachtsman, a great passion of Askew before him, when the latter had opportunity to lay down his tools and get out on the water in spirited, racing sail vessels. Following the captivating material about Askew, Duddy takes up the subject of the yachts *El Sueño* and *Audrey B.*, and Arctic trading schooner *Anna Olga*, all of whom had both storied and checkered service. *Audrey B.*, well known to readers familiar with Arctic exploration, began her life as a rum runner.

Having introduced readers to the means by which adventurers, fur traders, and others travelled in the early 1900s along the coastlines of Western Canada and the Arctic, and up numerous treacherous rivers, Duddy turns to the fur trade, which opened up the vastness of northern Canada to citizens of the fledgling country.

George has great interest in this subject, as well as maritime matters and yachting, because his father, after immigrating to Canada, was employed by the Hudson's Bay Company. His work included running a trading post in Fort St. John, where George was born in this northern town on the Peace River. To assert that trappers, traders, vessel crews, and other employees of the HBC were hardy individuals, is an understatement. The conditions under which they worked were often brutal, even more so in winter. Those who became "iced in" and couldn't escape frigid, Arctic wastelands (my term), were said to have "wintered over." Providing they had adequate shelter, heat, and food, and could avoid life-ending encounters with nature, they greeted spring—bringing melting of ice, and longer days—with renewed spirits and love for the vast countryside and their chosen vocations.

George Duddy, who is ideally suited by background, temperament, and intellectual curiosity, has devoted considerable work to researching notable Canadians—some well known to readers of a certain age, and some quite obscure—to whom successive generations owe much, and to vessels essential to expansion into the North. The information gleaned, including some hard sought details, are dovetailed and woven into an important and informative book.

I visited British Columbia, and ports in Alaska during my naval career, but confess I knew little about the geography of Canada, and the storied history of some of her sons and daughters. Those detailed herein, ventured much, and accomplished much, with very little—while exploring and expanding into new regions in this northern neighbor of the United States.

David D. Bruhn
Cdr. USN (Retired)

Foreword

Photo Foreword-1

But a few reminders of the exciting and remarkable life of George Francis Hume Askew.

When George Duddy was researching material on the life of George Francis Hume Askew, he contacted my cousin Rodger Askew to see what information he might have about our grandfather. Rodger enlisted my help and I was pleased to take up the challenge of providing personal vignettes of family history and associated photographs in collaboration with my other cousins.

Photo Foreword-2

Francis and John Askew as young children. They are aboard the *Hereanthere*, at Maple Bay, Vancouver Island, with George on the pier, crouched down, tying up the boat.

George's older of two sons, Francis Victor, married Josephine (nee Murphy) and had four children: Margaret, Doreen, Martin and Rodger. Francis, or "Frank" as he was known, apprenticed as a boatbuilder and spent his working life plying his trade in Vancouver. Younger son John Douglas Askew married Wendy (nee Ashfield) and had one child: Kathryn (me). He also apprenticed as a boatbuilder and worked for a variety of large and small boat yards in Vancouver, and then Sidney on Vancouver Island.

The five of us came into our grandfather's life when he was in his final decade. We remember gathering for many celebrations as a close family.

Photo Foreword-3

Taken during a Christmas dinner at John and Wendy's house in Vancouver circa 1957 (three years after George's death). Adults left to right: Marion Arnould (Frank and John's first cousin), John Askew, Josephine Murphy Askew (wearing hat) and Wendy Ashfield Askew. Children left to right: Doreen, Martin (with glasses), Kathryn (on lap), Margaret (in front of lamp), Roger (front).
Frank Askew photograph

Margaret (centre back) knew our grandfather for nine years and has vivid memories of him moving upstairs into her parents' home on Adanac Street in the late 1940s, not far from the house where he had lived for 40 years and raised his sons. Margaret worked as a registered nurse and had two children: Jennifer and Matthew Terhardt.

Margaret and her younger sister Doreen (front left) would accompany their grandfather on the bus to the Vancouver Yacht Club in Coal Harbour where he'd treat them to hot dogs. Once he even let Doreen find her own way home when she was about five, to her mother's horror! Doreen worked as a practical nurse and had three children: Michael, Douglas and Tessa Correa.

Martin (at front second from the left) was about three with blurry eyesight when he recalls visiting our grandfather in hospital but not being able to see him well. He worked in land and water transportation management and had two children: Lauren and Scott Askew.

My own recollection (centre on my father's lap) of grandfather is lifting a paper bag of his favourite "humbug" candies high up to where George was tucked into bed after one of his strokes when I was just over two years old. My work included being an elementary teacher and political organizer. My two children are Penny and Jill Gotto.

The youngest of us, Rodger (seated centre front), was just fourteen months old when George died. Rodger carried on our grandfather's and our fathers' love affair with boats as a marine engineer. In his retirement Rodger was asked to survey three of our grandfather's vessels; the *Arthur C. Clarke* (previously the *Leola Vivian*), the *Hereanthere* and the *Cresset.* He says it gave him goosebumps to put his hands on timbers that George had placed there long, long ago. Rodger had five daughters: Kyri, Brianna, Morgan, Jessica and Stephanie Askew.

Photo Foreword-4

Medals won by George for swimming, rowing and sailboat racing.

There were traces of George's life in the homes where we grew up: silver cups and medals from his swimming, rowing and sailboat racing days, a delicate pocket scale for weighing gold dust, an old Seth Thomas ship's clock from the *Hereanthere*, browning, curled photos of his boats, and of his boatbuilding adventures, blueprints of sternwheelers, his passport, and gold rings with nuggets brought back from the Klondike.

There was something mysterious about George Askew. He'd been 46 and 49 when his sons Francis and John were born, so he was always "the old man" to them growing up, absent up north from early spring to autumn most years, and then larger than life in the winters when he returned to his family in Vancouver. Francis and John were just 34 and 31 when he died and there were SO many parts to his life that they never thought to ask about.

The five of us are grateful that George Duddy applied his curiosity and writing skill to exploring the life work of George Askew, hammering out a boatbuilding saga of which we are in awe. We've followed the author's research excursions with surprise, delight and approval, adding what snippets we could to help frame and then paint our grandfather's life story. We're so proud to read about the grandfather we hardly knew, and we welcome this history to pass on to our children and our grandchildren. Thanks to George Duddy for his generous gift of time in surfacing this incredible tale.

Kathryn Askew
BA, Dip. Ed, MA
Comox, BC

Foreword

My great uncle is Ernest James (Scotty) Gall, who left Scotland in 1923 to start a new job with the Hudson's Bay Company in Canada at a remote post on Herschel Island. I, like many others, often know little about a particular forefather as a result of broken links in passed down written or oral family history. When I was a child growing up in Glasgow, Scotland, his sister (my grandmother), never spoke about him. She never kept any of his letters and my mother only knew that her uncle lived and worked in Canada. The only information I had about Scotty Gall at the time was from local newspaper articles that mentioned a voyage through the Bellot Strait. By my 50th birthday, I still knew nothing of Scotty's life in Canada, or about the Canadian Arctic wilderness, or indeed, the lives of people who lived there.

Photo Foreword-5

As a young boy Scotty Gall lived in Ballindalloch railway station on Speyside, Scotland. Courtesy of Iain Grant Cameron

My introduction to the author came about in 2010, when I set about to share what little information I had on my great uncle. George contacted me and he passed along excellent information about Scotty that I never knew about. Together, we pieced together Scotty's life, and his work, and realised what an adventurer and humble man he was. With George's keen determination to see it done, we managed to honour Scotty's achievements with a plaque, installed along the Explorers Walk on the wall of the inner harbour in Victoria, B.C., alongside other remarkable adventurers, such as Sven Johansson, and Captain J. J. Moore. I am very grateful to George for all of this incredible work and perseverance over several years to get Scotty, and his motor schooner *Aklavik,* the recognition they deserve as a vital element in the development of Canada's north.

George has been an inspiration to me, for finding out the full history of the life of Scotty Gall, and other fascinating information. For instance, I always thought that life above the Arctic Circle was almost non-existent until George showed me that even in weather conditions that are alien to me, people not only survive but live full lives in the bitterly cold Arctic, these being the very same extreme conditions in which my great uncle also thrived.

We became good friends as a result of our distant communications, and meeting twice at his home, some 4,500 miles away from my own in Scotland. George has a great passion for all that he researches, no matter the subject. He is meticulous in his approach, and double-checks everything, before committing to the written word. I have assisted him, in a very small way, with some of his maritime-related research.

With this book, George tells the true stories of hearty ships like the *Aklavik, Audrey B., Anna Olga* and yacht *El Sueño*, to name but a few, along with the incredible stories of people like George Askew who built sturdy ships and then sailed in them, and those of my own great uncle, Scotty Gall, who went to the Arctic seeking adventure and fortune, and found both.

Well done freen and slange var.

Iain Grant Cameron
Ellon, Aberdeenshire, Scotland
2021

Foreword

I will confess to being an Arctic armchair explorer, one of those ilk who travel by dogsled, endure blizzards, and listen to the sickening crunch of ice against a wooden ship's hull, all from the cozy and safe comfort of my home. My curiosity as to what propelled so many to face such adversity, such uncertainty, is insatiable. I am simply fascinated (at a safe distance) by the struggles of those who chose the Arctic to make their fortunes, to live out their lives, and sometimes, to unexpectedly leave their bones behind.

In reading *Called by the North* and learning the stories of the individuals who headed to the Arctic, to build ships, to navigate treacherous rivers and wind-whipped lakes, to risk small fortunes for potentially much larger ones, I began to re-think my idea of the Arctic as being a dark, frozen, far-flung region. Instead, through the pages of George Duddy's book, I began to see it as one full of diversity, teeming with potential, and full of life; in fact, full of lives. In telling the stories of mostly lesser-known adventurers—though no less important in history—he brings us a glimpse of their life in the Arctic, to see how fur trade operations were conducted, to learn who the personalities involved were, and to appreciate the stamina required to either make a big splash or sink without remark.

There were hardships for those who risked being iced-in for a winter with inadequate supplies, or those undertaking a voyage on seas covered by jagged ice and in white-out conditions, but these were not deterrents to those who struggled to make a living from such a harsh environment, and are testimony to the toughness of these important but little-known northern personalities.

The story of opening up the Canadian Arctic truly stems from the efforts of citizens from many nations: from the Inuit who helped the early explorers survive; to the many Arctic-sharing nations who found the land mass at the top of Canada full of arctic fox and trading opportunities; to those who brought a semblance of order to the growing settlements through RCMP detachments and HBC post stores.

Many enterprising Americans who came seeking fortune from the truly last wild frontier, invested in fur, and later, mineral extraction. Without doubt, the influx of Americans—and their money—aided in rapid development, but it also warranted a close watch by Canadian authorities, certainly of no appetite to repeat the worry of American expansionism as experienced in the mid-1800s along the British Columbia and Washington State border. However, if not for the risk-taking and investment of American-funded exploration, the Canadian Arctic would have struggled to become what it is today. Indeed, the contribution of stalwart people from many countries and walks of life all left their mark on the land of the midnight sun.

I've travelled the Arctic region vicariously with George as my guide, stepping in the faded snowshoe prints and dogsled tracks of those who took a gamble, headed north, and endured conditions and privations most of us cannot imagine. I trekked alongside trappers, traders, shipbuilders, and navigators, who ventured north with courage and changed forever the landscape of the Canadian Arctic.

The book you now hold will take you there, as well. Finally, we are able, in one comprehensive work, to learn about, and appreciate the interrelated efforts of many, mostly unknown individuals who gave so much of themselves, to expand the Canadian frontier northward to the Arctic Circle and beyond.

Lynn J. Salmon, Marine Historian and Writer
Vancouver Island, BC, 2021

Acknowledgements

Unlike a novel where the achievement is the work largely of one person, this book could not have been written without the collaboration and assistance of many people. The level of assistance I have been rendered is extraordinary. I attribute this mainly to a perception that those assisting firmly believe, as I do, that the remarkable true stories of northern heritage embodied in this book deserve to be brought to the public realm in a freshly coherent way.

Photo Acknowledgements-1

John Horton

Working from the cover inward, the reader will first notice that the content is enveloped in the fine artwork of acclaimed marine artist John Horton, OBC, CSMA, FCA.

The painting commissioned for the cover, *Meeting at Gjoa Haven*, depicts an often overlooked but significant event in Canada's Arctic history. On 6 August 1930, two Hudson's Bay Company vessels, *Fort McPherson* and her sister ship motor schooner *Fort James*, met at King William Island at Gjoa Haven. As *Fort James* had sailed from St. John's, Newfoundland, and the *Fort McPherson* had sailed to the Arctic from Vancouver, the two ships became the first-ever Canadian-built and registered ships to complete the navigation of the Northwest Passage. John Horton, drawing from actual Arctic experience, has captured this important moment in all its quiet beauty. Further details on the life and career of John Horton, including his contact information, can be found on his website https://johnhorton.ca/.

Photo Acknowledgements-2

Meeting at Gjoa Haven by John Horton, depicting L-R: *Fort James* and *Fort McPherson.*

This book could not have been published without the help of two very special persons. Although encouraged by colleagues to publish several years of research, my early inclination—at the age of eighty plus—was to *not* undertake such a monumental project. However, the task was taken out of my hands, and I was lifted-up by two amazing friends who knew how to go about the task of making it happen. In addition, they have cheerfully provided ongoing encouragement throughout this effort.

The first is USN Commander David Bruhn (retired), a prodigious and current writer of naval history. His in-depth examination of WWI and WWII naval events, as well as maritime action in both Korean and Vietnam waters, are covered in over twenty books that look at the involvement of not only the US Navy but also that of Britain, Canada, Australia, New Zealand, South Africa and other navies. Following his naval career, in which he commanded the mine countermeasures ships USS *Gladiator* and USS *Dextrous*, David then taught at high school and was a track coach for ten years, and is currently a USA Track and Field official. His experience has helped shape this book into coherent and chronological order, and I could not have proceeded without his unfailing eye for detail. Information about his many books and other useful items can be found at: http://www.davidbruhn.com/.

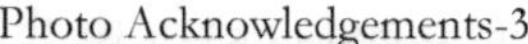
Photo Acknowledgements-3

David D. Bruhn, circa 2006

I have also been blessed by having Lynn Salmon as the other vital facilitator for the preparation of this book. She has leant her social conscience and helped modify language and references which, although acceptable in the past, are today considered offensive. Together with David, her cheerful and positive disposition has helped me over many barriers in reaching the finish line.

Photo Acknowledgements-4

Lynn J. Salmon, circa 2019

She writes about the marine history of BC and her articles have appeared in the *Western Mariner* and the *Times Colonist*, and she is also co-author of *Around the World in a Dugout Canoe* (with John M. MacFarlane). She concluded a fifteen-year career as a radio officer with the Canadian Coast Guard in 2016, shore-based work that kept her close to the water and the marine industry. I call her the "Lady of the Lantern" as she has taught us not to "hang lanterns": a writing term to not shine light on events in advance of where the reader should properly encounter them. Her involvement with fine-tuning the text has brought the words to life.

Lynn Tosello, the final editor, lent her eagle piercing eyes to the project, succeeded in getting Queen Victoria and King William back to their appropriate Arctic islands, and generally made the text crisper.

The Chapters on George Askew could not have been so fully rounded without the full participation of all of his grandchildren who provided much information and many photographs. Thanks go to Margaret, Martin, Rodger, and Kathryn. Kathryn's extensively researched family tree, editorial assistance, and contribution of a foreword have been most appreciated. Her skill as an English teacher has instilled in us the proper rules for capitalization of the word "arctic" based on the strange logic that has evolved in the writing community.

Photo Acknowledgements-5

Kathryn Askew

My thin remaining ties to a Scottish heritage rest with my endearing friendship with Iain Cameron, Scotty Gall's great nephew, who lives in Ellon north of Aberdeen in Scotland with his wife Janis. The book's journey started out with our joint rooting out of his history. Thanks, Iain, for your participation over the years and with your help for this latest endeavour. We often joke that it all came about as a result of Iain stamping about on the grave of a distant relative of mine and stirring up the ghosts of our families to get on with the job. That relative was Rob Roy MacGregor.

Photo Acknowledgements-6

Iain Grant Cameron

Over the years that the book was conceived and during its writing, I have received outstanding support from many archives that are ascribed on photographs and noted elsewhere. I would like to especially highlight these individuals who have taken particular interest in the work: Robin Weber, NWT Archives, Yellowknife (Robin is granddaughter of Ray Ross, a well-known HBC post manager mentioned in the book); Edward Atkinson, Nunavut Archives; James Gorton, HBC Archives, Winnipeg; Leah Edgar, Aslynn Prasad, and Duncan MacLeod, Vancouver Maritime Museum, Vancouver; Brittany Vis, Maritime Museum of BC; Victoria and Heather Sjoblom, North Peace Museum, Fort St. John, BC.

Thanks are also extended to many individuals who also have provided material and information to the project over several years, or otherwise influenced this book via their work, writing, or deeds: marine artist Bo Hermansen; Nauticapedia.ca colleagues (for photographs and research) Ron David, Roger Craik and Simon Bancroft; Gordon Norberg; daughter of Arctic hero Cecil E. Bradbury, Cecily Hinton; Canadian history writer Janice Cavell; (late) Arctic navigator Sven Johansson; Scotty Gall's neighbour Wilma Saville; Anna Gall's great nephew, Kevin Fagerstrom; former Delta archivist Catherine McPherson; La Have Museum Society Nova Scotia representative Kathy Sillivan; late marine writer S. C. Heal; Canada Transport ship registrations, Paul Sandhu; Burnaby Archivist Library and Archives Canada, Suzanne Sulzberger; Ottawa contract Archives Canada researcher Ken McLeod; friend, Steve Oura; Tarfran live-aboard residents Jeff and David Tarris, and Pauline Pilkington; retired lakehead shipyard official Dave Benedet; Canada's History online manager Tanja Hütter. Also recognized are those who contributed over the long book period but somehow were omitted from this list.

The book would never have been achieved without the loving support of my partner Helen O'Neill, and that of my children: son Blair, daughter Janice and her husband Chad, and their sons Eric and Toby, and son David and his partner Kim.

Two final tributes need to be included. To my lifelong friend Chris Gardner, now from Dunrobin near Ottawa, who found the little HBC history with Scotty Gall's inscription that prompted my history journey of this book ten years ago. Thank you, Chris, but please don't go looking for any additional little books in small Ontario town bookstores.

And finally, I am especially grateful to John M. MacFarlane (FRGS), friend and colleague, with whom I have had the privilege to work on the Nauticapedia Project over the past several years. It was John who first suggested I assemble my research into book form. Widely recognized for the breadth and depth of his nautical history of British Columbia, he is Curator Emeritus of the Maritime Museum of British Columbia and the author of many books and publications including *Shipwreck!*, *Paddlewheelers of Western Canada and the US*, and *Around the World in a Dugout Canoe*. His awards include the Sovereign's Medal for Volunteers, as well as the Maritime Museum of British Columbia's S.S. *Beaver* Medal for Maritime Excellence, and in 2019 was appointed an Honorary Member of the Company of Master Mariners of Canada. In 2020 he shared the John Lyman Book Prize of the North American Society for Oceanic History for his and Lynn Salmon's book, *Around the World in a Dugout Canoe*. His unwavering commitment to sharing BC's nautical heritage has been an inspiration to complete this book.

Photo Acknowledgements-7

John M. MacFarlane

Thank you, John, for seeing the value in my project, for your mentoring and invaluable assistance, and for allowing use of material from your articles. His nautical heritage site, offering extensive information on Canada's Pacific, western and northern nautical history and heritage and other topics of general maritime interest, may be accessed at: https://www.nauticapedia.ca/.

Preface

Photo Preface-1

Northern Lights as seen from Mackenzie River, San Sault Rapids, November 1979.
NWT Archives N-1995-002-8096 (Rene Fumeoleau Fonds, 24 November 1979)

Enterprise, entrepreneurial endeavour, and plain old-fashioned curiosity drew many to the seemingly limitless opportunities of the north in western Canada at the turn of the twentieth century. Those who took a gamble to embark on the adventure of a lifetime led extraordinary lives; some accomplished remarkable feats; but some just found a new home and a satisfying life.

Two marine transportation systems for the fur trade opened the north and the adjoining Arctic to development and settlement, and transformed Canada's perception of itself. One of these is the inland route down the mighty Mackenzie River system and the other, a short-lived ocean route from Vancouver and San Francisco around the Alaskan Peninsula. Although they drew attention to the area, for the most part, the changes were not the result of famous sponsored-explorers such as Amundsen and Stefansson whose derring-do in the icy north captured the imagination of a generation. Instead, the accomplishment of opening the north—making it accessible to the outside world—resulted from work of ordinary people who were called upon to carry-out extraordinary feats of survival while simply earning their living as fur trade employees, shipbuilders, navigators, and trappers. Many risked everything on their own initiative, quietly, anonymously, and without guarantee of success.

Map Preface-1

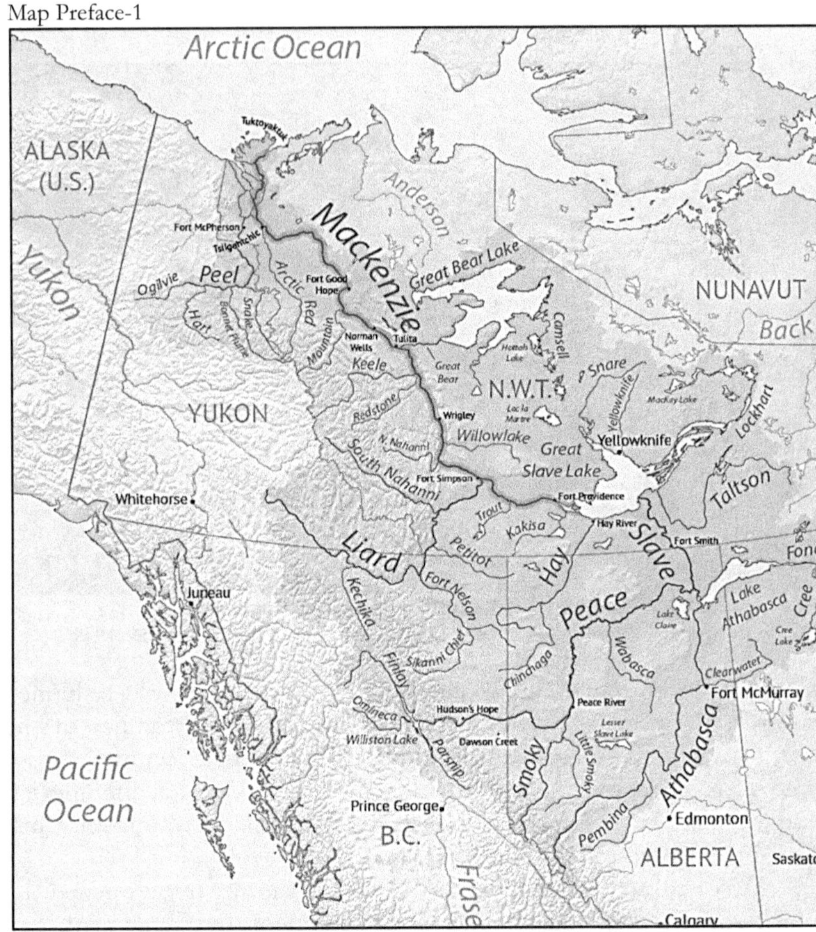

Mackenzie River Basin; for millenniums this river system has provided a pathway from the interior of North America to the Arctic Ocean via the Athabasca, Peace, Slave and Mackenzie rivers and connecting lakes
https://commons.wikimedia.org/wiki/File:Mackenzie_River_basin_map.png
(Author: Shannon1)

At the start of the twentieth century the Mackenzie Basin transportation system already boasted steam-driven vessels. For generations the fur trade had operated in harmony with the Dene nations within the vast river and its tributaries, constituting the longest river system in Canada and the second largest drainage basin in North America after the Mississippi. At the mouth of the Mackenzie and along the coast both westward and eastward, the Inuit people of the western Arctic, the Inuvialuit, had been in contact with traders inside the delta and whalers at Herschel Island for many years. In sharp contrast, Canada's central Arctic (rudimentary-mapped by early explorers) was virtually unknown.

Photo Preface-2

SS *Grahame* at Fort McMurray, Athabasca River, circa 1890s (first steam vessel on the Mackenzie River system). Glenbow Archives photo NA-4035-98

Isolated by vast tracts of tundra and frozen ocean, its sparsely populated nomadic Inuit peoples lived in almost total isolation (as they had for thousands of years) well-adapted to their survival on the harsh land. Yet a rapidly shrinking and inquisitive world inevitably imposed its values and curiosity on people who otherwise may have been content to remain as they had been; the disruption to their lives was most definitely accelerated by events that saw ships and outsiders drawn to their tundra and waterways.

Unexpectedly, a fashion craze for the previously almost worthless pelt of the arctic fox sky-rocketed the price of fur garments. As a consequence, trappers and traders infiltrated deep into Arctic areas to obtain fox along with other animal fur. The Inuit of the central Arctic adapted as they always had and became skilled and wealthy trappers, just as their cousins the Inuvialuit of the Mackenzie Delta had already done a few years ahead of them. Growing interest in—and dependence on—outside goods (examples include motor schooners and gramophones, not to mention staple items such as food and ammunition), created business opportunities for the traders and required increased transportation of imported goods by ships from the south. For the Inuit, there was no looking back; their lives and traditional lifestyle were forever changed.

Transportation was critical but it was one part of a much larger interdependent enterprise that saw missionaries, police and government officials follow the fur trade as it progressed eastward across the Arctic. In the vast remote northern regions at the time, no one could transport needed equipment, materials, and supplies if it weren't for seasonally open rivers, lakes and sea routes. Without the shipbuilder and his ships, needed access along river and sea routes was impossible; without ships' crews, trade goods and other materials could not be delivered; and without such items, the trader could not procure fur from the trappers.

Those who ventured into the north had to face the isolation and hazards of locations among the remotest in Canada. Some were fortunate and could return south in the winter, like ships' crews and shipbuilders, and just like migratory birds, they were drawn north again as summer arrived. Others, like traders and trappers (and their wives and children) spent long, dark, frigid winters at remote trading posts, lucky to receive mail once or perhaps twice in the period. What compelled these hearty dreamers to head north? Fortune, curiosity, perhaps even desperation. Initially, the remote land was wide open to those who could get there; for those tough enough, it was full of opportunity and challenge. The land, at times seemingly impassable and inhospitable, provided a living for some, despite its harshness. It captivated them, and became their permanent home, where their descendants still live today.

The men and women in this book were particularly suited for their endeavours in the northern and Arctic wilds. They had goals, they had grit, and at times, they had luck. But not always. Such were the whims of the region; a tide that brought supplies to a distant shore could also just as easily bring an ice barrier to prevent access of a supply ship to a polar sea. Ships sank, traps were found empty, rail lines were left unfinished mere miles short of the destination. Despite these hurdles, stalwart northerners nudged the region into the 20th century, connected through the ships they built and sailed and fur posts they established.

Adventurers like Scotty Gall, who was hired in Scotland, came to Canada as a young man looking for work and exciting activity. He left the Arctic decades later with the distinction of being the first person to navigate his ship, the *Aklavik*, through Bellot Strait. I first 'met' Scotty through chance, connecting with a living relative who was also interested in learning more about him. Together, we were able to develop his story more fully, and give recognition to his many important feats. Another 'friend' of discovery was George Askew, an unassuming and hard-working shipbuilder who constructed river sternwheelers and barges, and tugs and pioneered the technology behind "tunnel-boats." He built—and raced—yachts for the Royal Vancouver Yacht Club members as well as for himself. His innovative work, and long years dedicated to shipbuilding revolutionized river travel and made it possible for supplies to reach far-flung outposts.

My endeavour to consolidate story fragments into lucid accounts, and meld histories and personalities into a single captivating work, has been a progressive journey for me. My closest connection to the North is through my father who was an employee of the HBC, having started his career in 1923 (the same year as Scotty Gall) as an apprentice at Oxford House, Manitoba, and retired many years later in 1944 as manager of the Company store in Fort St. John, BC (where I was born).

Photo Preface-3

My father, George S. M. Duddy, as a young Hudson's Bay Company apprentice attired in winter garb, circa early 1920s. He is standing in front of HBC Oxford House post buildings (also shown in the lower photograph), located in northeast Manitoba. The post was established in 1798. The "little fur trader" in the upper right is the author at the HBC Store in Fort St. John, British Columbia, circa 1941-42.

More recently, I have had the pleasure of becoming acquainted with and collaborating with museum curators, archivists, citizen researchers, family descendants of key characters in the book, a modern-day Arctic navigator, descendants of Arctic personalities, and marine historians. All have enriched this book via their perspective and insights, and generously-provided material for inclusion in it. I find these northern characters fascinating, and hope to bring a voice, and recognition of their feats, to subsequent generations.

BOOK CONTENT AND STRUCTURE

Called by the North offers readers a deep insight into the history of the fur trade-seasonal inland marine and ocean shipping that connected Canada to its northern regions in the Mackenzie Basin and the western and central Arctic during the first half of the twentieth century. Prominently featured are notable vessels involved and the lives and outstanding feats of many of those who built and sailed them, while driving them to the remotest accessible points in North America.

The book comprises seven historical studies, as shown in the table of contents, which highlight supporting and overlapping achievements of remarkable and accomplished individuals. The studies are related, but offer unique experiences that will lead readers into unexpected but interesting areas. Examples of these include shipbuilding in the small town of Poulsbo in Washington State, populated by Norwegian immigrants; a champion San Francisco racing yacht struggling up the Yukon River to the Klondike goldrush propelled by steam engines fitted in it for this endeavour; and the ship's engineer of a "rumrunner" who volunteered to spend Christmas in jail in Brooklyn, New York. Much as an anthology, related chapter groups can be read in any order.

GEOGRAPHY PRIMER

The following five maps will assist readers unfamiliar with Canada's and Alaska's vast northern regions, and the Northwest United States to better understand geographical areas described in the book. After considering this graphic information, readers may also consult the Canada section of the book's index, which associates all the locations mentioned in the book with their appropriate province or territory.

The convention used in this book for locations in northeastern Canada is to identify them as is done today as "Nunavut" rather than previous to 1999 as being in the "Northwest Territories (NWT)." In 1999, Nunavut was created by subdividing the then existing larger NWT.

Map Preface-2

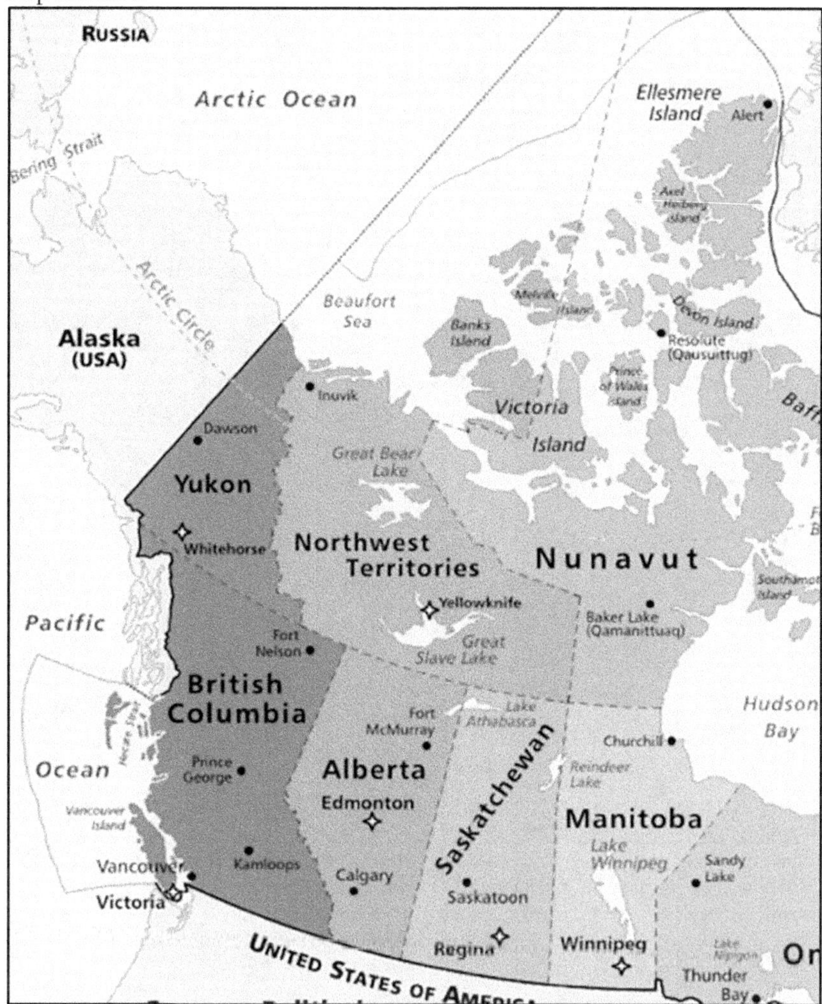

Western Canada, Eastern Alaska, and Northwestern United States
Atlas of Canada: Drawn and adapted by E. Pluribus Anthony uploaded to Wikimedia Commons

Map Preface-3

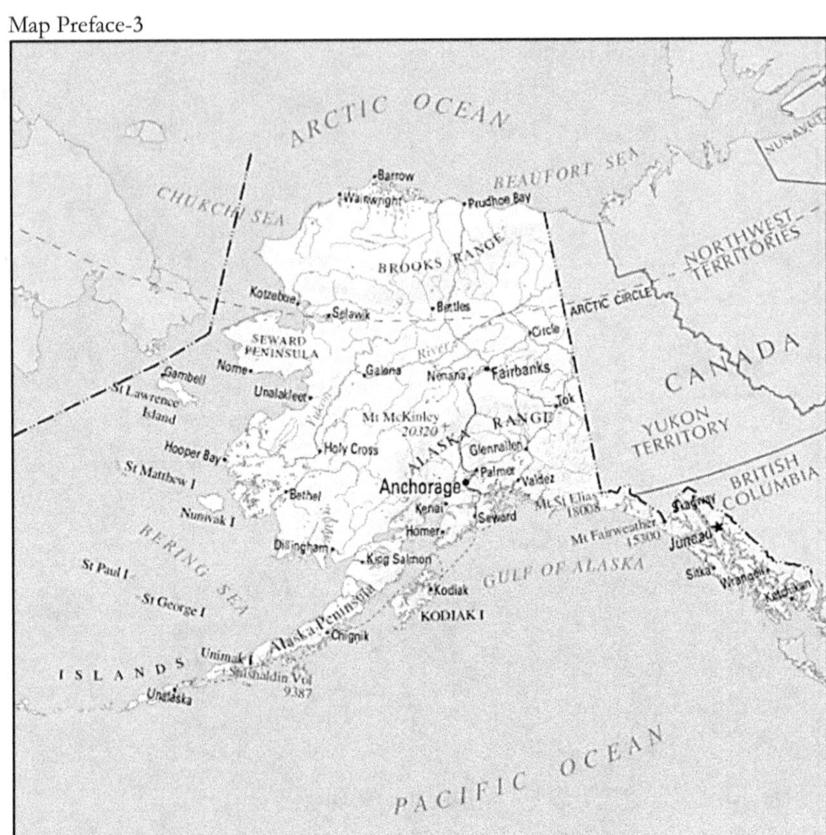

Western Canada and adjacent Alaska and Russia to the west-northwest; passage to the North was by sea around Alaska via the Bering Strait, Chukchi Sea, Arctic Ocean, and Beaufort Sea; or by inland transit of Canadian rivers and lakes.
National Atlas of the United States uploaded to Wikimedia Commons

Map Preface-4

Eastern Alaska to the left of dotted line on the map; western British Columbia to the right of the line, and the Yukon Territory above the border with British Columbia https://maps.lib.utexas.edu/maps/united_states/alaska_90.jpg

Map Preface-5

Canada's Yukon Territory
https://maps.lib.utexas.edu/maps/united_states/alaska_90.jpg

Map Preface-6

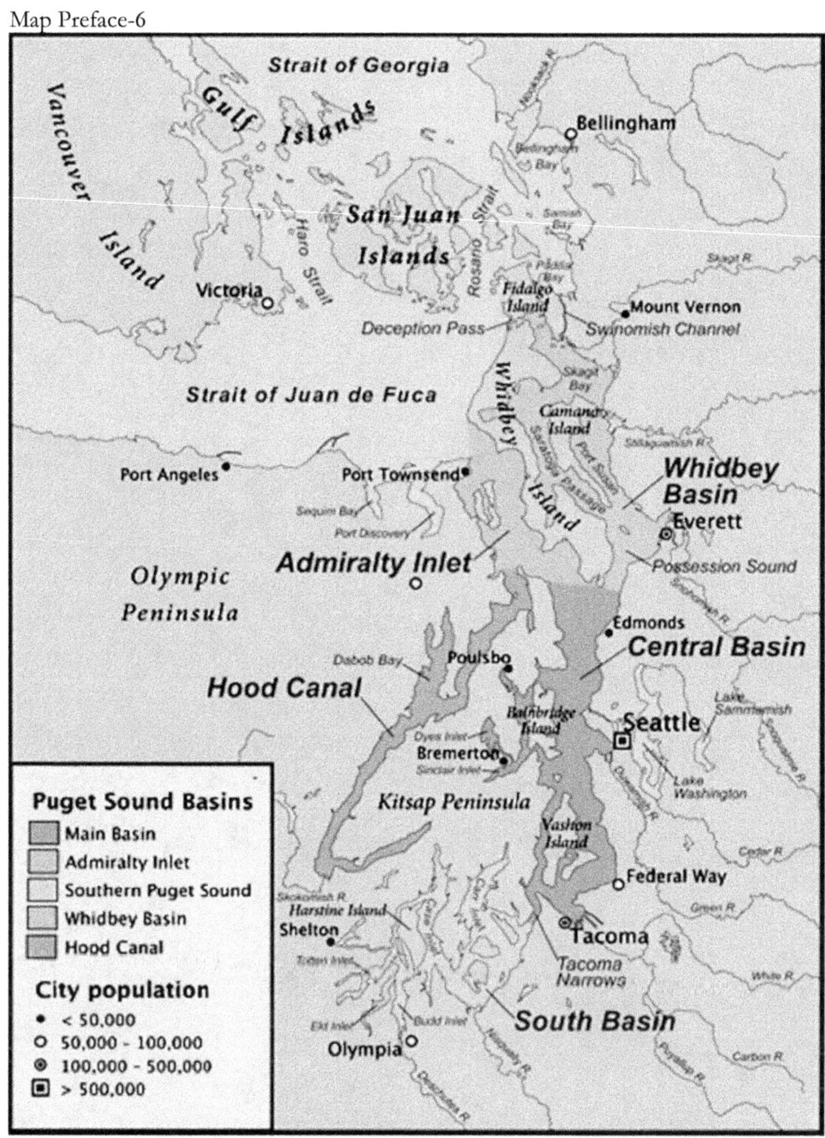

Southwest British Columbia and, across the Strait of Juan de Fuca, the Puget Sound area of northwestern Washington State, have close maritime ties to one another https://commons.wikimedia.org/wiki/File:Map_pugetsound.png

1

George F. Askew, Master Boatbuilder

Photo 1-1

George Askew sporting a watch fob made from gold nuggets he collected in the Klondike. Kathryn Askew collection

INTRODUCTION TO GEORGE ASKEW

Anyone delving into the history of western Canada's northern rivers, lakes, and seas cannot escape coming into contact with the name George Askew. He constructed, or worked on, a great variety of vessels that included sternwheelers, propeller-driven freight craft and tugs, Arctic trading vessels and barges. In addition to the Pacific coast, these vessels worked on the Yukon, Fraser, Peace, Athabasca, Slave and Mackenzie rivers and even in the Arctic Ocean. As well, in coastal waters, his legacy of fine craftsmanship can be found in commercial vessels and fine yachts, both power and sailing, some of which are still afloat today. His career in boat and shipbuilding—from his apprenticeship in 1889 to his retirement in about 1944—extended some 55 years. This period spanned most of the industrial booms along the major river basins in western Canada and Alaska during the first half of the twentieth century, a period of time that relied on the use of water transportation to open up settlement and access for resource extraction.

George passed on his love of shipbuilding to his sons Francis and John by involving them in his work and both eventually ran their own boat building businesses. An athlete, sportsman and keen yachtsman, George was awarded an honourary life membership with the Royal Vancouver Yacht Club in 1950. He built some of the best-known boats in the club, and in 1929 was part of the crew of the yacht *Lady Van* that wrestled the Lipton Cup away from the Seattle Yacht Club. He lived a full life and died in 1953 at 81 years of age.

Burgees of the Royal Vancouver Yacht Club (L) and the Seattle Yacht Club (R)

EARLY LIFE

> *G. F. Askew has issued a challenge to sail the* Scud *against any yacht in Victoria for $250 a side.*
>
> —*Victoria Times*, 4 October 1893.

George Askew, born in 1872, spent his early days at Chemainus on Vancouver Island where his father Thomas George Askew, a veteran of the Cariboo Gold Rush, had established a sawmill. In 1868 his father married Isobella (Isabel) Julia Curtis, an immigrant from England who arrived on the bride ship *Tynemouth* with her mother Frances Curtis, via passage around South America. Together, Thomas and Isobella had eight children, including young George. In 1880, when George was only eight, his father died. His mother tried to keep the sawmill business going, but because a shipment of spars was blocked by controlling Dunsmuir interests, she was forced to sell out. In 1881, while Isobella was still fighting to save the business and with no school in the Chemainus area, George and his older siblings were sent to the interior town of Lytton, in British Columbia, to live with their grandmother and her husband, merchant Jean Jules Boucherat (known to George as "Papa Jules"), to attend school there.

Photo 1-2

Askew homestead at Chemainus, on the east coast of southern Vancouver Island; a British sloop, thought to be HMS *Rocket*, is in the foreground. Martin Askew collection

Before the completion of the Canadian Pacific Railway (CPR), travel probably meant by steamer up the Fraser River to Yale, a British Columbia town on its bank, and thence by road over the famous dizzying Cariboo Wagon Road. This involved passage near the contractor Andrew Onderdonk's constructions and explosions as the CPR railway grade was carved out of the precipitous canyon-rock mass. Surely George's travels and experience in that canyon were an exciting and memorable time for a young boy. It was also probably his first experience with sternwheelers; an early encounter with vessels for which he would later become so famous.

By 1883/84 George and his siblings were living with their mother on Pemberton Road on the outskirts of Victoria, BC. This property had been purchased from the proceeds of Thomas George Askew's forays into the interior gold fields about 1862. The small cottage had been improved over the years, and with a final upgrade by Isobella after her husband's death it would last the family for the next 25 years until her death in 1905. In 1889, after completing high school at Central School, George entered into an apprenticeship with J. J. Robinson, known as one of Victoria's foremost boatbuilders. The city's shipbuilding and iron working industries, aided by the neighbouring naval base at Esquimalt, were at the centre of that industry on Canada's west coast.

Photo 1-3

J. J. Robinson Shipwright and Boatbuilder, Victoria BC. George Askew on the left. Kathryn Askew collection

Photo 1-4

Painting by Bo Hermansen of the British sloop HMS *Cormorant* in dry dock at Esquimalt on 21 July 1887. The ironclad battleship HMS *Triumph* can be seen in the background.
Courtesy of Bo Hermansen

The establishment of the Esquimalt Marine Railway by William Fitzherbert Bullen in 1896, the opening of the first graving dock at Esquimalt in 1897, and the establishment of Alexander Watson Jr.'s new shipyard in Victoria provided a vibrant environment for George to learn and hone the skills of a shipwright and ship designer following his apprenticeship. It is not known if George was actually employed by Watson, but the latter's methods and approaches to construction of sternwheelers for remote river locations were certainly an example for him. Later, George did work on many of Watson's vessels in the Yukon and on the Skeena River.

ATHLETIC INTERESTS

Victoria also provided George a home for his recreational interests, pursuits and prowess. The James Bay Athletic Association (JBAA) helped him to develop proficiency and win awards in swimming, rowing and canoeing. Membership in the fledging Royal Victoria Yacht Club (then located in its first home on a float in the James Bay area) allowed him to develop the contacts and access to yachts in which he proved to be an outstanding and award-winning helmsman. He was so confident in this ability that as reported in a 4 October 1893

Victoria Times newspaper article, he put up a $250 challenge for anyone to outsail him in a race with the yacht *Scud* which he would pilot.

George was particularly well-versed with this vessel, having survived a knock-down when attempting a retreat from an aborted race, having been caught in an overpowering gale in August of that year. He and the other crewmen—his brother Walter, James Watson and Dan O'Sullivan all strong swimmers from the JBAA, and initially all thought drowned—had survived by clinging to the overturned hull, awaiting rescue.

Photo 1-5

James Bay Athletic Association (JBAA) Crew Amateur Champions of BC, 1891. Members (l to r) Dan O'Sullivan, F. A. Jackson, George Askew, and F. S. Widdowson. Askew family collection & BC Archives photograph J-00900

In June 1897, before George left to join the Klondike gold rush, he piloted William Fitzherbert Bullen's yacht *Ariadne* to victories over challengers, some from as far away as Seattle. *Ariadne*, a large yawl-rigged vessel requiring a crew of twelve to fully manage her large sail plan, had been launched from Bullen's Esquimalt Marine Railway yard in 1896. In the *Victoria Daily Colonist* article of 26 June 1897, the yacht was described as "the largest as well as the swiftest in all the Northwest country." It is conceivable George even had a hand in her construction; he had worked at Esquimalt.

Photo 1-6

Yacht *Ariadne* near Victoria, built by William Fitzherbert Bullen.
Image B-03119 courtesy of the Royal BC Museum

In 1897 George, along with thousands of other fortune hunters, made his way to the Yukon on the wave of the Klondike Gold Rush. Family members believe he was outfitted in Edmonton, and took the difficult all-Canadian route via Edmonton, Peace River Landing, and down the Peace and Mackenzie rivers to Fort McPherson in the Northwest Territories, crossing over the mountains and down the Porcupine River to the Yukon River. Little is known of his gold mining experiences. He did bring back several large nuggets, which were afterwards fashioned into two large rings, one for each of his sons. A report in the *Victoria Daily Colonist* of 5 March 1899, indicates that he spent the end of 1898 on a failed claim near Dawson City—a town on the Yukon River inseparably linked to the Klondike Gold Rush—with partners from Victoria. Soon after he found a ready market for plying his shipbuilding skills at Whitehorse.

By the turn of the century Whitehorse was developing as a summer shipbuilding and repair centre for construction and maintenance of the large fleet of sternwheelers and barges that the White Pass Railway was consolidating through its subsidiary British Yukon Navigation Company (BYN). Even while employed with BYN, Askew appears to have been able to participate in prospecting. He is quoted in the *Victoria Times* of 31 December 1901 as owning several promising claims in the Big Salmon area east of Hootalinqua on the Yukon River.

Photo 1-7

Klondikers carrying supplies ascending the Chilkoot Pass, a high mountain pass, whose summit in the Boundary Ranges of the Coast Mountains of Alaska and British Columbia marks the international border between the United States and Canada, 1898. Askew entered via a different means, but this photograph suggests there were no easy routes to the Gold Fields, if many seeking riches chose this method to get there. University of Washington Library photograph ChilkootPass_steps.jpg uploaded to Wikimedia Commons

2

Working in the Yukon for the British Yukon

George Askew is home from Dawson where he assisted in repairing the steamer Bonanza King.

—*Whitehorse Daily Star*, 19 July 1907.

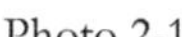
Photo 2-1

Whitehorse dock and shipyard, 1903.
Yukon Archives photograph YA #5537

Robert D. Turner's important book *The Klondike Gold Rush Steamers – A History of Yukon River Steam Navigation*, details rapidly expanding shipbuilding that occurred throughout the Pacific Northwest, Unalaska Island in the Aleutians, and at the mouth and along the banks of the mighty Yukon River. Water transport provided by this major commercial episode supported and supplied the early armada of gold-seekers, known as "stampeders," and the industrial alluvial and hard rock mining that followed them.

Photo 2-2

Engraving of "Ounalaska" (Unalaska), Aleutian Islands, 1879. The naval exploration vessel USS *Jeannette* was in the harbor, in August, while en route to the Arctic.
U.S. Naval History and Heritage Command photograph #NH 92112

The British Yukon Navigation Company (BYN) was a subsidiary formed by the White Pass Railway in 1901 to extend its transportation system deep into the Yukon to Dawson City. Eventually, in 1913, through its US-incorporated subsidiary, the Alaska Yukon Navigation Company (AYN), access was continued into the Fairbanks area (in the interior region of Alaska), and even to St. Michaels (on the central west coast of Alaska), near the Yukon River's mouth. BYN started off small but eventually absorbed many lesser competitors until it became the dominant carrier on the upper Yukon River and was a major player on the lower half (from its source in British Columbia, the Yukon River flows through the Yukon and continues westwards through Alaska).

George Askew is not specifically mentioned in Turner's book, but he was familiar with and worked on many of the vessels and dozens of scows and barges. He worked for British Yukon from 1899 to 1909, finishing there as foreman shipwright with his reason for leaving as "to accept a better position." He must have initially worked for one of the companies that were taken-over, as BYN was not incorporated until March 1901. He seems to have been based at Whitehorse but travelled to other locations, as necessary, for repair and maintenance work. A notification in the *Whitehorse Daily Star* of 19 July 1907 indicates George was "... home from Dawson where he assisted in repairs of the steamer *Bonanza King*."

For many of the BYN employees the work was seasonal which allowed them to "come-out" for the winter after the vessels were hauled out and put into winter quarters before the Yukon River froze. The maintenance workers were back in early spring for an intense effort to overhaul, paint and otherwise prepare the vessels for launching once break-up had occurred and the river was safe for navigation. This arrival and departure of personnel was possible after 1900 because of the completion of the White Pass Railway, which added to the already existing steamer services to the Port of Skagway, in southeast Alaska, along the popular sheltered route, the Inside Passage.

Photo 2-3

Decades later, destroyers USS *Dallas* (DD-199), USS *Long* (DD-209), and USS *Wasmuth* (DD-338) are moored abreast one another at Skagway, Alaska, with snow-capped mountains in the background, 1937.
Naval History and Heritage Command photograph #NH 109565

Many of the vessels that ended up in BYN were rooted in the shipbuilding industry that George had been involved with in Victoria. No doubt George had participated in the innovative lightning-speed construction of three "brand-new" BYN vessels at Whitehorse in the spring of 1901, just about the time the BYN was formally incorporated.

These speed-built vessels SS *Dawson*, the *White Horse* and the *Selkirk*, had been built at Whitehorse with parts hauled in over the recently completed White Pass Railway.

The hull frames, specially designed for vessels in the upper Yukon River service, were prefabricated at Victoria by Alexander Watson and shipped to Skagway. Other materials for the new vessels, including upper works and machinery, were stripped from three former Vancouver-built CPR vessels that had been towed to Skagway: the SS *Ogilvie*, *McConnell*, and *G. M. Dawson*. These sternwheelers had been built in Vancouver by the Canadian Pacific Railway for the failed "all Canadian" route to the Klondike via the Stikine River. When purchased by the BYN, they were virtually new. George's unseasonable departure from Seattle to Skagway on the steamer SS *Dolphin* as reported in the *Victoria Daily Colonist* of 28 September 1900, may have been related to the ordering of hull parts from Watson.

Whitehorse newspaper reports make it clear that George did not suffer from lack of athletic activities during his time there. Besides some prospecting, as previously mentioned, he actively participated in organizing and playing baseball games including challenges with teams from neighbouring communities such as Skagway. As reported in the *Whitehorse Daily Star* of 20 August 1909, in his final year with BYN, he managed to take off six summer weeks to visit Victoria, Vancouver and Seattle where he attended the Alaska-Yukon-Pacific Exposition.

During these heady years of prospecting, exploring and boat-building in the north, George was always in touch with his family back in Victoria. He supported his mother in ensuring his five sisters "married well" and waited until all his siblings had married and moved away from home before seeking out a marriage partner himself. The first of his four wives crossed his bow in Whitehorse. In 1898, Jennifer "Jennie" Ardrie Bigger had sailed to Dyea, Alaska, about nine miles west of Skagway, where her parents Henry and Elvira had established an outfitting business for miners preparing to ascend the Chilkoot Pass. Her family moved on to Whitehorse when the gold rush ended, and Jennie met and married "Mr. Spragge" who died sometime before 1908. By 1909 Jennie had returned to Portland, Oregon, with her parents, but George had set his sights on Jennie and the two were married in Vancouver in July of 1909.

3

River Boats for the Grand Trunk Pacific Railway

The material for the two new hotels being built for the Grand Trunk Pacific construction on the Fraser River from Tete Jaune Cache to Fort George is being prepared at New Westminster, British Columbia, at the local ship yards of G. S. Askew.

—*Edmonton Journal*, 29 December 1911.

Photo 3-1

Grand Trunk Pacific steamers at Prince Rupert.
Prince Rupert City & Regional Archives & Museum of Northern B.C., Wrathall collection, JRW164

While George was still employed with BYN in the first three months of 1909, and before the navigation season on the Yukon began, he was concurrently employed at Prince Rupert, the port city newly established as the western terminus of the Grand Trunk Pacific (GTP) railway in 1910, located on British Columbia's northwest coast. He worked at the Hays Creek ways for Captain Sanborn, the Superintendent of Transportation for Foley, Welsh and Stewart, principal contractor for the GTP. This work involved modifying the stern of the steamer *Skeena*—to improve her backing ability through rapids (*Victoria Daily Colonist* article, 29 January 1909)—and removing and replacing her engines with more powerful ones.

The captain of the *Skeena* at the time was Captain George Magar, who would be George Askew's neighbour at the West Peace River shipyard where he would build the riverboat *D. A. Thomas* in 1915 and 1916. (The *Skeena* was then known as the "Burns Boat" as it was almost exclusively used to transport that meat firm's products to railway construction crews from its slaughter house at Hazelton, BC.)

Askew's experience at the Hays Creek ways probably led him to taking on additional employment with GTP including the building of a shipyard and maintenance of its vessels. An article in the 29 October 1909 *Whitehorse Daily Star* indicated that George had moved to Prince Rupert to establish new ship ways for that construction firm's fleet of river steamers intended to supply construction projects along the Skeena River in British Columbia.

The ways and shipyard in which George was involved, along with his home, were established at Dodge Cove on Digby Island opposite Prince Rupert, where the land was suitable for landing and storing sternwheelers. The 1911 Census indicated that George and his new wife Jennie were living at this location and that his employer was indeed Foley, Welch and Stewart.

While a sternwheeler steamship service already operated on the Skeena River prior to start of construction of the railway in 1908, Foley and his partners, in order to support railway grading and bridge projects at multiple locations, acquired their own fleet of steamers. These vessels in 1909 consisted of the aforementioned *Skeena* (built by D. McPhee at Coal Harbour, Vancouver, in 1908) and the nearly identical "sisters" (built by Alexander Watson Jr. in Victoria in 1908 and 1909), *Distributor*, *Omineca*, *Conveyor* and *Operator*.

The construction of the GTP progressed from two fronts: one starting in the west proceeding eastward along the Skeena River; the other from Edmonton westward, traversing the Rocky Mountains. (Edmonton is sited on the North Saskatchewan River in Alberta.) At the end of 1911, with steel laid and the as-yet uncompleted major bridge at Skeena Crossing, the end of steam boating on the Skeena was in sight.

The eastern heading under Foley, Welch and Stewart was becoming less in need of water transportation. However, the western one, which under Stewart had barely crossed the divide from Alberta to BC, and was approaching Tete Jaune Cache on the upper reaches of the Fraser River, was still in desperate need for just such a resource. Accordingly, *Operator* and *Conveyor,* instead of joining their sisters for the winter on the Dodge Cove ways, were sent south to the lower mainland for cannibalization of their machinery and other parts for use in the new hulls to be constructed at Tete Jaune.

George was in charge of this work. While the vessels were registered with new numbers, they retained their original names. The construction of the second *Operator* and *Conveyor* were the first large vessels attributable to him. As reported by the *Edmonton Journal* of 29 December 1911, hull parts for the vessels were prefabricated at "his" shipyard in New Westminster (the oldest city in western Canada located in the Lower Mainland region of British Columbia) and shipped by rail to Edmonton for forwarding to the end of steel which was approaching Tete Jaune.

As he would encounter in later situations at Peace River and Waterways, Alberta, the final delivery of steamer parts to river assembly was exceedingly difficult. At Tete Jaune, for example, the hauling of a 25-ton boiler with horse teams over 25 miles on tote roads (unpaved and rough roads meant only to facilitate moving supplies and equipment to remote camps) took a week and tragically, resulted in a death of a workman (*Passenger and Merchant Ships of the Grand Trunk Pacific and Canadian Northern Railway* by David R. P. Guay, page 123).

In addition to the assembly of the two steamers, six scows were built to work with them. Details of George's involvement with these vessels' employment in the completion of the GTP line to Fort George and then later south of there, on the construction of the Pacific Great Eastern Railway PGE, are not fully known but it seems to have occupied most of his time in 1912.

Before leaving this segment of his life history, it is noted that George was also involved in the construction of smaller craft while residing in Prince Rupert. While the building date is obviously incorrect, the Royal Vancouver Yacht Club history reports that his sloop *Ardrie* (named for his wife, which was her middle name) was built there in 1915. (The date cited is wrong because the vessel was winning races in Vancouver in 1914 and early 1915. Other data, a note on a photo indicates she was built in Prince Rupert much earlier in 1908).

Importantly, for his later reputation as a prime builder of shallow draft river craft, was his involvement in the construction of a tunnel boat for William John "Wiggs" O'Neill.

This boat, the *Kit-ex-chen* (various other spellings exist including *Kitexchan* – means "men of the Skeena"), as reported in the *Prince Rupert Daily News*, was launched from the Cow Bay boatyard of Hugo Johnson in August 1911. It was used by O'Neill to ferry train passengers arriving at the still uncompleted bridge at Skeena Crossing to Hazelton. Several years later, in an 18 March 1921 article in *The*

Vancouver Daily Province newspaper (hereafter, generally referred to as the *Province* for simplicity's sake), a reporter disclosed this information obtained from George about tunnel boats: "... designed and built his first tunnel motor boat for 'Wiggs' O'Neill, on the Skeena River in 1911, so that these boats are now no experiment, but an established success." It appears that a one-year discrepancy about the building date of the boat likely resulted from a memory lapse on George's part, and did not reflect the building of two separate boats.

Photo 3-2

William "Wiggs" O'Neill's tunnel boat, the *Kitexchan*, going up the Skeena River in Hazelton, BC.
Bulkley Valley Museum, photograph P0747

"Tunnel boats" as referred to herein, are low-draft propeller vessels designed to operate in shallow waterways. They have a cavity (or cavities depending on the number of propellers) moulded into the bottom of their hulls that extends in the rear half of the hull, and is designed to house the shaft and propeller in such a way as to safeguard them if the vessel touches bottom or is grounded. Water drawn into the tunnel, at least to its load draft height and expelled from the rear of the tunnel, allows the vessel to maintain way in only inches of water.

4

River Boats on the Peace River

Photo 4-1

Askew residence at 1925 Union (later Adanac) Street, Vancouver.
Vancouver Archives photograph CVA 786-68.19

ESTABLISHMENT OF A NEW HOME IN VANCOUVER

In 1913 George and Jennie moved from Prince Rupert to Vancouver where he built his home, which he lived in for most of the rest of his life, at 1925 Union (later Adanac) Street. Jennie only shared it with him for two years. In Vancouver, even with frequent absences, George was able to resume his earlier joys of competitive sailboat racing. He became a member of the Royal Vancouver Yacht Club in 1913. During the next two years he actively participated, and enjoyed frequent successes, with his sloop *Ardrie*, winning the cup for B-Class sloops for the Labour Day Race of 1914. In 1915, the day after winning the Commodore Cup (racing from Galiano Island to Point Grey), he filed for divorce from Jennie. The petition was granted without contest on June 30, 1915. Jennie Askew returned to Portland and was still living with her parents in 1920.

RIVER BOATS ON THE PEACE RIVER, 1915-1916

> *Mr. George Askew who is here today from Peace River Crossing, where he superintended the building of the vessel [*D. A. Thomas*], states that she is 190 feet long and 37 feet beam. She has a speed of 16 miles an hour. She was laid down in the fall of 1915 and completed in May of this year. She will operate for 650 miles on the Peace River, with Peace River Crossing as a base.*
>
> —*The Vancouver Daily Province*, 25 November 1916

Photo 4-2

River boat *D. A. Thomas.*
Provincial Archives of Alberta photograph A 5099

In 1915 George received one of his most important shipbuilding contracts. David Alfred Thomas, a wealthy Welsh industrialist (seeing huge potential in the Peace River country in farming, coal, oil and tourism as railways pushed into northern Alberta) decided to get into transportation in a large way. (Thomas was later Baron Rhondda, a one-time honour extending only to the death of his daughter, awarded in 1918 for his war efforts in procuring munitions).

The inspired vision of D. A. Thomas and his well-financed associates was to speculate on a new northern railway running from the mouth of the Nass River (at Nass Bay in British Columbia) to Prince Albert, Saskatchewan with river steamers and tramways on the lower Peace and Slave rivers. Thomas was particularly interested in finding sources of oil for the Royal Navy as they actively converted vessels away from coal.

Photo 4-3

Coaling party on board the light cruiser HMAS (ex-HMS) *Encounter.* The griminess of the men and the state of the ship's deck, which must be made spotless, testify to the filthiness of the task and its unpopularity.
Australian War Memorial photograph 300630

To do so, Thomas instigated the drilling of several exploratory wells in the Peace River area in northwestern Alberta. As reported in an article in the *Province* of 15 October 1915, one near Vermilion Chutes was down to 300 feet, approaching 400, where oil was expected to be struck. Unfortunately, these big dreams were interrupted by WWI. After Thomas' death in 1918, local governments lost their enthusiasm for pursuing these endeavours post-war with his daughter Margaret (then known as Lady Mackworth).

George was engaged to construct the largest and most luxurious sternwheeler ever built on the Mackenzie River system at Peace River, Alberta, as well as a much smaller tunnel boat intended to serve as both a transportation vessel and a river tug. The former, which became famous and fortified George's reputation as a fine builder of river steamers, was named in honour of its owner, the *D. A. Thomas*, but would have mixed success. Its smaller and more successful cousin was named *Lady Mackworth* in honour of Margaret (who as part of the Thomas award received this title.) Both vessels were originally part of the fleet of Thomas' Peace River Development Company (PRDC), but eventually came to be owned via a succession of sales by the HBC through its Alberta and Arctic Transportation Company (A&AT) subsidiary.

As the sternwheeler was nearing completion at a shipyard on the west side of the river, the construction of the new railway into Peace River underway at the time stalled, barely in sight of the town, and awaited the completion of a large viaduct over the Heart River. The owners spared no expense in construction of the vessel, right down to purchasing the finest linens and silver for the dining room. Although used machinery was available, new boilers and engines were purchased and superior Douglas fir and cedar lumber were brought in from the coast. Because the railway remained incomplete, all material, including the two heavy boilers and the paddle wheel-shaft, had to be dragged down the steep slope and across river ice from the end of steel near the bridge site. This movement proved a Herculean task. Prior to the completion of the major railway bridge across the waterway in 1918, access to the West Peace River shipyard was either across the ice in winter or by reaction ferry in summer. (This cable-type ferry uses the reaction of the current of a river against a fixed tether to propel the vessel across the water.)

The construction of the vessel from the initial grading of its building site through its launching, and even manning with its first crew, is unusually well-documented in a series of 35 photographs taken by William Meikle, and available for online viewing at the Provincial Archives of Alberta website (as of 2021).

The *Lady Mackworth* was a prototype for many other subsequent successful shallow-draft vessels built by George and copied by others on the Mackenzie River system and elsewhere. Like the *Kit-ex-chen* designed for William John "Wiggs" O'Neill, *Lady Mackworth* was of tunnel design so her screws would not come in contact with the river bottom if grounded. This is what the aforementioned *Province* article reported about this vessel:

> Another vessel which Mr. Askew has superintended is the gasoline craft *Lady Mackworth* which is 58 feet long and 11 feet beam. She will navigate the river in the fall and early spring when the waters are low. She draws only nine and a half inches of water and is a twin screw job. The material used in these vessels was all obtained from Vancouver.

It is noteworthy that later in 1920, when Lamson and Hubbard took over David Alfred Thomas' assets, this vessel was taken down the Peace

River over the Vermillion Chutes (Falls), down the Athabasca River and over Smith Portage to provide valuable service on the lower river. It is not known if George was involved with or made this journey.

Photo 4-4

Men lowering *Lady Mackworth* down Vermillion Chutes.
Askew family collection

George's neighbour at the West Peace River shipyard was Captain George Magar, formerly the captain of the *Skeena.* As noted in the 1916 Census for the area, Magar, along with his wife and daughter, were George's immediate neighbours at West Peace River. In 1915 Magar was responsible for building a smaller sternwheeler, the *Northland Call,* at West Peace River for the Peace River Navigation Company, a business created by James Cornwall in which Magar and two others were partners. The vessel used machinery salvaged from James Cornwall's upper Athabasca River steamer of the same name (*Northland Call*). Magar owned a sawmill in the area and was captain of this vessel. The second *Northland Call* was reportedly unsuccessful, and Cornwall was unable to extend his influence in shipping to the upper Peace River.

The vessel's unsuccessful employment was influenced by a damaging rock-striking accident in 1915, Cornwall's departure that same year to join the army for WWI, and Magar's death in 1916. *Northland Call* operated in 1917 but not the following year when the PRDC was the only operator on the upper river. Eventually in 1920, PRDC purchased the vessel, upgraded it and renamed it the *Hudson Hope.* The sternwheeler was part of the PRDC assets that the Canadian subsidiary of Lamson and Hubbard purchased in early 1920.

The Lamson and Hubbard Trading Company was engaged in the fur trading business in the Canadian North, with over fourteen outposts in the Athabasca-Mackenzie River district in Alberta and the Northwest Territories during the early 20th century. It was in direct competition with the Hudson's Bay Company, and engaged in river transportation. The trading enterprise was formed primarily to service Lamson and Hubbard's isolated fur trading posts along the Mackenzie River, but also to provide commercial service through its subsidiary Alberta and Arctic Transportation Company (A&AT) incorporated in 1921.

Lamson and Hubbard beaver felt top hat and associated hat box

Photo 4-5

River boat *D. A. Thomas* nears completion behind Captain George Magar's *Northland Call* at West Peace River, 1916.
Provincial Archives of Alberta photograph A10157 (William Meikle)

At Peace River Landing George stayed at the hotel on the east side of the river across from his boatyard. There he became acquainted with Agnes Martin who served in the restaurant and cooked for hotel customers. Agnes was raised in the Kawartha Lakes area north of Toronto. Her mother had died when Agnes was eleven and she and her older sister Catherine left school to raise the six younger children while their father worked as a cabinet maker. No stranger to hard work, Agnes cooked her way across Canada in various railway camps, reaching Bickerdyke, Alberta, in 1911 where she ran a boarding house for railway workers pushing track through to Tete Jaune.

By 1916 she was working at Peace River Landing where homesteading tracts had been released by the Dominion Government. As winter settled in later that year, Agnes (38) travelled with George (44) back to the coast where they married in November. From all accounts, theirs was a solid marriage and it's possible that adventurous Agnes accompanied George north from time to time. Their sons, Francis and John, were born in November 1918 and October 1921, respectively; both in Vancouver.

Tragically, after giving birth to John by caesarean section, Agnes contracted an infection and died just four days later. George's sister Julia Arnould arrived to help with the children and took them to her farm in Sardis. Julia and her three teenage daughters cared for them over the following three years, while their father went north, again.

VANCOUVER SHIPYARDS, 1916 AND 1917

After returning from the Peace River with Agnes, George worked at both the Wallace Shipyard in North Vancouver and at Western Canada Shipyards in Vancouver. Wallace at that time was working on six huge wooden *Mable Brown*-class lumber auxiliary schooners that, per Tim Colton shipbuilding records, were delivered, beginning with the *Mabel Brown*, in March 1917 and completed with the *Marie Barnard* in September 1917.

The work at Western Canada Shipyards in Vancouver involved construction of six 2300-ton wooden freighters for the World War I effort, beginning with the delivery of *War Nootka* in January 1918 and completing with the *War Tanoo* in August 1918. The construction of these vessels involved tasks where someone with George's skills and experience would find ready employment. Based on his later commitments and these delivery schedules, it can be concluded that prior to leaving for a new assignment in St. Michaels, Alaska, in mid-1917, he worked at Wallace Shipyard. During his return home in the winter of 1917-1918, he worked for Western Canada Shipyards, then returned to St. Michaels in mid-1918.

5

St. Michaels, Alaska 1917-1918

The Shipyard crew is working on the Klondyke *and will finish her this season. She is in very bad shape and the repairs are extensive. Askew figures that he will have her ready for opening Navigation all except caulking, and is doing considerable necessary work on the* Sarah, *that otherwise would have to be done next June before she could sail.*

—From AYN Manager William Taylor's Weekly Report, St. Michaels, Alaska, 12 October 1917 (courtesy Yukon Archives, Whitehorse).

Photo 5-1

Canadian Arctic Expedition (CAE) ship, the motor schooner *Polar Bear*, hauling onto a slipway at St. Michaels, Alaska, September 1918.
Canadian Museum of Civilization photograph JH 50682 uploaded to Wikimedia Commons

During the summer navigation seasons of 1917 and 1918, George rejoined the BYN Co. serving as shipyard superintendent for their subsidiary Alaska Yukon Navigation (AYN) at St. Michaels, Alaska, near the mouth of the Yukon River. Similar to BYN operations at Whitehorse, their subsidiary operated on a seasonal basis with the majority of the ships' crews and shipyard workers present only in the summer months. At the time, most of the work force came in from Seattle on the Alaska Steamships large liner SS *Victoria* (ex Cunarder SS *Parthia*). They came in early June, on the initial seasonal voyage to Nome and St. Michaels in western Alaska—along with hundreds of miners bound for Nome, about 125 miles northwest of St. Michaels—and returned to Seattle on the last voyage out in late October.

Photo 5-2

St. Michaels, Alaska, circa 1905.
University of Washington: Special Collections photograph 6553 uploaded to Wikimedia Commons

Photo 5-3

Nome, Alaska, in 1907.
Birds-eye view of Nome Alaska 1907 jpg. Wikimedia Commons

Although George's job application was made on 15 March 1917, his employment, seemingly because of immigration approval difficulties, did not start until 1 June of that year. It was early enough to join the annual migration on the *Victoria*; thus, it is likely that he travelled aboard her both in the 1917 and 1918 seasons. The ten-day voyages would have given George an opportunity to meet prominent Nome mining personalities such as Louis Lane. The *Vancouver Daily World*, 3 June 1918 edition, reporting on *Victoria*'s sailing that day, stated "On the passenger list are a number of mining operators who are going to Nome and camps of the Seward peninsula for the season's work." George apparently spent the winter of 1917-1918 in Vancouver as evidenced by the birth of his son Francis in November of 1918, so he likely made four voyages on that vessel.

The port of St. Michaels is situated on Norton Sound, an arm of the Bering Sea near the Arctic Circle. At the time, although the port contained many derelict river steamers from the earlier frantic Klondike gold rush days, it was still used as a trans-shipment point for the company for unloading ocean ships from the south onto their river steamers for supply of the Fairbanks area of Alaska, until the Alaska Railway was completed in 1923. According to shipyard reports, George was much involved in the maintenance of very large sternwheelers—including the two monsters 223-foot *Sarah* and her sister *Susie*—which BYN had taken over from former US operators. These included the Alaska Commercial Company and the North American Transportation and Trading Co., which had operated their vessels on the Yukon River as far as Dawson in the gold rush.

Photo 5-4

Steamboat *Sarah* on the Yukon River, circa 1898.
From Wikimedia Commons (WARNER 499)

FAMED EXPEDITION SHIP *POLAR BEAR*

During the summer of 1918, George was involved in the repair of Vilhjalmur Stefansson's Canadian Arctic Expedition (CAE) motor schooner *Polar Bear* at St. Michaels. He is quoted in the *Vancouver Daily World* article of 24 March 1919 that he was the former shipyard superintendent of White Pass and Yukon Railway at St. Michaels, and had outfitted the *Polar Bear* after haul-out and repairs. Captain John Hadley and thirteen other members of Stefansson's CAE crew—after enduring a miserable winter exposed and grounded on Alaska's north slope—had heroically freed the vessel and sailed first to Nome and then to St. Michaels. Being unable to proceed to her home base in Esquimalt, *Polar Bear* was hauled out by George.

As reported in the *Oakland Tribune* of 6 November, twelve members of Hadley's crew took passage on the final 1918 voyage of *Victoria* to Seattle. It was not a happy passage on the storm-battered ship; three persons died and were buried at sea of sickness or heart failure. They were not part of the 153 of the 709 passengers who were infected with the Spanish Flu, one of whom died off Cape Flattery. The *Seattle Star* 6 November 1918 edition headline blared out the news, "17 AMBULANCES MEET ALASKAN 'FLU' STEAMER."

INTRO TO / ACQUAINTANCE WITH LOUIS LANE

The *Polar Bear,* which George hauled out, was built and owned by Captain Louis Lane, an individual whose continuing dreams of entering the fur trade would provide George with his next two years of employment. Constructed by the E. W. Heath Company of Seattle, and powered by a three-cylinder gasoline engine, the 81-ton schooner was modelled after Gloucester fishing schooners. *Polar Bear* made two trading voyages to the Siberian Arctic, then a whaling voyage in 1913. During her second whaling voyage in 1914, she encountered members of the CAE several times, and was subsequently purchased by Stefansson in 1915.

After the collapse of whaling interests, American firms turned their attention to the fur trade, and in particular, the arctic fox, an abundant resource of soft, white fur. Captain Lane, son of American mining magnate Charles D. Lane, soon became well aware that participants in the Arctic fur trade, pioneered by American firms (such as Liebes and independent traders) and even the staunch old HBC, were realizing huge profits from it.

In 1916, with Chicago dairy products tycoon and adventurer John Borden, Lane built the *Great Bear* in Seattle, a large 175-foot three-masted schooner equipped for Arctic service, which was described as "the staunchest ice ship afloat." Ostensibly the vessel was to carry relief supplies to Stefansson's beleaguered expedition but clearly there seemed to be other uses for such a vessel. Unfortunately for the venturers, their new vessel was wrecked on Pinnacle Rock near St. Matthews Island in the Bering Sea on 10 August 1916. Fortunately, all on board, including Borden and Lane's sister Ila, were rescued after a two-week stranding on the island.

It is likely, through his involvement with the *Polar Bear* (and the fact that Lane owned a large mine, together with his brother Tom, at Nome adjacent to St. Michaels), that George became acquainted and subsequently well-associated with Lane. About this time, an old Boston-based American fur trading firm, Lamson and Hubbard Company, was making ambitious plans for expansion into Canada. Well-financed, they were planning on establishing a fur trading organization that would operate in the Arctic and extend down the Mackenzie River to compete head-on with the HBC and other Canadian firms. It is reported that they had started to establish posts in western Canada as early as 1917. It is known that Lane was associated with this firm as early as 1918. His draft card, dated 12 September 1918, states his position as Pacific Coast Manager of Lamson and Hubbard, and that he was based in San Francisco.

6

Working for Lamson and Hubbard, 1918-1920

Much credit is due Mr. George Askew the builder of the S.S. Distributor, *who has turned out a splendid boat under the most trying circumstances.*

—*Edmonton Journal*, 28 August 1920.

The veteran shipbuilder and prospector has "mushed" three times into the great north country and knows every tree along the great Mackenzie. On his last trip he covered a distance of over 300 miles on foot and it was then that he was in the Fort Norman district when the oil was first struck.

—*Vancouver World*, 8 January 1921.

Philip Godsell's book *Arctic Trader* and the journals, letters and photographs of adventurer Norman Robinson reveal that American fur traders, lead by well-financed Boston-based Lamson and Hubbard Company—emboldened by almost unfettered access in the western Arctic—entered into strong titanic competition with established Canadian firms in the Mackenzie watershed and other parts of Canada. As noted by Godsell, the Alberta and Great Waterways Railway (A&GW) provided Lamson and Hubbard a relatively easy means of accessing the fur trade in western Canada, in spite of its dilapidated and unfinished condition at the time. The main thrust of their forays began about 1918 and extended to 1924 when, in essence, its Canadian operations failed and all of the shares of its transportation subsidiary, the Alberta and Arctic Transportation Company, were purchased by the HBC.

In the *Vancouver World* newspaper article previously referred to, George announced he was on his way to Edmonton and thence down the Mackenzie to join Captain Louis Lane to help establish a new American-owned fur trading concern in the Mackenzie Valley and the Arctic coast, to compete with the HBC and other Canadian fur trading companies. Although it was not stated in the article, the firm was indeed Lamson and Hubbard. George's involvement would entail building a motor tug, a large river steamer, and a two-masted schooner. The first two vessels turned out to be the motor tug *Canadusa* (constructed at Waterways, Alberta, in 1919) and the large steam sternwheeler SS *Distributor* (built at Fort Smith, Northwest Territories, from 1919-1920). It is not known what type the third vessel was, or if it was actually constructed.

Photo 6-1

Alberta Great Waterways Railway, 1920, problems building on muskeg.
Provincial Archives of Alberta photograph A3892

Photo 6-2

Hudson's Bay Company tug *Canadusa* pushing a barge filled with supplies.
Provincial Archives of Alberta photograph A1537

Obviously, the planning for the operation had been in place for some time as it was announced by the company in a *Winnipeg Free Press* article of 10 April 1919 that "...no less than 17 carloads machinery and fittings [had] gone forward to Fort McMurray and on their way to Fort Smith." The plan was to send all of the cars to the end of steel on the A&GW railway which, still under construction, was short of its objective. (Fort McMurray was in Alberta, and Fort Smith, 235 miles to the north, in the Northwest Territories.)

This forwarded material included lumber, preassembled ship parts and machinery, and the two large tractors and six wagons that Lamson and Hubbard would use in modernizing transportation at Smith Portage on the Athabasca River. In preparation for construction of a new vessel, the *Distributor III*, the boiler and engines and other equipment from her predecessor *Distributor I* (of Skeena River fame and reused for *Distributor II)*, were part of these shipments. (*Distributor II* had operated on the Thompson River for Canadian Northern Railway construction.)

The transportation must have been a formidable task in its own right. At the time the railway, although started before WWI, had never really been completed. Trains ran as far as Lac La Biche and ties and track extended to a location above the Clearwater River where it was entered by the Christina River, then known as Cache 23, about 12 miles upstream of the eventual depot at Waterways (now a neighbourhood on the southern edge of the Fort McMurray urban service area).

This final portion of track—which extended over muskeg and had not been stabilized or properly ballasted—was not capable of carrying heavy trains and already had resulted in deaths when a locomotive turned over into the muskeg. (Muskeg is a type of northern landscape characterized by a wet environment, vegetation and peat deposits.) Final delivery of needed materials carried in train cars were more successful as a winter operation when the ground was frozen and when loads could be hauled on sleighs by horse teams along the river. It was therefore necessary to get this train of goods moved over the unstable roadbed, down the slope to the Clearwater River and along the ice of the river while everything was still frozen.

Photo 6-3

Wooden vessel *Distributor* under construction.
NWT Archives photograph N-2002-005-0078 (Norman Robinson)

No details remain how this was carried out, nor the extent of George's involvement, but the results are known. By the end of 1919, the *Canadusa* (probably carried to the Clearwater River in knocked-downed sections) had been assembled and launched at Waterways and supplies and materials for the construction of the *Distributor III* (hereafter referred to as *Distributor)* had been moved from Waterways down the Athabasca and Slave rivers and over Smith Portage to allow construction of the vessel to commence.

A building site had been prepared, and accommodation and supplies for the crew that were to build and launch the large ship were in hand. An article "Rivals for Fur" by Arthur Ray in the Canadian history magazine *The Beaver* noted in the April-May 1990 edition that "Accordingly, in the spring of 1919 Lamson and Hubbard began construction of a stern-wheeler for use between Fort Smith and Fort McPherson [in the Northwest Territories]." This information indicated that parts of the hull had been erected by the end of the 1919 season. It is not known whether George returned to Vancouver over the winter of 1919-1920.

A 12 March 1920 *Edmonton Journal* newspaper article indicated a Vancouver-based, eleven-man shipbuilding crew was mobilized and was being sent to Fort Smith. They must have been a hardy lot as they had to mush by dog sled more than 300 miles down the frozen Clearwater, Athabasca and Slave rivers, and over the Smith Portage, to reach the construction site to continue the work started in 1919. It is very likely that George was part of this gruelling mush.

Progress at Fort Smith was swift, enabling *Distributor* to be launched, in front of local and company dignitaries, on 3 August 1920 by Miss Alma Guest of Lamson and Hubbard's Edmonton office (described in the *Edmonton Journal* of 28 August 1920). *Distributor* was finished to an extent that she was able to complete a "shake-down cruise" to the Arctic and back before winter haul-out at Fort Smith. It was probably on this cruise that George experienced the oil gusher at Norman Wells and obtained the samples that he returned with to Vancouver (*Vancouver Daily World*, 8 January 1921).

Details of George's travels during 1920 following the haul-out of the *Distributor* are as yet unknown. He did not return in 1921 when a crew was sent in to add cabins on the "Texas deck" and complete final finishing, as he obtained new assignments from the HBC (Alexander Watson apparently took over the work).

Distributor was an exceedingly successful and popular vessel for various owners. Although the duration of her service was exceeded by the smaller and older "sister" SS *Mackenzie River*, *Distributor* was probably the best-known and loved of all Mackenzie River vessels. Thousands of passengers of all northern pursuits, as well as many tourists and adventurers, helped to spread the vessel's fame, including Canada's Governor General. At one time the main deck was used as a court room for a murder trial. There were no materials that left or entered the Arctic which did not occupy the freight deck or the commodious barges pushed or carried alongside.

Throughout World War II, with her "sister" and dozens of other vessels, *Distributor* did yeoman's work, particularly for the US Army, by supporting the construction of the Canadian Oil (Canol) pipeline that ran from Norman Wells to Whitehorse. In the early days of her service, mountains of cordwood were gobbled, previously cut and stacked alongside the river, and in later years, the boiler was warmed by burning numerous barrels of Norman Wells crude.

Photo 6-4

Captain Don Naylor of the *Distributor*, 1936.
Hudson's Bay Company Archives, Archives of Manitoba
By Richard Hourde while on assignment for *The Beaver magazine*, 1987/271/NB22

7

Working for the Hudson's Bay Company, 1921-1924

The little craft only draws about six inches of water light and about eight inches loaded. Capt. Askew laughingly stated that on a good rainy day the ship might be able to find her way along Granville Street without much difficulty. She may have some difficulty in negotiating the tunnels on her way over the Rockies, however, for there is only about half an inch to spare in width in complying with the regulations of the railway.

—*Vancouver World*, 28 March 1921, announcing shipping of motorboat *Weenusk*.

George's subsequent employment with the Hudson's Bay Company (HBC) allowed him to develop and perfect the designs for tunnel boats—that were copied by others and which became the standard of river transport and tugs on the Mackenzie and other river systems throughout the world, and afforded him the opportunity to build his last large steam sternwheeler.

In 1921 he did not return to Fort Smith to complete cabins on the "Texas deck" or other work on the *Distributor*. With his wife pregnant with their second child, he accepted a new position with the HBC. Under newly appointed Fur Trade Commissioner Angus Brabant, the HBC was mounting a huge effort—in essence a corporate fight-to-the-death—to resist Lamson and Hubbard and its partners' intrusion into their traditional business and trading area. The HBC also wished to prevent the newcomers from gaining dominance of the river transportation business, which in the face of Norman Wells oil finds, was attracting huge interest.

In a partnership deal, Lamson and Hubbard had combined their transportation assets (including those purchased from the David A. Thomas estate) together with those of the old BX Corporation, which formerly operated river steamers on the upper Fraser River in BC, into a new corporation, the Alberta and Arctic Transportation Company (A&AT).

This large fleet, together with the announced rebuilding of the BX Company vessel *BC Express* at Waterways (that apparently never happened) by Alexander Watson, posed potentially dangerous competition to HBC's aging fleet on both the upper and lower main stem of the Mackenzie River system. On the upper Peace, the HBC no longer had any operating vessels as, after retiring the original SS *Athabasca River*, they had contracted out their transportation needs to the Peace River Development Company.

BUILDING ELEVEN VESSELS IN CITY

Ships Valued at Close to Quarter Million Dollar Mark Being Constructed for Hudson's Bay.

Work Commencing in April and Continuing Until Late in Fall.

Eleven vessels, ranging in size from gas boats to big stern wheelers over 200 feet in length, with a total value of well over $200,000, will be built in this city for the Hudson's Bay Company for operation on the Mackenzie River during the coming spring and summer months, according to information given The World by an official of the company who is making arrangements for the commencement of the work.

While several of the boats will be "knocked down" here and shipped up the Mackenzie, where they will be completed, at least six vessels will be completed here and shipped. The big ship which is being constructed at the B. C. Marine Ways for the Hudson's Bay Company will probably carry four small schooners, each forty-two feet in length, on her decks when she goes north in a few months.

The building programme has as its most important item a 210-foot stern wheeler. It was announced in The World a few days ago that two of these ships would be built, but, according to later information, it has been decided to build only one large ship for the present. This vessel will be worth probably $80,000 or $90,000 when completed.

Commence in April.

There are the four schooners referred to and a big gas boat for the Peace River. This craft will be about sixty feet in length and will be completed here. A big scow will be built here and assembled up north. A barge is also on the programme to be built and knocked down here. The remainder of the work planned will include power schooners and gas boats.

Work on the big order will be commenced in April, and it will be well into the fall before the work is completed. A shipyard crew of from fifty to one hundred men will be given steady employment. A larger payroll may be necessary if the work does not proceed as rapidly as planned.

Easily Converted.

It is interesting to note that the big stern-wheeler is to be fitted with furnaces which will permit the use of wood, coal or oil. The ship will be convertible in ten minutes' time. The oil used will, of course, be that obtained in the north, the ships being operated in that vicinity.

As to the location of the yard where the ships will be built, while plans are not yet complete, it is understood that two sites are being looked over. One of these is in the East End of the city, on Burrard Inlet, and the other is on False Creek. This detail of the work will be completed within the next few days. The work is not being let out by contract, the Hudson's Bay Company having their own shipyard officials.

Progress of HBC Shipbuilding in Vancouver was important news.
Vancouver World, 8 January 1921

In an article in the *Vancouver Sun* of 29 December 1920, Captain Tom P. O'Kelly, assistant Chief Commissioner, announced the intended construction of two sternwheelers stating that "Mr. George Askew is now preparing the plans for these vessels. They will be built, if reasonable tenders are received, on the shores of Burrard Inlet, one being for the Athabasca and Lower Peace and the second one designed for the Mackenzie River Trade." The latter vessel was never built. (Burrard Inlet on the southwest mainland coast of British Columbia, constitutes Vancouver Harbour, with arms extending into neighbouring mountainous terrain.)

A follow-up announcement on the progress of HBC's overall Vancouver shipbuilding program, that included vessels for their northern river system and the Arctic, was published in the *Vancouver World* of 8 January 1921 (see preceding page). The article reported that the number of large sternwheelers—originally announced as two—for the time being had been reduced to only one.

George's new employment was fortuitous. It provided him with several years of good work as the HBC expanded its Arctic fur trade, along the western Arctic coast and even into Siberia, and replaced and upgraded their Mackenzie basin fleet (which supplied their established posts along the Mackenzie system). Through the end of 1923, his employment arrangements as "General Superintendent of Steam and Motorboat Building" apparently were for ship design and construction supervision, while actual fabrication and assembly in the field was by HBC contractors or their employees. This allowed George to spend more time in Vancouver, enjoy time in his home with his young family, and to rejoin his friends in the RVYC in boating activities, especially in sailboat racing.

In 1921, George delivered his first HBC vessel that was intended to re-establish their transportation capability on the upper Peace River. As previously mentioned, HBC's transportation needs in this area had been contracted out to the PRDC since the retirement of HBC's original SS *Athabasca River* in 1918. However, Angus Brabant (HBC) could not let this continue with Lamson and Hubbard in control after the sale of PRDC's vessels to the new joint-venture subsidiary A&AT.

Brabant's solution was George's 60-foot motor boat *Weenusk*, a low-draft tunnel boat of the *Lady Mackworth* and *Canadusa* type, with cabins for passengers and a capability of pushing a barge for larger freight. The *Province* of 18 March 1921, informed its readers that the new vessel was built in Vancouver with coast wood, then shipped to Peace River by railway—a process that George advocated for smaller vessels and parts for larger vessels.

Photo 7-1

Motor boat *Weenusk* with barge *Fort Vermilion* (by Askew) at Peace River 1922. Glenbow Archives photograph NA-639-2

In late March 1921, as the new vessel was being dispatched by rail to Alberta, George was interviewed by the *Vancouver World.* His response to a reporter's question regarding the vessel was that he was more concerned about the railway tunnel clearances than the draft. As previously noted, the vessel barely met railway clearances, there being only one-half inch to spare. Following building at Chappell Brothers Shipyard in Coal Harbour and testing in Burrard Inlet, the vessel had been taken to the CPR steamship dock and lifted onto a rail flatcar for shipping. Three cars were involved to provide the proper clearances and also because a considerable quantity of lumber was being loaded (presumably for barge construction). *Weenusk* was a very successful vessel and served for many years. (Five 75-foot barges attributed to Askew were also assembled at Peace River, Fort McMurray and Fort Smith that summer.)

Two slightly smaller 48-foot tunnel boats, built to George's design, and two associated barges quickly followed the first delivery. They were for HBC's fur trading venture to Siberia. The names lettered on the bow "Собепь" and "Весенъ" appear to be similar to the Russian words for "Sable" and "Spring" according to Galina Sanaeva, Professor of Russian Languages at the University of Victoria, but may also have been names sounding like "Sobel" and "Vesen."

The vessels were constructed by shipwright P. McMillan, also at Chappell Brothers Shipyard, at Coal Harbour. The boats and barges left Vancouver on 19 May 1921 as deck cargo on the motor vessel *Casco* which HBC had chartered to pioneer this new Siberia venture. The enterprise is described in a well-illustrated article by John MacFarlane

(Nauticapedia.ca, 2020) titled "The Hudson's Bay Company Venture in Siberia." A September 1938 article from *The Beaver*, "Trading into Siberia" by L. R. M. Beavis, Master Mariner, also describes this short and ill-fated experiment on the Kamchatka Peninsula.

Photo 7-2

Barge under construction at Peace River, the man is thought to be Askew.
Courtesy Ron David family collection, circa 1921-1930

Photo 7-3

Kamchatka launches alongside motor vessel *Casco*.
Courtesy of the Brabant collection

With expertise in wooden ship design and construction, access to competent shipyards in Vancouver and improving rail access to the Mackenzie system, George was well-positioned to provide vessels, and vessel parts, made from desired west coast lumber. For a period, it was a halcyon time, but then on 9 October 1921, just four days after the birth of his second son John Douglas Askew, his wife Mary Agnes died from complications arising from the birth. In order that he continue with his work, George had to call upon his sister Julia Arnould and her family in Sardis to care for his two young boys.

George's next assignment was construction of a replacement for the deteriorating sternwheeler SS *Fort McMurray* built in 1915. Her successor, the SS *Athabasca River II*, was a 148-foot vessel (not quite the 210-foot vessel mentioned in the clipping above), very similar to the SS *Distributor*. She was built of superior coast lumber and equipped with machinery from HBC's retired Skeena River steamer the SS *Fort Simpson*.

While veteran HBC Mackenzie River Captain Haight took a crew to Prince Rupert to recover boilers and engines, George drew up the plans and oversaw the fabrication of hull components and preassembly on the Canada Lumber Company ways (located in Vancouver at the foot of Smythe Street, near Cambie Bridge, in False Creek). Because the railway was still incomplete into Waterways, George again had to contend with a final difficult delivery in winter for hull parts and machinery. As before, this action involved sliding the valuable freight down the slope from the railway to the Clearwater River, and hauling it on the river ice with teams of horses.

Photo 7-4

George Askew with son Francis in framing of *Athabasca River* before shipping north. Askew family collection

Photo 7-5

Extraction of boiler from *Fort Simpson* (previous photograph) at Prince Rupert, and installation in *Athabasca River* at Waterways.
Askew family collection

Athabasca River was soon assembled and, with much fanfare and publicity, launched on 3 June 1922. She proved to be a very successful and reliable vessel and served the HBC on the Waterways to Fort Fitzgerald, Alberta, route until after World War II.

Photo 7-6

Launching of *Athabasca River*, June 1922.
Askew family collection

A 14 November 1922 *Province* article mentioned the busy and successful first season of operation of the *Athabasca River*. In a caption below the photo of the vessel (as well as extolling the success of George's tunnel boats and the superior BC quality wood and its longevity in comparison to locally milled Waterways' wood), there was mention that Askew had also been busy with non-HBC work. It was not stated whether the craft he built were for HBC's customers or for George's personal clientele:

> While in the North last summer Mr. Askew built a number of sail and auxiliary craft for the [Inuit] at the mouth of the Mackenzie and received orders for several more. The operators of boats [praised] the superior qualities of B.C. fir as boat material, and now all specify this timber …

In 1923 with the railway still not complete into Waterways, George's next task in upgrading the HBC's fleet was to assemble four new Vancouver-sourced vessels at Waterways. One vessel the *Fort Nelson* was an 81-foot tow barge for use on the Athabasca River. Another, a 41-foot gasoline motor boat *Fond du Lac*, was for use on Lake Athabasca. The other vessels, respectively, would be put into service on the Mackenzie system downstream of Fort Smith and on the Arctic Ocean. The first of the northern vessels was a 60-foot shallow draft motor boat/tug of tunnel boat design, the motor boat *Liard River II*. This boat replaced a short-lived steam-driven sternwheeler of the same name which had been wrecked in 1921, while employed pushing supply barges on the Liard River and other waterways downstream of Fort Smith in the Northwest Territories.

Like many of George's other vessels, the new *Liard River* was very successful, with long service. In 1933, in validation of her design and shallow-draft, she was the first HBC vessel to navigate up the notorious rock-strewn rapids of the Great Bear River to haul supplies to the developing mines of Great Bear Lake. This lake, in the Northwest Territories, is the largest such entirely within Canada, located astride the Arctic Circle.

Photo 7-7

Motor boat *Liard River*, June 1923.
Louis August Romanet fonds, UAA-1972-081-007-001-009-523, University of Alberta Archives, Edmonton, Alberta, Canada.

The other northern vessel was the 51-foot deep-draft motor schooner *Aklavik* ordered for use on the Arctic Ocean to support the HBC's expanding fur trade in the western Arctic. In 1937, under trader Ernest James "Scotty" Gall, she gained fame as being the first vessel ever to navigate Bellot Strait in the Northwest Passage.

Photo 7-8

Vessel framed in Vancouver shipyard believed to be the motor schooner *Aklavik*. Askew family collection

Photo 7-9

Aklavik under Scotty Gall's command completing first navigation of Bellot Strait. From Wikimedia Commons. Original Source believed to be Hudson's Bay Archives, Archives of Manitoba, View of HBC *Aklavik* from RMS *Nascopie*, 1937, Prentice G. Downes fonds, ca 1937, HBCA 1984/31/

According to the Vancouver Directory for 1923, George worked for Coughlan shipbuilders that year. In the spring of 1924 Lamson and Hubbard finally "threw in the towel" over the expensive battle with the HBC. The surviving company (HBC) acquired all of the shares of the A&AT Company, inheriting their mostly modern fleet of river craft, all of which were retained except for the older sternwheeler SS *Slave River* (formerly an HBC upper-Athabasca River steamer), which was disassembled near Waterways.

The exuberance over the oil discoveries at Norman Wells abated significantly after 1921, slowing investment in drilling and transportation. This resulted from difficulties in bringing the high-quality oil to market, and the high cost of maintaining oil leases pending development. (This type oil was burned in diesel engines that had been started and warmed on conventional fuel.) These factors contributed generally to a hiatus for the need for shipbuilding in the Mackenzie River basin for George and other builders, until the economy picked up again after the Great Depression. In the meantime, they turned to other pursuits.

Photo 7-10

First Imperial Oil well, Norman Wells, Northwest Territories, 1920.
Glenbow Archives photograph NA-503-4

When he returned home to Vancouver for the winter of 1923, George decided he needed help raising his sons Francis, 5, and John, 2. He advertised for a housekeeper and offered the job to a German divorcee from Milwaukee, Wisconsin, Ella May Schneider Hubbard, who was just seven years his junior. The arrangement was clearly a success. George and Ella were married on New Year's Eve of 1923, and the boys developed a lasting love for their new mother. She guided them through their school years, cooked wonderful meals at the family home on Adanac Street (formerly Union), sent the boys off with generous picnic lunches when they sailed the gulf islands with George on weekends and became the glue that held the family together when George was "up north."

8

Contract Work for HBC in 1926 and 1930

George Askew Vancouver contractor for the Hudson's Bay Company reached here Tuesday from the Pacific Coast to take personal charge of the building of one or more flat bottom vessels to take the place of the D. A. Thomas. *Askew is building a flat bottom vessel, gasoline powered, of 50 tons, capable of hauling one or more grain barges in the river trade.*

—*Edmonton Journal*, 5 June 1930, from Peace River, Alberta.

Despite overall depressed shipbuilding opportunities in the Mackenzie basin, two construction opportunities opened for George that are worthy of mention. Unlike his previous employment, this work was by direct contract between George and the HBC. The first opportunity occurred in 1926. In accordance with an article in the *Edmonton Journal* of 7 August of that year, George was awarded a $20,000 contract to build a "gigantic" 300-ton capacity covered barge to be used with the SS *Distributor* on the lower Mackenzie.

The 133-foot vessel (nearly as long as *Distributor* to which she would be made up, and propelled by the 151-foot vessel) *Barge 300* also offered cabins for passengers. In addition to providing extra passenger capacity, use of the barge increased *Distributor*'s freight capacity from 250 to 550 tons.

The barge was prefabricated in Vancouver and transported knocked-down (disassembled) to Waterways by rail. As soon as navigation was open after spring ice break-up on the Athabasca River, the vessel components were taken by river transport to Fort Fitzgerald and then over Smith Portage to Fort Smith. There, they were assembled and the resultant vessel launched. The large barge had a successful life until 1938, when it was wrecked on a rock near Fort Simpson with the loss of a large cargo of Arctic supplies. Fortunately, as reported in the September 1938 issue of *The Beaver*, all passengers were saved when they were able to scramble onto the *Distributor*. Additionally, the HBC through expedient action, was able to ship duplicate vital supplies in time for delivery in the summer Arctic season.

Photo 8-1

Sternwheeler *Distributor* and *Barge 300* in 1936; three men boarding the barge via a makeshift walkway leading from the shore, are wisely wearing bathing suits.
First published in *The Beaver* June 1943; digital image HB-001578 by Richard Hourde

The other opportunity occurred in 1930, when the HBC decided to retire the *D. A. Thomas* from the upper Peace River. She was navigated down the Vermilion Rapids and Chutes and, while suffering some damage en route, eventually reached Fort Fitzgerald, Alberta, under her own power. There, she lived out her days as a grain-store warehouse. To partially replace the capacity of the *D. A. Thomas* on the upper Peace, George was given a contract to design and build a motor vessel and barge(s) to provide replacement passenger and freight service.

The replacement (a wooden vessel presumably also prefabricated in Vancouver) was named *Buffalo Lake*. The 91-foot twin propeller-driven craft, which looked like a cross between a sternwheeler and a tunnel boat, was fitted with heavy-duty Vivian engines that were reported to be "gas guzzlers." Their appetite for large quantities of fuel—in the face of the Depression-shrunken economy—resulted in the vessel being "out-of-commission" (usable, but not used) from 1932-1939. In 1939 the offending engines were removed and the high-quality vessel became *Barge 87*.

Buffalo Lake was the last wooden, powered-vessel launched on the Peace River for the HBC. The honour of being the final vessels built fell to river tugs *Weenusk II* constructed in 1940, and *Watson Lake* built in 1946. They were both steel vessels but incorporating the tunnel-design pioneered by George. The latter tug served only until 1952, when all marine transportation was withdrawn by the HBC. An interesting history of river transportation in this area appears in the March 1953 issue of *The Beaver* magazine "An Era Closes" by Norman Soars.

Photo 8-2

Launching of *Buffalo Lake* on east bank of the Peace River. *Weenusk* is astern of her. Askew family collection

9

Yachts and Commercial Vessels Built in Vancouver, 1924-1939

LADY VAN *CAPTURES THOMAS LIPTON CUP… Sailing with Mr. [Jack] Cribb on the last race were Norman Gyles, George Askew and [Harold] Harry Jones.*

—*Vancouver Sun*, 4 July 1929.

Photo 9-1

Location of former Askew shipyard below Burrard Bridge. Main building shed and ways were near the east end of the large white building to the left in this photograph. City of Vancouver Archives photograph CVA 586-683

In conjunction with contracted shipbuilding, George also had his own boatbuilding business. Beginning in 1924, when he built his own personal sailboat, the *Doris*, and was able to spend more time in Vancouver, the focus of this business became centered on the construction of smaller commercial boats and yachts for individual owners. George never wanted for a location to ply his trade, whether it was in the heart of Vancouver or at the edge of some northern river, if he had an order to fill.

Photo 9-2

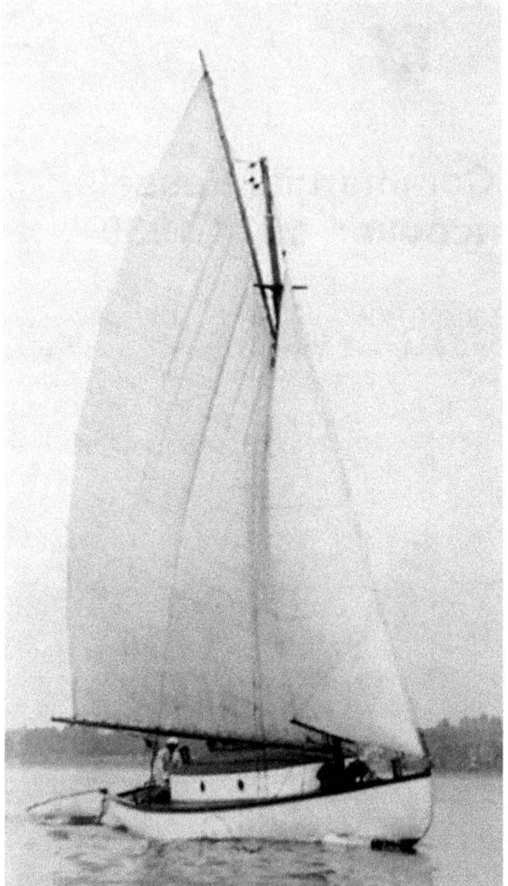

George's yacht *Doris* built 1924.
Askew family collection

Starting in 1926 (as evidenced in *Wrigley's British Columbia Directory*) and continuing until 1937 (*Sun Directory*), George had a boatbuilding business at 1050 Beach Avenue in Vancouver. (His former yard is the present location of the aquatic centre just west of the Burrard Bridge.) According to family lore, the yard was foreclosed on in the mid-thirties. As reported in the *Vancouver Sun* of 15 February 1938, a rezoning application was made on behalf of Home Oil Company, which had a marine bulk storage at the adjacent 1068 Beach Avenue site. Following an order from the Fire Marshall for the buildings on both sites to be demolished, the company sought to have both properties rezoned in order to erect a concrete warehouse.

Map 9-1

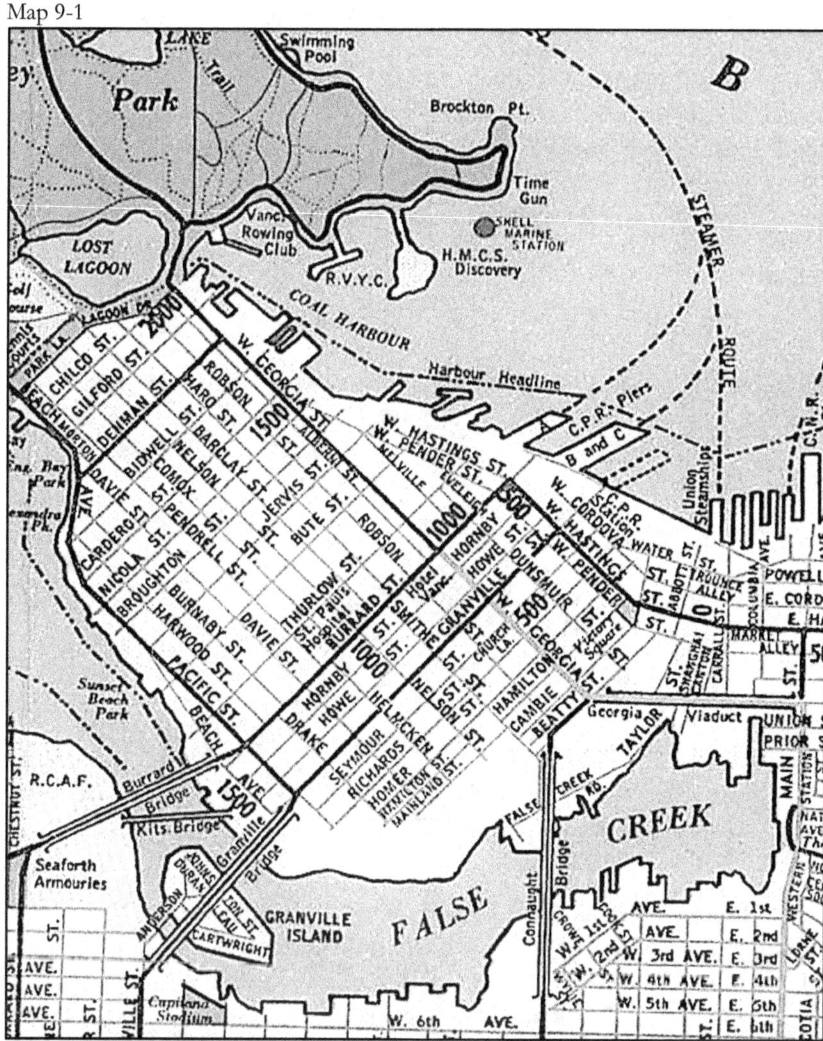

Downtown Vancouver BC portion of Shell Oil Street map of Greater Victoria, BC and Greater Vancouver, BC, circa 1948. Askew shipyard (demolished) was at east end of Burrard Bridge on north side.
City of Vancouver Archives, AM 1594 - LEG 1335.4

As evidenced in Appendix A, many of the vessels constructed at George's boatyard were fine sailing yachts and motor yachts for associates at the Royal Vancouver Yacht Club that are celebrated in the annals of that organization. Particularly notable are the forty-foot yawls *White Wings* (*Westward Ho*), *Nelmar*, and *Hereanthere* and a cutter *Cresset*. *Hereanthere* became George's family yacht, and served as his son Francis' home during his WWII army service at Esquimalt. George saved it from the shipyard foreclosure proceeding by placing it under the ownership of his cousin Marian Arnould in 1936.

A 39-foot power cruiser, *Leola V*, built for his friend and colleague engine-builder William Vivian, was used by Vivian to showcase his engines. The 61-foot *Yukon Rose* was another fine example of George's expertise in low-draft tunnel boats.

Photo 9-3

Yukon Rose on trials in False Creek, Vancouver.
Askew family collection

George won a competition to design and build *Windor,* a star-class racing sailor for the Los Angeles Olympic Games. She placed third.

During his tenure on Beach Avenue, George's neighbour to the east was the Burrard Bridge construction project, which was completed and opened in 1932. His boatbuilding contribution to the project was fabricating forms for the four boat-prows, one on each side of the north and south main portal structures. These towers host busts of Captain George Vancouver and Sir Harry Burrard-Neale crafted by sculptor George Lister Thorton. Vancouver was the Royal Navy explorer who charted much of the Pacific Northwest coast. He named the inlet (Burrard Inlet) where the City of Vancouver is located in honour of Burrard, a famous British admiral and high-ranking member of the British aristocracy.

Photo 9-4

North end of the Burrard Bridge; bust on the right is of Sir Harry Burrard, situated nearly above the old Askew boatyard.
Photo courtesy of Simon Bancroft

There was a reduction of ship and boatbuilding activity after the early 1930s with little interest in commercial vessels, let alone building yachts, as the Great Depression touched every corner of the coast. It is hard to judge if maintenance work helped, but many yards suffered and many more failed.

During this period George revelled in many successes in his passion for sailboat racing, including building and racing 53-inch racing models (sailed like pond models in the harbour accompanied by rowboats), 15-foot kitten-class dinghies, and the famous R-class boats of the Royal Vancouver Yacht Club. It was in 1929, when he sailed with his friend and long-time colleague Jack Cullen aboard *Lady Van*, that the RVYC finally wrested the Lipton Cup from *Sir Tom* of the Seattle Yacht Club. Cullen, the lead challenger, formerly apprenticed with George as a shipwright when they both were working on GTP steamers on the Skeena River. Of course, sailboat racing didn't pay the bills, and during this period while searching for a means of income, George again looked to the North.

Photo 9-5

Yacht *Lady Van,* winner of the Lipton Cup in 1929. George is on left, the others are Jack Cribb, Harold (Harry) Jones and Norman Gyles, order not presently known. Askew family collection

10

The Great Bear Lake Shipbuilding Boom, 1934

$100,000 CONTRACT FOR CITY – BOATS FOR GREAT BEAR LAKE

—Headline, *Vancouver Sun*, 20 April 1934.

The progression of mining, a result of mineral discoveries in the Great Bear Lake region, from exploratory to production phases, provided early relief from the dirge of the Great Depression in the Mackenzie Valley. In the early 1930s both silver and radium concentrates were beginning to be produced from the area. A 21 August 1931 headline from the *Regina Leader Post* extolled: "20 Tons, Valued at $8,000 a Ton, Sent South From Great Bear Lake" the first such shipment made.

While bush pilots and their aircraft materially facilitated the mining boom, it became apparent that increased water-borne transportation was required to service the mines. Vessels were needed to bring in equipment, supplies, and vital fuel that was then available from the Norman Wells finds, and haul out the mineral concentrates produced. Providing such service was a formidable task. Passage from the Mackenzie Valley up the Great Bear River provided a marine link to Great Bear Lake, but it was a shallow, rock-strewn route hostile even to the small-draft vessels that were able to navigate it.

It wasn't smooth sailing once vessels successfully arrived at the lake as the mines were mostly located on the eastern shore. These had to be reached across one of the largest and deepest lakes in Canada, one open to wind and large waves. The initial solution, before a bypass road around the worst of the rapids could be constructed (including the associated pipeline and storage tanks) was to use shallow-draft vessels on the river. On reaching the lake, their cargos were then transferred to deeper draft vessels providing both hatched-holds and wide deck space. In this way, vital fuel supplies were carried using thousands of barrels, all the way from Norman Wells to the mines.

HBC's *Liard River* and another privately-owned vessel, the schooner *North Star*, had demonstrated the feasibility of navigating the river. In 1933 *Liard River* transited the river, crossed the lake, and brought in supplies, but larger capacity, in more suitable vessels, was required.

Photo 10-1

Motor tug *Liard River* and her barge near the head of the rapids on the Great Bear River.
NWT Archives photograph N-1981-002&Item_Number=0009

Competing factions to supply the mines and take away product resulted in a huge shipbuilding program in 1934 at both Fort McMurray and Fort Smith. The Arctic Transportation division of HBC was one of those involved, and the Northern Transportation Company (which was almost concurrently being morphed out of a division of White Eagle Silver Mines) was the other. As reported in the *Vancouver Sun* of 20 April 1934, George's Vancouver shipbuilding business was able to obtain a $100,000 contract for supplying two vessels and two barges.

These were a 70-foot motorized sternwheeler (registered initially simply as *Sternwheeler*, but later known as *Silver Queen* that would operate on the rivers); a 91-foot deeper draft tunnel boat, *Great Bear* for use on Great Bear Lake; and two 71-foot shallow draft barges (N.T. *Barge 3* and *4*), probably designed for use on the Great Bear River.

Photo 10-2

Sternwheeler *Silver Queen* pushing a low-draft barge loaded with empty barrels for oil wells, at foot of rapids road, August 1937.
Library and Archives Canada/4-584e-1937-MM

As evidenced by an *Edmonton Journal* article of 3 April 1934 an even larger order of vessels, valued at $122,000, was obtained by George's rival, the Northern Boat Building Company out of Edmonton under Captain John Matheson. This order included two large 81-foot tugs, and an 80-foot shallow-draft barge for the HBC, as well as three 90-foot deep-draft barges (one motorized) and two scows. (The deep-draft barges and scows were for the same White Eagle Silver Bay mines group as George's order.)

With the exception of the *Great Bear* (built at Fort Smith), all of George's vessels were assembled and launched at Waterways, sailed to Fort Fitzgerald, then taken over Smith Portage by trailer and launched for service at Fort Smith. Matheson's vessels were assembled at a shipyard at Fort Smith, high on the river bank, and dragged down the slope for launching.

Richard S. Finnie, noted northern historian and photographer, witnessed and recorded all the hectic activities of northern transportation and shipbuilding in a series of syndicated newspaper articles in the summer of 1934. By early August, new ship construction—along with rapid launchings—increased congestion at Fort Smith. At this time, huge amounts of fur trade freight, increased by the additional requirements for the Great Bear Lake mines, streamed across Smith Portage.

At Normal Wells, thousands of barrels of petroleum products were filled in anticipation of the new vessels taking them to the mine sites. Finnie, always ready to document with first-hand experience, hitched a ride on Matheson's new *N.P. Barge 1* down the Mackenzie, ensconced in her cargo hold, to record the initial arrival.

On the Bear River (where George's new *Great Bear* took over as a pusher tug, joined by HBC's new *Hearne Lake*, a similar barge and series of smaller craft), the competitors began a heroic struggle with their powerful engines and winches and miles of cable and dug-in "dead men" (log anchors in filled-in pits in the ground) to ascend the shallow, rocky stream not welcoming to vessels of their draft. Eventually, in spite of a series of mishaps and bruised hulls, the larger vessels were able to reach the lake.

With the assistance of other members of the new fleet and existing vessels, the Great Bear Lake mines received all their freight, including fuel and supplies that would enable them to operate through the coming winter. It was an epic achievement attributable to the shipbuilders and the crews of the vessels. Finnie recorded his experiences on the river as part of his newspaper articles and followed up with a magazine article, "Battling the Great Bear," on the same topic in *The Beaver* issue of March 1935.

Photo 10-3

Eldorado Mine, with tunnel boat *Great Bear* and barge unloading at Mill Sites, Great Bear Lake, NWT, 1935.
Library and Archives Canada/photograph 3398155

11

The Pre-war Years, 1935-1939

Departing on the same train with the Sorel [Québec] crew was a party of 17 Vancouver ship builders also employed by the Northern Transport company for the building of barges in the north. They plan to construct five steel (sic) barges with tonnage approximately 700 tons in all. It was explained by George Askew who will be in charge of the work.

—*Edmonton Journal*, 6 April 1937.

Following his work for the Northern Transportation Company in 1934, and the loss of his Beach Avenue property about 1937, things appear to have been dismal for George as Canada worked itself out of the Depression. An illustration of the bleakness of the situation in Vancouver appeared in a 16 February 1935 *Vancouver Sun* article about the Boeing boat and aircraft building firm in the city, which indicated that their normal number of employees of 250 were down to only 50. There were only two entries during 1935 and 1936 related to George, who was often featured in local news. The *Vancouver Sun* announced on 9 November 1935 that he was that year's recipient of the RVYC Bird Rock trophy, after running his prized yawl *Hereanthere* on a rock in Porlier Pass, resulting in a ruined keel and a badly damaged centerboard. The following year, an article in the *Province* on 8 June 1936 informed readers that he was building a 40-foot tunnel boat for Lamb Lumber Co. to be used for handling logs on Mohun Lake on Vancouver Island.

One of the factors that helped improve the economy in western Canada in the 1930s was the continuing expansion of the mining industry in the north, particularly on Great Bear Lake, Great Slave Lake, and Lake Athabasca where finds at the Goldfields camp were being developed. On Great Bear Lake, the mining companies continued to vastly increase production, straining the capacities of available water transportation. At the time, radium—sought-after for cancer treatment and other purposes—was the most valuable material in the world, fetching upwards of $70,000 per gram before the Great Bear mines began production, reducing the value to $25,000 per gram (*Edmonton*

Journal, 26 March 1938). For every gram produced, enough pitchblende ore had to be mined and processed at Great Bear Lake to ship six-and-one-half tons of concentrate to the refinery in Ontario (*Edmonton Journal*, 31 August 1934). To support the mining and processing operation on the lake, vast quantities of fuel had to be moved from Norman Wells up the Great Bear River and across the lake.

In 1936 contractors for the federal government finally completed a portage road around the upper rapids of the Great Bear River, allowing inbound freight and outbound ore to be transported by truck around this impediment. Also, the means of quenching its thirst for fuel from the source at Norman Wells—which had been supplied by the transportation of fuel in thousands of barrels on river barges—was being improved. In 1937 a pipeline was to be constructed alongside the new road with storage tanks at each end. Two other tanks were to make up the system. One of these was to be located at Fort Franklin, Northwest Territories (to receive bulk shipments from river barges and to load deeper-draft lake barges) and the other tank was to be a receiving one at the mine site at Port Radium. The intent was to replace the two-way barrel transport on barges with tanker barges on both the lake and the rivers below the portage road.

In late 1936 newspapers announced that the Northern Transportation Company (NTCL) was being taken over by the Labine-led El Dorado Gold Corporation, the largest mine operator on Great Bear Lake. (Gilbert Labine was the discoverer of the rich Great Bear Lake deposits and a principal of the corporation that was developing them.) In other news, well-known local bush pilot Matt Berry (who, together with his mechanic Rex Terpening, had just been lauded for an amazing Arctic rescue of Roman Catholic missionaries) took over the field management of the transportation company, and a major investment in new marine assets was in the works. Because transportation needs for the lake had nearly doubled between 1934 and 1935, and almost tripled by 1936 (*Edmonton Journal*, 25 September 1937), NTCL, with the financial backing of El Dorado, initiated a major ship and barge acquisition program. It involved contract-procured ships and barges constructed by the company's own forces.

George and his sons were a part of this undertaking. George may have been, in fact, the field superintendent. The *Edmonton Journal* of 6 April 1937 noted the departure of crews, including seventeen Vancouver shipbuilders, with those from a Québec-based ship supplier. The *Journal* announced that George had control of five vessels of the barge building aspect of the work in the field. It is suspected that his involvement in the project may have extended into advising on design. An article in *Pacific Motor Boat* of October 1944, titled "George Askew; His Riverboats Have Pioneered Canada's Far North Frontier," informed readers that:

> Askew has designed several other vessels for the Northern Transportation Company in addition to the sternwheeler now been completed. [The sternwheeler in question, launched in 1944 was named the *George Askew*, obviously an honour to him and a reflection of his regard by the company.]

The total program included the acquisition of the first steel vessels used on the river, the *Radium Queen* and *Radium King*; the low-draft wood passenger-boat and tug *Radium Lad*; and seven wooden barges. Two of the barges (one under the ownership of Imperial Oil) were built to house steel tanks for bulk-tanker service. The steel vessels of twin tunnel-type were designed by well-known eastern ship designers Milne, Gilmore and German. They were built at Les Chartiers Industries Ltee (forerunner of Marine Industries Ltee) shipyard in Sorel, Québec, and then cut-up and shipped by rail to Fort McMurray to be reassembled by a team sent from Québec: *Radium Queen* at Fort McMurray and *Radium King* at Fort Smith. The *Radium Lad* and the two tanker barges, one for Imperial Oil and one for NCTL, were apparently built (as confirmed by an ad placed in Edmonton newspapers) by George's competitor Captain John Matheson. The remaining barges must have been built under the direction of George Askew. (See Appendix A.)

The program had one major setback with the apparent loss of one of the barges, built by Matheson of Northern Boat Building Company, for use on Great Bear Lake. The 132-foot tanker barge (the largest vessel constructed to date with a capacity for 72,000 gallons of fuel) apparently never made it up the river to the lake. An article in the *Windsor Star* of 4 May 1938 cites great difficulty winching the monstrous craft through the upper river rapids. Near the end of the season, while still hundreds of yards from safe water at the upper end of the rapids, the barge struck a great boulder that damaged one of the tanks.

The effort of getting through the rapids was then abandoned and the barge was dragged up on the shore for the winter. Although the article expressed optimism it could be repaired and put into service in 1938, there are no further references to the incident or the outcome suggesting a desire to hide the fiasco and subsequent large financial and tactical loss. Further evidence of its destruction: no barge of this size appeared in ship registration records (Blue Book 1940); perhaps this was the missing *Radium Barge 7* that fails to appear between *Radium Barges 6* and *8*. An *Edmonton Journal*, 10 March 1939, article disclosed that

Northern Transportation had ordered a new steel barge for the service from Standard Iron Works in Edmonton, named *Radium Barge 10* (curiously, a *Radium Barge 9* does not appear to exist).

Map 11-1

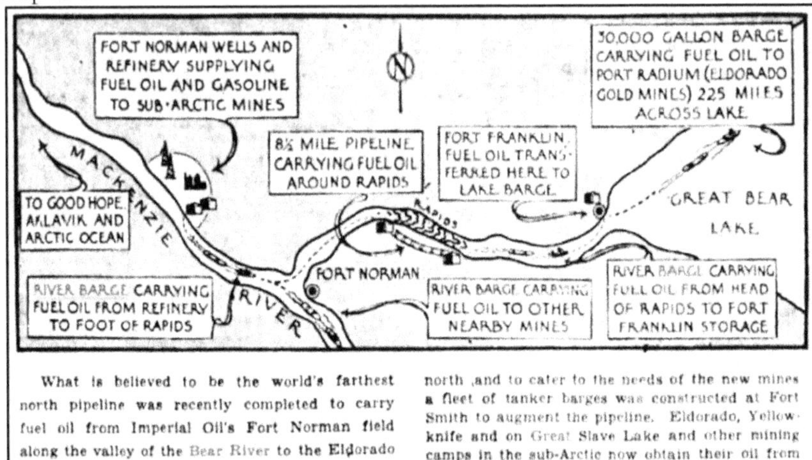

What is believed to be the world's farthest north pipeline was recently completed to carry fuel oil from Imperial Oil's Fort Norman field along the valley of the Bear River to the Eldorado radium-silver mine. During the past six years tremendous development has taken place in the north ,and to cater to the needs of the new mines a fleet of tanker barges was constructed at Fort Smith to augment the pipeline. Eldorado, Yellowknife and on Great Slave Lake and other mining camps in the sub-Arctic now obtain their oil from the Fort Norman wells. The map shows the route covered.

Illustration for supply of petroleum products to Great Bear Lake Mines.
The Vancouver Daily Province, 22 December 1937

Photo 11-1

Northern Transportation's steel vessel *Radium Queen* pushing a barge, Waterways 1942.
Provincial Archives of Alberta photograph A14449

A need for new ships to support the mining industry continued to exist in the Mackenzie district in 1938 as other companies vied to catch up to NTCL efforts of the previous year. That year, George started off with a new client and ended helping an old one. The Consolidated Mining and Smelting Company (CMS), developing gold mining properties in the Yellowknife area on Great Slave, in the Northwest Territories, decided to obtain its own marine resources for this service. (This enterprise was short-lived; the tug and two barges obtained for transportation of materials and equipment on the lake were sold to HBC's Mackenzie Transport the following year.)

The vessels, which became part of HBC's fleet, were built by George. The *Edmonton Journal* of 29 March 1938, disclosed that boats and barges "will be constructed by Askew, boat builder of Vancouver, who is expected to arrive here Wednesday." Francis and John, respectively his 20- and 16-year-old sons, joined George (then age 66) on this new project. It is not known where necessary parts for the vessels were fabricated (the Marpole yard, later used for other of his work, is a possibility). A deep-draft, 62-foot tug *Porphyry* (selecting a mineral-themed name) was duly assembled at Waterways, launched on 18 June with a specially flown-in bottle of champagne, and sent on its way to pass Smith Portage for work on Great Slave Lake. Ship registration records also indicate that two 94-foot long, 28-foot wide, 7.9-foot draft barges (CMS *Barge 102* and *Barge 103* respectively) were also constructed at Fort McMurray in Alberta.

Photo 11-2

Port quarter view of the tug *Porphyry* at Waterways Shipyard.
Askew family collection

Photo 11-3

Barge at Waterways Shipyard.
Askew family collection

While George was busy at Fort McMurray, disaster befell one of his former creations, HBC's huge freight/accommodation vessel *Barge 300,* striking a rock in the Mackenzie River below Fort Simpson and sinking. All passengers managed to make it aboard *Distributor* but the barge and the vital cargo carried was lost. A replacement barge—an even larger one of 500 tons capacity and fittingly named *Barge 500*—was soon procured. HBC barge data sheets credit J. A. Davis as the builder and George as the designer.

George's contacts and influence in Vancouver likely helped in securing the vast quantities of coast lumber and timber required for construction. Incredibly, the enormous barge was launched just six weeks after the sinking of its predecessor, in time for the last northern trip by *Distributor* that fall. George's presence for the launching of the 165-foot behemoth (as evidenced by family photos), probably attests to his help in the swift construction. The HBC's data sheet reveals that the larger replacement vessel cost $35,330; comparable, if increased size is considered, to the $20,000 value of George's contract for *Barge 300* in 1926.

Vancouver-based workers contributed to this achievement. An article in the *Edmonton Journal* of 20 August 1938, titled "Boat Builders End Big North Season," announced the return to Vancouver from Fort Smith of 35 boatbuilders, and noted, "One of the big jobs completed by these men was construction of a 600-ton barge (sic), largest craft ever constructed in the north." A well-illustrated article by H. N. Petty in the March 1939 issue of *The Beaver,* titled "Mackenzie River Transport" describes the event, as well as the activities of other HBC vessels, many of them George Askew creations.

Photo 11-4

Building of *Barge 500.*
The Beaver, March 1939 issue

Prior to 10 September 1939 (the date that Canada entered WWII) opportunities for boatbuilders like George, using the traditional material of west coast-sourced wood, were coming to an end in the Mackenzie basin. Steel became the preferred material as evidenced by an article in the *Edmonton Journal* of 10 March 1939. Matt Berry, of NTCL, announced an order for "two new all-steel boats and an all-steel barge equipped to carry oil in the hull, which would be the first of its kind on northland rivers and lakes."

The boats would be the *Radium Express* and the *Radium Cruiser* (of the tunnel, low-draft variety pioneered by George), supplied by Russell Brothers of Owen Sound, Ontario, while the barge was *Radium Barge 10* supplied by Standard Iron Works of Edmonton. Although nothing has been found in the record, it seems likely that this vessel was a replacement for the large wooden tank barge that failed to make it through the upper rapids of the Bear River at the end of 1937—and indeed the huge wooden vessel had been written off.

With the economy improving, and appetites for pleasure craft reviving in 1939, George was able to find employment closer to home. The decade ended for George with the construction of the 65-foot power cruiser *Leola Vivian.* This was the second yacht that George built for William Vivan, the first being the *Leola V*, designed by Thomas Halliday, and launched in 1928. It is not clear where the new vessel was built, but photographs suggest an old boatbuilding yard in Coal Harbour. Her completion was heralded by this announcement in the *Province* of 7 October 1939, as Vivian made plans for a trial voyage to Victoria:

One of the handsomest private yachts on the Pacific Coast has this week been added to the Vancouver fleet. It is MS *Leola Vivian*, 65 feet long, 14.6 feet beam, and 100 percent British Columbia built. Frames, keel, ribs, planks, decks, house, were grown here and fabricated here, and the engines are Vancouver-built.

Photo 11-5

Yacht *Leola Vivian.*
Askew family collection

12

The War Years, 1940-1945

Local Yard Building 15 Boats for Watson Lake.

—*Vancouver Sun*, 5 March 1941.

Photo 12-1

Askew shipbuilders at Dease Lake 1941, left to right, Francis, George and John. Askew family collection

In 1940 George was part of one of two separate Vancouver groups (the other was headed by R. Crowe-Sword) advocating to the Canadian government for construction of wooden freighters in local yards for WWII, using local material and available labour, based on prior experience in WWI. The vessels, built of readily-available local wood, would help supply the desperate need for wartime shipping in the face of restricted steel supply. George's group proposed 340-foot vessels with central island structures, powered by engines manufactured locally by Vivian Engine Works. William Vivian, his co-proponent, advised 8-cylinder diesels, developing 2,000 hp.

Diagram 12-1

A British Columbia Answer to Submarine Losses

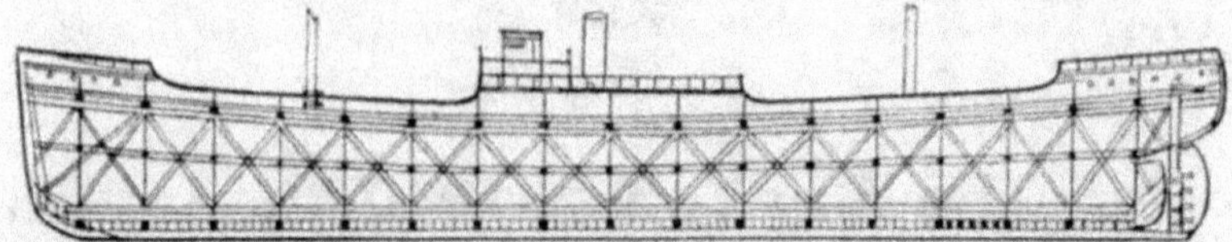

This type of wooden freighter—designed by George F. Askew of Vancouver, veteran shipbuilder, to replace Britain's mounting submarine losses—would be 340 feet in length, 49-foot beam and would carry about 3700 tons of cargo.

City Shipbuilder Ready to Turn Out Wooden Freighters Quickly, Cheaply

Proposed wooden freighter design
Vancouver Sun, 29 November 1940

Both argued that such vessels could be constructed in half the time and for half the cost of equivalent steel ships to no avail. They were not able to convince Ottawa of the merits of either of their proposals. George then turned his attention to other pursuits that could help the war effort.

Even before the United States entered the war (which took place after the attack on Pearl Harbor in 1941) Canada recognized the need for northern defence, and had started construction of a series of airports across northern Alberta, British Columbia, and the Yukon. These aviation facilities would eventually become known as the Northwest Staging Route. The construction of the airfield near the town of Watson Lake, in the Yukon, was particularly difficult to support owing to poor access. The answer was to use the old fur trade supply route from Wrangel, Alaska, up the Stikine River to Telegraph Creek.

From Telegraph Creek the existing supply trail to Dease Lake could be used, then returning to water transportation the freight could be taken down the lake to the Dease River, and thence up the Liard from the juncture with the Dease, finishing again by land with a cat road (a rough bulldozer-hewn road) to the site at Watson Lake. Thus, a transportation route already existed to Dease Lake (in the Northern Interior of British Columbia, south of the Yukon border) that could be improved to move the required 1,300 tons of freight and construction equipment, but to complete the process a fleet of river boats and barges would be required.

A 5 March 1941 article in the *Vancouver Sun* describes the work for building a 70-foot sternwheeler, two tunnel boat launches, and twelve scows at a shipyard at 1224 West 77th Ave, then knocking them down and transporting them to Dease Lake for assembly, starting about 20 April. George was in charge of this work and took a small crew, including his two shipwright sons Francis and John, to Dease Lake to assemble and commission the fleet. This would afford him an opportunity to be together with his sons and work with them before both set off to war: Francis with the Canadian Army and John with the Royal Canadian Navy.

The vessel parts were expeditiously fabricated then disassembled in Vancouver, shipped, and successfully reassembled into vessels at Dease Lake, allowing the construction equipment and material transportation for the airfield to proceed. United States immigration documents indicate the construction party departed Telegraph Creek on 21 July for Juneau, travelling down the Stikine on the US river boat *Hazel B2*, on their way home to Vancouver. For George and his two sons, their time at Dease Lake had to have been a pinnacle of their combined shipbuilding experiences, seeing the fruits of their city labour quickly spring to life in a beautiful wilderness setting, before the full toil of the war tore into their lives.

Photo 12-2

Completed river boat with cargo for Watson Lake airport construction, 1941.
Askew family collection

Soon after arriving home, Francis, then age 26, took up wartime duties with the Canadian Army following the federal government's National Resources Mobilization Act of 1942, to provide a force for home defense. On his way east, he received new orders and returned to the coast and ultimately spent his service life living with his new wife on the family yacht *Hereanthere* in Esquimalt Harbour, supervising the Army's fleet of coastal vessels. John, at the age of 23, was already a member of the Royal Canadian Naval Volunteer Reserve. He, too, was able to do his service on the coast, tasked with impounding fishing vessels from "enemy alien" Japanese-Canadians, then with making repairs to a Russian submarine at Nanaimo, and then with overseeing the construction of Liberty boats for the war effort in Kelowna. He retired after the war with the rank of Chief Petty Officer.

Within a month of returning from Dease Lake, George was faced with a serious loss. Ella May, his wife of seventeen years and stepmother to the two boys, passed away at home on 21 August 1941 at age 59. This was a big blow to both George and his sons.

The Askew family have always referred to the property at 1224 West 77th Ave as George's "Marpole" shipyard but according to Vancouver directory records, from 1942 to 1944, it was a Vancouver Tugboat Company (Vantug) shipyard before the tug operations were moved to the foot of Denman Street. In 1942 they operated five tugs and a fleet of eighteen large scows (*Vancouver Sun*, 18 February 1942). George is listed as foreman in 1942 and superintendent in 1943 and 1944. This contrasts with 1941, when the Watson Lake work was carried out, and the property seems to have been listed as occupied by private residences. Both before and after the war, the Askew family had a close relationship with Harold Jones, of Vantug, through the RVYC. After his war service, Francis worked for them at their Denman Street location.

Vantug's chief occupation was moving surplus wood waste, known as hog fuel, from saw mills to other industrial sites that consumed it for boiler fuel. During a time in which news was often suppressed because of wartime security requirements, it is not clear exactly what the employment arrangements were, but work other than expanding and maintaining their fleet appeared to have occurred at the site.

The first news of George's involvement with this firm was in the above-mentioned *Vancouver Sun* 18 February 1942 article that indicated the construction of a new tug under the supervision of George (and Don Sinclair), and designed by Thomas Halliday, a well-known Vancouver naval architect. The 85-foot tug *La Garde* was launched on 13 August by Miss Beverly Jones, daughter of Harold Jones (the president of the company) and, after completing trials in November 1942, was quickly put into service.

Photo 12-3

Tug *La Garde.*
Courtesy of Roger Craik, Maple Ridge, BC

In 1942, with the Japanese attack invasion of the Aleutian Islands in June, and the attack on Pearl Harbor the previous December (1941), a huge construction boom in British Columbia, Alberta, and the Yukon was launched. The US Army was struggling to build the Alaska Highway. They also needed fuel supplies from the remote Norman Wells oilfields on the lower Mackenzie River, and constructed the Canol pipeline from there to Whitehorse, Yukon. Although no direct information has been found that the Marpole yard participated, it is clear that George was involved. He is credited with building the 66-foot sternwheel tug MV *Alcan* (*Harbour and Shipping*, August 1948) and associated barges acquired by the US Army for ferry use as well as for construction support for building the large suspension bridge at Taylor on the Peace River.

It is likely that the vessel used at Taylor would have been prefabricated at the Marpole shipyard. Perhaps a hastily-issued Canadian passport, dated 22 June 1942 with a 10-day entry permit into the United States, was related to arrangements that George had to make with the US Army who was his client for these vessels. US and Canadian entry stamps, dated respectively 22 June 1942 at Blaine, Washington, and 24 June 1942, indicate these arrangements were quickly made, indeed.

Photo 12-4

Sternwheel tug *Alcan* and barge on the Peace River.
Library of Congress photograph 287871704

Although it remains a matter of speculation, the Marpole yard may have also been involved in the supply of prefabricated components for barges on the Canol Project. It had assembly space, was next door to sawmills producing high grade lumber, had access to rail and marine transport (for project shipping that was done through Prince Rupert) and, as argued by the earlier proponents for wooden freighters, had a supply of aging but highly-skilled workmen experienced in wooden-vessel construction. Regardless of their origins, dozens of wooden and steel barges were assembled at Fort McMurray for the US Army beginning in the summer of 1942. A wartime news black-out existed until well into 1943 so photographs and reports were not published until afterwards, often upwards of more than a year after events occurred (*The Beaver* magazine, September 1943).

The barges were for the transportation of the mountains of material, equipment, and supplies needed for the Canol Project, transiting down the Athabasca, Slave, and Mackenzie rivers.

Photo 12-5

Vessel believed to be the *Athabasca River*, pushing river barges loaded with US Army vehicles and supplies.
Askew family collection

In 1943, on one of his many jaunts across the Strait of Georgia to his childhood haunts in the Gulf Islands aboard the *Hereanthere*, George met and befriended Helen Williams Power who was working at The Green Lantern Hotel in Chemainus. She would become his fourth wife. Helen had emigrated from England to Montreal, at the beginning of World War I, married and had four children before moving west to BC. She and George were married in Coal Harbour by the Reverend John Antel, of the Columbia Coast Mission, aboard George's boat on December 31, 1943. John Askew served as best man. This marriage would last until Helen's death from cancer in 1952.

George's final wartime work, to be his last ever, was in 1944 at the age of 72. The Northern Transportation Company commissioned him to build a motor-sternwheeler for service on the shallow Great Bear River. Unknown to most at the time, this was part of the "Highway of the Atom" which was supplying material for manufacturing the atomic bombs that ultimately put an end to World War II. A headline in the *Edmonton Journal* of 5 April 1944 announced "20 Go North to Construct Boat." After his crew assembled the new ship at Waterways, the vessel was sailed north to Fort Fitzgerald and then taken over the Smith Portage on a massive trailer to Fort Smith. There, it was re-launched and began its working life. The owners, recognizing the huge contribution that the long-experienced builder had made to their company and the north—and knowing it was the end of the lauded builder's career—graciously named this vessel the *George Askew*.

Photo 12-6

Sternwheeler *George Askew*.
NWT Archives photograph N-1981-002-0041

13

Retirement, 1945-1954

A Real Old Salt is George – They honored a real old timer at the Royal Vancouver Yacht Club general meeting Thursday, making George Askew, shipbuilder, pioneer and yachtsman, an honorary life member of the club.

—*The Vancouver Daily Province*, 25 March 1950.

Photo 13-1

George Francis Askew holding his grandson Martin in front of his home in Vancouver, 1951. City of Vancouver Archives photograph CVA371-154

With the war drawing to a close, it was a good time for the 72-year-old shipbuilder to retire. George's "second home" at the RVYC was nearby with many of his old cronies still around and thoughts of racing, suspended during the war, were in the air. There was time for recollections of a full life; his success with his 15-foot sailing dingy *Native Daughter* and his participation as an advisor and a crewman on the J-class *Lady Van* (that finally wrested the Lipton Cup from Seattle's *Sir Tom* in 1929) would likely often be the subject of conversation.

The *Vancouver Sun* reported on George being made an honorary life member by the RVYC in its 24 March 1950 edition.

FABULOUS BACKGROUND

Geo. Askew Made RVYC Life Member

Royal Vancouver Yacht club members last night honored an old timer. They made shipbuilder George Askew, skipper of the Here and There, who joined the club in 1913, an honorary life member

Jack Cribb filled in a little of the fabulous Askew background for the younger members and told of the apprenticeship he served under him when Askew was building sternwheelers on the Skeena. He claimed he first met George in 1908 in the Yukon and considered him old then.

One Sunday they were working on the sternwheelers the "old man" showed the young toughies on the crew up when he swam the icy Skeena and dared the rest to follow. The next week Jack tried and made it one way but couldn't get back.

Roy Ginn told the meeting that George Askew was a member of the Royal Victoria Yacht Club in 1898. Harry Wylie, an honorary life member, recalled cruises in one of Askew's early ships, the centreboard sloop Doris.

Later Askew built some of the best known ships in this area, the Westward Ho, formerly owned by Commodore Barney Johnson, Alex Marshall's Nelmar and Doug Urry's Cresset.

Juvenile Boys Start Cup-Ties

Some thirty-two Juvenile soccer teams will start the first round of the Mainland Cup Saturday.

In first division the twice postponed Collingwood vs. St. Andrews game will finally get underway at Collingwood or Norquay Park.

Division 1 (Mainland Cup Round One)—Time, 2:15: Transfer vs. Westerns, Powell or Templeton, Lear; Collingwood vs. St. Andrews, Collingwood or Norquay, Bludell; Capilanos vs. Gibbs, Kensington, Parker; South Hill vs. N. S. Kiwanis, Sunset, Gurney.

Division 2 (Provincial Regional Round)—Time, 1:00: Prices vs. South Hill, Powell, Coombes.

Division 3 (Mainland Round Two)—Time, 11:00: Collingwood vs. Bluebirds, Collingwood, Weisbrod; Kiwest vs. Marpole, Ambleside, Croll; Duecks vs. L. C. Merchants, Mahon, Robinson; Elite Taxi vs. Hale-co, Capitol Hill, Black.

Division 4 (Provincial Round Three)—Time, 11:00: Burrard Lions vs. Westerns, North Templeton, Blundell; **(Mainland Round One)**—Capital Hill vs. Kivans, Willingdon, King;

Sadly, in 1952, his wife Helen at the age of 63, passed away after fighting breast and lung cancer for three years. During this period, she resided in Nanaimo (on the east coast of Vancouver Island) with her daughter who looked after her. According to Vancouver City directories, from 1948 on, George lived with son Francis and his wife Josephine in the house they had built after the war under the Veterans Land Act at 2060 Adanac.

George died on 17 August 1953 at the age of 82 from pneumonia after suffering a second stroke and a brief stay in hospital. His funeral was held on 20 August 1953 in Vancouver and conducted by Rev. A. Greene. His remains were cremated but his ashes were not scattered until 1 September 1954 when a group of yachts assembled off Jericho Beach. As a retiring member of the RVYC "Eight Bells Club" the particular rites were duly followed by those in attendance, a truly fitting tribute to a man who had spent so much of his life on the water, whether for work or pleasure. It was an end of an era.

Despite the chronological reconstruction of George's life through his shipbuilding career, many aspects remain incomplete. For example, little has been found about his early travels during the Yukon gold rush and mushing on other northern rivers. There is some family lore that he was involved in the salvage of copper from the old Russian-built gun boat SS *Politkoffsky*, and of smaller boats that he built for the Inuit and other customers. George's possible involvement in barge construction in 1943 for the Canol pipeline project, that was hushed-up, remains a mystery. And then there were probably many small barges and scows that must surely have been built, but have not been found in the record.

George was blessed with a good mind, outstanding athletic abilities, and an aptitude for focused application of his talents. Perhaps a greater ability than his fine craftsmanship was his capacity to organize crews, materials and machinery, and have them transported to remote, carefully-prepared building sites where they could be transformed into huge vessels and successfully launched in the narrow seasonal windows that the North afforded.

His outstanding contribution included the development of transportation systems in western Canada that helped to open up settlement and development. He saw out the great age of the sternwheeler, which was initially a key driver in this enterprise with its ability to operate in the shallow waters of lakes and rivers. Then, through foresight and pioneering of an idea that others copied, developed the tunnel boat concept which allowed propeller-driven vessels to operate in these same conditions.

Canada's vast western geography was George's domain, and he often travelled to the extremes of its rivers and lakes to build and assemble his vessels. As *Pacific Boating* aptly observed, George was the "dean of river boat builders in the north country, he is probably the oldest boat builder in the Northwest."

Finally, in addition to be being well-remembered in the annuals of the RVYC, he left us a few fine examples of his exquisite workmanship and design that remain afloat, as of 2021: including his beloved yawl *Hereanthere*, the sailing vessel *Cresset* and the power yacht *Oliver Clark II*, formerly *Leola Vivian.*

Photo 13-2

Yawl *Hereanthere* not far from where she was launched.
Roger Askew collection

Photo 13-3

Oliver Clark II, originally launched as *Leola Vivian* in 1939.
Roger Askew collection

14

Yacht El Sueño, *bringing "the dream" to the Northwest Passage*

Photo 14-1

El Sueño (the former San Francisco racing yacht which brought trade to the Northwest Passage) standing out of Cambridge Bay, September, 1925, after establishing the first trading post on King William Island (today, part of Nunavut). Her voyage across Queen Maud Gulf was only the second vessel passage, the first being that of Norwegian polar explorer Roald E. G. Amundsen in the schooner *Gjøa.*
Library and Archives Canada/67-1925-L.T.B. (Lachlan Taylor Burwash)

While George Askew and his mates in Victoria had abandoned their favourite pursuits of competitive yacht racing and other sports to join the cadre of gold-seekers up north, drunk on dreams of pulling untold fortunes from Canada's Yukon streams, similar minded yachtsmen in San Francisco were doing the same, devising their own unique means of access. Yachts launched with great celebration and the breaking of champagne bottles sometimes later fade from memory having, in old age, been sunk or abandoned as derelicts in some backwater or on a lonely beach. The story of the schooner *El Sueño* is known in the western Arctic only through a number of history glimpses. While her complete life, like that of other mysterious ladies, may never be completely revealed, a compilation of scraps of her Arctic history, glimpses of places and times are evidence she had a very unusual and significant life.

EARLY DAYS AS A PROMINENT RACING YACHT

Photo 14-2

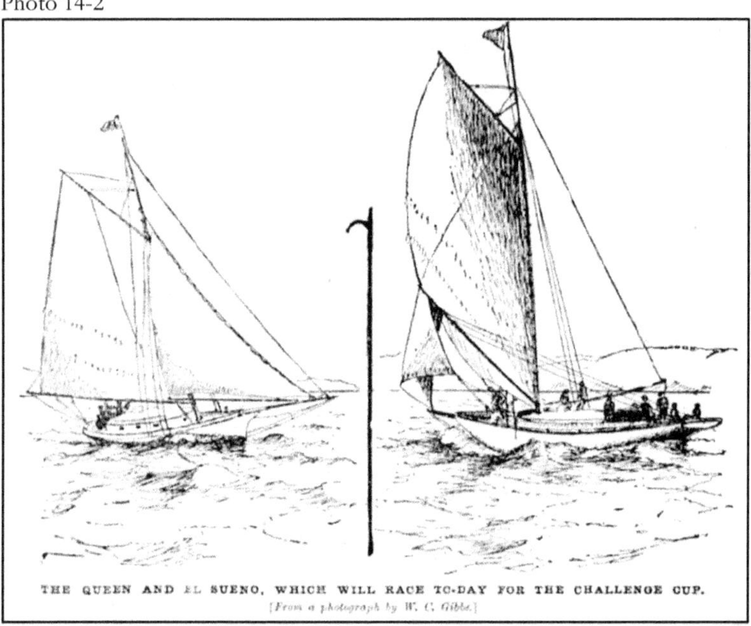

THE QUEEN AND EL SUENO, WHICH WILL RACE TO-DAY FOR THE CHALLENGE CUP.
[From a photograph by W. C. Gibbs.]

Sketch of the yachts *Queen* (left) and *El Sueño* (right).
San Francisco Call, 31 August 1895

El Sueño—meaning the dream—was built for San Francisco yachtsman and prominent Alameda real estate developer Joseph A. Leonard. Constructed at Alameda, California, in 1894 as a 44-foot sloop with a gasoline auxiliary engine, Leonard spared no expense in equipping her with the finest, most up-to-date furnishings and equipment. A particularly useful feature was a heavy, retractable metal centerboard that permitted her to operate in very shallow waters. As the most elegant and fastest boat in the Encinal Yacht Club, she served as flagship when founder Leonard was Commodore. In 1895 she became the first winner of the San Francisco Challenge Trophy, defeating the San Francisco Yacht Club's *Queen* by 11 minutes over a fifteen-mile course. This cup is still in challenge today and is considered to be second only to the America's Cup in prestige. Before the real estate market collapsed about 1898, resulting in Leonard losing his fortune, he and the yacht were featured items of many newspaper articles in the Bay Area.

Map 14-1

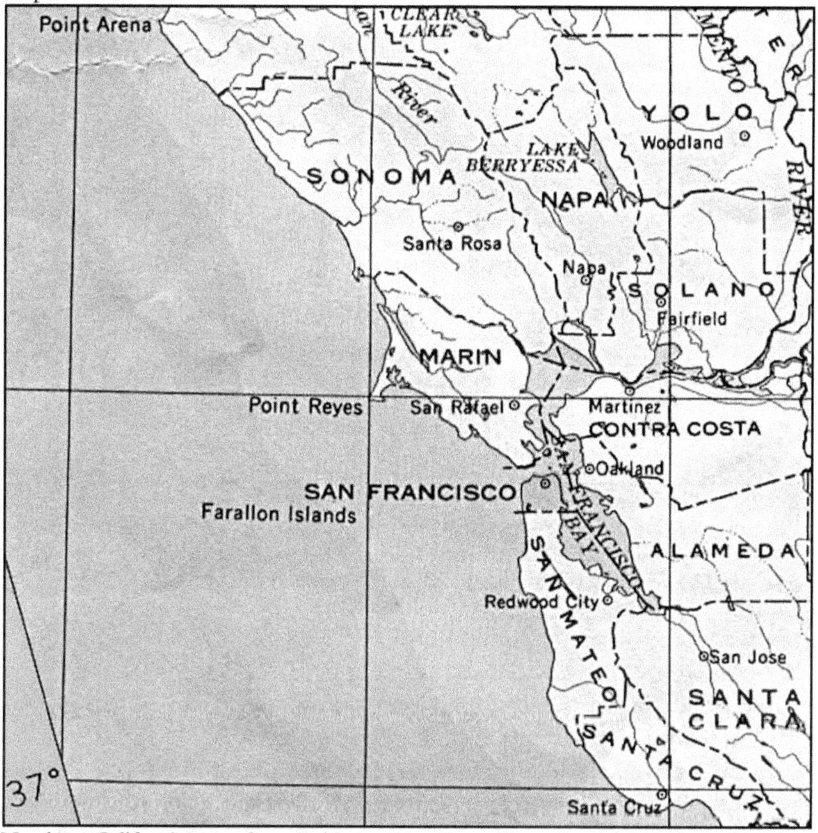

Northern California coast from Point Arena to Santa Cruz; the Encinal Yacht Club is at Alameda Island, adjacent to and directly south of Oakland; which is across the San Francisco Bay from the city of San Francisco.
https://maps.lib.utexas.edu/maps/united_states/california_north_90.jpg

NORTH TO THE ALASKAN GOLD FIELDS AND A VOYAGE ON THE YUKON RIVER

Photo 14-3

The gasoline-powered schooner *Bessie K.*, with the yacht *El Sueño* aboard, being brought over from Oakland Creek and docked at Mission 2. The yacht had been fitted with a 25-horsepower engine, and was expected to be the most comfortable boat that had yet made the trip up the Yukon to Dawson City.
San Francisco Call, 14 August 1897

By 1897 the interests of those in charge of the yacht (Leonard now had partners in her ownership), along with many other enterprises, had turned from match-racing to gold. On 14 July 1897, as the steamboat *Excelsior* arrived in San Francisco carrying half-a-million dollars of Klondike gold dust, stampeders rushed to the gold fields of the Yukon and Alaska, and entrepreneurs developed plans for making fortunes. No longer dreaming of winning races, *El Sueño*'s owners, along with associates and cronies at the yacht club, turned their attention to gaining access to the gold riches of the Yukon. It was risky, as were all schemes for extracting wealth from the alluvial deposits of the Yukon, but *El Sueño*'s owners had devised a unique plan. A prospecting party was to be engaged and they and the yacht would be loaded aboard *Bessie K.*, a larger motor schooner, to be transported to the mouth of the river at St. Michaels, Alaska.

There, the sailing yacht was to be converted to steam-propulsion, complete with a boiler and steam engine, while wintering at St. Michaels and then, in the following spring, proceed with the rush of river boats bound for the gold fields. Wood cut locally, or possibly coal, would be used as fuel.

In spite of delays, deck-loaded aboard the schooner *Bessie K.* (diverted to Port Angeles, Washington, for repairs), *El Sueño* reached St. Michaels on 16 October 1897, just as the port and the Yukon River were icing over. With the skipper of the *Bessie K.* anxious to sail for home before being frozen-in, it was necessary to hold the schooner's crew at gun point to keep her in port long enough to unload *El Sueño* and her supplies.

Photo 14-4

Third Street, Dawson City, Yukon Territory, circa 1899.
University of Washington photograph (Eric A. Hegg)
uploaded to Wikimedia Commons

Following the river break-up, *El Sueño* did not reach the goldfields of Dawson in the summer 1898 as planned. Instead, she ascended the Dall River to a wintering location approximately 990 miles from the mouth of the Yukon. From there, the remnants of her original eight-man crew were able to make overland forays across a divide to the Kuyukuk (now Koyukuk), a northern tributary of the Yukon River, where they staked a number of claims. It is not clear why the objective of Dawson was changed. Perhaps it was unobtainable in the short navigation season. More likely it was because by 1898, most of the population of Dawson had already left, migrating down river to the newly discovered gold finds on the beaches of Nome, Alaska. Also, apparently as a result of disagreements between Leonard and his associates about oversight of the expedition, Leonard was replaced by Captain McCullough as manager of the venture.

William Mills Coffee was the captain of the field party. The terms of his engagement are unclear but it was some sort of profit-sharing arrangement dependent on the venture's success. It seems some members of the field party were relatives or cronies of the investor group. Coffee kept a personal diary of their activities which he mailed home to his wife in installments. In addition to narrative descriptions, it also contained sketch maps of exploration areas and detailed accounts of funds expended. In 2005, his grandson Phillip Michael Coffee published the diary in a book titled, *El Sueño de Oro - The Dream of Gold.*

It covers the period from 21 August 1897, when Coffee left San Francisco on the schooner *Bessie K.*, until he returned on the steamer *Portland* on 24 August 1899. Unfortunately, a key part of it covering the ascent of the Yukon River from 1 June to 13 September 1898 was lost.

The diary is a firsthand account of the major difficulties faced by the party, living conditions, extreme winter prospecting ventures, and betrayals and desertions by party members. In the case of Coffee, it revealed a man of integrity, loyalty and compassion. He was innovative and possessed many skills. One example was his hand-hewing of a ship's wheel to replace the *El Sueño*'s original tiller-helm. It appears it was only because of his immense labour and ability to keep cranky steam engines repaired and fueled that *El Sueño* was able to safely ascend the Yukon River and return to St. Michaels in 1899.

Interestingly, a newspaper article indicates that Leonard joined Coffee's expedition late in the enterprise but had to return to San Francisco when he badly injured his foot.

Following this venture, and in the absence of official orders from the syndicate (Coffee did meet with Leonard, but at that point he had been deposed as head and had agreed to the sale of *El Sueño* for only fifteen dollars if all other offers failed), Coffee decided to try his luck in the new gold fields at Nome. Almost out of funds but still possessing supplies, he gathered some paying passengers and set off across Norton Bay. By this time all of the original party had abandoned the expedition. Coffee was left with only one loyal subordinate known as Mack. Mack was probably John Moack (a member of the crew listed as "Boat Keeper"), the only salaried member of the expedition.

Together they managed to stake a few claims along Nome's harbour-less coast before *El Sueño* grounded on a sand shoal in huge breaking swells that threatened to tear her apart. In spite of Herculean efforts on the crew's part, and even with the assistance of others, they were unable to free the vessel from the shoal. Coffee, who had earlier contemplated selling the vessel and her supplies for a price that may have garnered some return on the investment, now yielded to a much harsher "as is" offer and sold the vessel for $100 to Lord & Klopenberg. The fire-sale pricing of this formerly grand yacht—which originally cost upwards of $5,000 when built—drew huge criticism in the San Francisco press.

Following the sale of *El Sueño*, Coffee and John Mack returned to St. Michaels on the schooner *Fisher Bro.* After settling the syndicate affairs, they used the remaining funds to book passage on the steamer *Portland* for San Francisco. For his more than two years of grueling effort, Coffee arrived home on 24 August 1899 with 25 cents in his pocket. Like many other stampeders who were fortunate to return, his only reward was an adventure he would never forget—one which most men would not even contemplate.

A SHADOWY CAREER AS AN ALASKAN TRADER

Lord & Klopberg's purchase of *El Sueño* proved fortuitous for them. Immediately after grounding, the seas had moderated into a flat calm and they were able to float *El Sueño* off the sand bank. Further, they were able to sell the supplies left on board for more than the one hundred dollar purchase price.

ALAMEDA, May 3.—Joseph A. Leonard of this city has received word that El Sueno, the yacht which he once owned, is now engaged in smuggling on the Siberian coast. El Sueno was taken north on the schooner Bessie K. about two years ago. The Bessie K. had a tempestuous voyage, but finally reached St. Michael after being disabled. Leonard and his business associates got very little use out of El Sueno on the Yukon. She had been fitted up with double engines and well provisioned, but one day she was run on a sand bar. The manager of the expedition sold the yacht and her contents as she lay for less than $200. Three days later her new owners got her off the bar without having strained a plank, and after selling the supplies in Nome for more than the entire purchase price, the yacht was used for freighting.

Subsequently it was reported that El Sueno was a wreck, but she escaped from the rocks after an exciting cruise. Recently Leonard received the information that El Sueno was plying on the coast of Siberia as a smuggler.

Article titled, YACHT *EL SUENO* MAY BE A SMUGGLER.
San Francisco Chronicle, 4 May 1900

After her salvage and sale, *El Sueño* was pressed into a shadowy career as a freighting and fur trading vessel on the Alaskan coast and across the Bering Sea on Siberia junkets. She was reported wrecked several times but, like the proverbial cat, always seemingly returned to continue her service—or continued to be put back in service. One such erroneous citation, from the official list of *Alaska Shipwrecks - A*

Comprehensive Accounting of Alaska Shipwrecks and Losses of life in Alaskan Waters, claimed the vessel a total loss off Nome on 31 December 1903.

EL SUENO (1903) The 23 ton steamer ***El Sueno*** foundered off of Nome December 31, 1903 and became a total loss.

Sources: 1. *The H W McCurdy Marine History of the Pacific Northwest* (1966) Pg 94. **2.** *Shipwrecks of the Alaskan Shelf and Shore* (1992)

El Sueño's arrival at Nome, Alaska, in 1913 would seem to disprove reports that she had been lost in Siberia that year. Her whereabouts in the decade preceding this arrival demonstrate all earlier reports of her complete demise were inaccurate. One of her crew in 1913, and perhaps her captain, Alexander Allen (sometimes reported as Allan as in the following chapter) was at the helm when she arrived in Canadian waters two years later in 1915.

MISSING VESSEL ARRIVES AT NOME

El Sueno Survives Storm by Using Oil Bags—Niginik Was Wrecked and Abandoned by Crew Before Going Ashore.

(Associated Press, World's Leased Wire.)

NOME, Alaska, Oct. 16—The schooner El Sueno, reported wrecked on the Siberian coast, has arrived here with Messrs. E. L. McIntyre, Martin Lauritzen and Alexander Allen. She escaped by using oil bags during the big storm. The schooner that was wrecked at Cape Serge was the Nigilik. The Eskimos say she was abandoned by her crew before she went ashore. It is supposed the crew were drowned.

Vancouver World, 16 October 1913

15

Captain Allan's Fur Trapping Voyage to the Canadian Arctic

Photo 15-1

Vessels in the harbour at Herschel Island, August 1915. To the left is the Hudson's Bay Company (HBC) motor schooner *Fort McPherson* recently arrived from Vancouver after wintering in Teller, Alaska, while to the right in the foreground is the *El Sueño* and in the background the HBC-chartered power schooner *Ruby*. One of the two vessels in the immediate foreground is the schooner *Atkoon of Collingwood* belonging to a missionary party of the Anglican church.
NWT Archives/Catherine Hoare/N-2013-022

El Sueño arrived in the Canadian Arctic with Captain Alexander Allan (spelling of name sometimes Allen) in 1915. By this point, the vessel had been converted to schooner rig presumably to allow easier handling with a smaller crew, and a club (boom-like device for self-tacking) had been fitted to a foresail. Her arrival was noted in the Report of the Royal Northwest Mounted Police (RNWMP) for 1915:

> The auxiliary schooner *El Sueño*, Captain Allan in charge, arrived from Nome, Alaska August 20, and left for Cockburn point with a load of provisions for the Canadian Arctic expedition on August 23. Captain Allan intended to return to Booth Island [Nunavut], east of Cape Parry, and spend the winter trapping.

The report cited duties paid by five vessels at Herschel Island, *El Sueño*'s entry point to Canada, and one at which she disbursed $179.29

in customs fees. While at the island, Allan encountered Vilhjalmur Stefansson (of the Canadian Arctic Expedition, CAE) who had just returned from his famous ice expedition. Stefansson had been rescued from Banks Island, Northwest Territories, by Captain Louis Lane's schooner *Polar Bear*. As Allan had surplus cargo space available, Stefansson hired him to transport supplies to his southern party headquartered at Bernard Harbour. Also, as Allan was skilled at repairing and maintaining marine engines, Stefansson engaged him to go over the engines of the expedition vessels at Bernard Harbour.

Bernard Harbour, a bay on what is now the Nunavut mainland, is situated on the Dolphin and Union Strait. Formerly a Hudson's Bay Company trading post, and later a former Distant Early Warning Line site, it is currently a North Warning System site (utilizing early-warning radar for the atmospheric air defense of North America).

The photograph on the preceding page, and a subsequent one showing *El Sueño* in winter quarters, are from an unpublished work documenting the Arctic exploits of William Hoare when he was with an Anglican group attempting to establish a mission station in the Coronation Gulf area (today, part of Nunavut) from 1914 to 1918. The work also includes his later experiences with the church, and when he was a wildlife field worker for the Canadian government in the Arctic, together with the related Arctic experiences of his wife. (Their remarkable stories, documented by William Hoare's diaries and photographs, are contained in a two-volume document titled *Adventures Unlimited*, by Catherine A. Hoare, available from the Archives of the Northwest Territories in Yellowknife, Exhibit N-2013022.)

Photo 15-2

Schooner *El Sueño* leaving Bernard Harbour, under sail in late autumn in 1915. This was presumably Allan heading back west on his trading and trapping mission. Photograph taken by Fritz Johnson, Canadian Museum of Civilization accession 42324 uploaded to Wikimedia Commons

Returning from Bernard Harbour, Allan encountered the missionary party of the Anglican church—Herbert Girling, Gabriel Elton Merritt, William Hoare and Pouchina ("an [Inuit] helper")—whose schooner *Atkoon of Collingwood* had also been at Herschel Island. The *Atkoon* was disabled near Clifton Point (Amundsen Gulf, in what is now Nunavut), when Allan stopped to offer assistance, even though his own vessel, *El Sueño*, had been badly damaged. (No details of this damage are mentioned in the Hoare diaries.)

Photo 15-3

Schooner *Atkoon of Collingwood* beached near Clifton Point, 15 March 1916. Wikimedia Commons

In the late winter of 1916, Allan and his wife travelled by dog sled to spend Easter with the church party at "Camp Necessity" beside their beached vessel at Clifton Point. Hoare and Merritt then returned with them to Pierce Point (now commonly known as Pearce Point, Amundsen Gulf, NWT) where *El Sueño* was in winter quarters. Along the way the group encountered Allan's fur trapping partners Nels Holmes and Captain Steen, presumably two of the four partners. (Amundsen Gulf is located between Banks Island and Victoria Island and mainland Canadian Northwest Territories).

The next summer, while trying to advance east to Bernard Harbour, the missionary vessel was completely destroyed by fire and her crew were forced to spend the winter of 1916-1917 at another winter camp. During that winter they came across Pete Norberg at his winter trapping cabin and almost shot him mistaking him for a bear. This must have been forgiven, as their account mentions Pete's assistance to them at a later time.

Photo 15-4

El Sueño in winter quarters at Pierce Point, 1916 (now more commonly known as Pearce Point, Amundsen Gulf, NWT). From *Adventures Unlimited* by Catherine A. Hoare

An entry at page 275 in the 1916 RNWMP Report chronicles Allan's and the missionaries' activities during the winter of 1915-1916:

> The Rev. Mr. Girling, Church of England mission, arrived at Bernard harbour on Oct 9, his boat, the schooner *Atkoon* having been driven ashore in a storm near Clifton Point on September 4; all his party are safe and the schooner undamaged; he returned to Clifton Point on November 10. Capt. Allan of the schooner *El Sueño*, who brought supplies here this summer, is wintering at Pierce point, with four other men, trapping.

A last report of Allan is contained in the RNWMP Report of 1918. In July 1918, Allan was travelling with companion Gonzales from Kittigazuit to Herschel Island by whaleboat. Gonzales was a former CAE member who had been fired by Stefansson in 1917. While en route they rescued Superintendent Phillips and Corporal William Andrew Doak of the RNWMP. The pair had been travelling by whaleboat from Aklavik to Herschel Island along with Constable Cornelius. The boat had been wrecked ten miles east of the island. All eventually reached Herschel Island safely including Cornelius who had set off on foot in an attempt to get help. Tragically, Doak, along with Hudson's Bay Post Manager Otto Binder, were later murdered by an Inuit, Alikomiak, at Tree River, NWT (now Nunavut). At trial, held at Herschel Island in 1923, Alikomiak and Tatamigana (another accused murderer) were found guilty. They were subsequently hung in 1924. The trial continues to generate controversy to the present day.

It appears that at the time of the rescue of the police officers, *El Sueño* had been sold to the Hudson's Bay Company. According to his 17 September 1918 diary entry, when William Hoare arrived at Bernard Harbour that summer, he became aware of the sale of the *El Sueño*:

> The *Challenge* has gone east with Pete Norberg as skipper and trader. The Hudson's Bay Company had bought the *El Sueño* for $2,000 without engine.

Challenge was a small schooner owned briefly by the CAE, sold in 1917 to a partnership of Otto Binder, Harold Noice and A. A. Carroll for use in fur trading. Carroll was a former employee of Northern Traders, a rival of the HBC, while the others were former members of the expedition. Stefansson reported the vessel was subsequently wrecked while in winter quarters on the mainland coast of Amundsen Gulf. Both Carroll as manager at Herschel Island and Binder at Tree River, became HBC employees. It is not clear about Noice, who was obsessed with collecting native artifacts. He was the individual who rescued Pete Norberg, when the latter was a trader at Kent Peninsula, from an angry dispute resulting in Norberg getting crushed in a fur press.

Photo 15-5

Shoreline of Tree River looking east, and Hudson's Bay Company store or residence interior at Tree River, Northwest Territories, 1926-1927.
NWT Archives/Ray Ross fonds/N-1992-124: 0037 and N-1992-124: 0040

Sometime after the loss of *Challenge* and the collapse of the partnership, Norberg turned to the HBC, beginning a long association with the company.

16

Hudson's Bay Company and Voyage to King William Island

By 1918, under District Manager Chris Harding, HBC fur trading posts had been established eastward from Herschel Island as far as Bernard Harbour. Harding's only means of transportation prior to the purchase of *El Sueño* was the stalwart motor schooner the *Fort McPherson*. His successor, Herbert Hanley Hall (son of Robert Hanley Hall, a former fur trade commissioner), continued the push eastward into the Coronation Gulf area under the local leadership of Inspector C. H. Clarke. Before this the gulf had been mainly the preserve of independent American traders such as Captain Christian Klengenberg and Joseph F. Bernard, nephew of Captain Pierre (Peter) Bernard. (Christian was also called Charles or Charlie, and was sometimes referred to as "Klink," because his surname was originally Klinkenbeg. At times, he commanded schooners and was addressed as Captain.) By 1920 posts had been established as far east as the Kent Peninsula, while the Northern Traders Post at Tree River had been purchased and opened as an HBC company post under Otto Binder.

Prior to the erection of post buildings at Kent Peninsula, trading from the schooner *El Sueño* had commenced. The Kitikmeot Heritage Society records that Kent Post was established by C. H. Clarke and fellow HBC employee Rudolph Thorvald Johnson in 1920. Though details are vague, it is likely that Pete Norberg initiated trading using the schooner as their trading post. The RNWMP Report of 1920 described an encounter with him during the winter of 1919-1920:

> Constable Brockie's patrol to Kent Peninsula, where he found the *El Sueño* wintering and Mr. Peter Norberg established as a trader for the Hudson's Bay Company, is chiefly noticeable for his friendly dealings with the [Inuit].

When the *Lady Kindersley* made her maiden voyage to the Arctic in 1921 it was the farthest post to be visited by any HBC supply ship from the Pacific Coast. En route at Bernard Harbour she encountered Pete

Norberg with *El Sueño*. While they were there Norberg, together with HBC employees C. H. Clarke and Tom O'Kelly and his wife Frances, were witnesses at a wedding. Afterwards Norberg piloted the *Lady Kindersley* to Tree Island towing the *El Sueño*. He then sailed the schooner from Tree Island after she had been loaded with supplies for the Kent Peninsula Post.

Norberg continued to work in the eastern gulf area until the spring of 1922. Reported to be manager of the Kent Peninsula Post, he left Tree River Post on 22 April to help Royal Canadian Mounted Police (RCMP) Constable Stevensen escort charged murderer Alikomiak to the west for trial. The trip consisted of a 726-mile-leg by dog sled to Kittigazuit, followed by a further 125-mile voyage by native schooner to Aklavik. In an interview reported in a 1929 article in the *Victoria Colonist*, Norberg indicated that he spent the winter of 1922 in Winnipeg. It is not clear if any of his children accompanied him. Caroline, his youngest, lived with relatives at Old Crow in the Yukon while Agnes and Johnny attended residential school at Hay River.

It appears likely that Norberg visited Old Crow on his journey down the Mackenzie in the summer of 1923 as he is reported to have joined Scotty Gall and the other members of HBC's new motor schooner *Aklavik* at Fort Simpson after "coming over the mountains." There, he took charge of the vessel and helped her navigate through the difficult and shallow Sans Sault Rapids. Norberg continued with the vessel to Aklavik where Henry Bjorn took over for the final leg to Herschel Island. HBC's District Manager Herbert Hall had arranged for the building of the vessel for Arctic service, along with other vessels, at Fort McMurray by Vancouver shipbuilder George Askew.

EXTENDING FUR TRADING TO KING WILLIAM ISLAND, A RECORD - PIONEERING VOYAGE

Prior to an inspection trip of Arctic trading posts for Fur Trade Commissioner Angus Brabant in 1923, Hudson's Bay Company Inspector Philip Godsell had been informed that the company wanted to extend its coverage eastwards from the Tree Island and Kent Peninsula posts by establishing one or two posts on Victoria Island, and also to send an expedition to King William Land (today, King William Island, Nunavut) to establish trading. This island, about 110 miles long and 100 miles wide, is in the Canadian Arctic Archipelago, between Victoria Island and the Boothia Peninsula. Reaching the island meant navigating across Queen Maud Gulf, a feat that had only previously been accomplished by Roald Amundsen in 1905 with the schooner *Gjoa* that had been equipped with an engine. The distance from the Tree

Island Post to King William Island is approximately 420 miles, and in a region not to be trifled with as evidenced by an earlier expedition in these unforgiving waters.

King William Island is where the Franklin expedition of 1845 had come to grief. British Naval officer Sir John Franklin with 129 sailors on two ships, HMS *Erebus* and HMS *Terror*, entered the Arctic to search for the Northwest Passage—a vital sea route between the Atlantic and Pacific oceans. The ships became ice-trapped, and all perished, including many who had abandoned their ships in a desperate attempt at escape, only to die ashore.

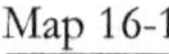
Map 16-1

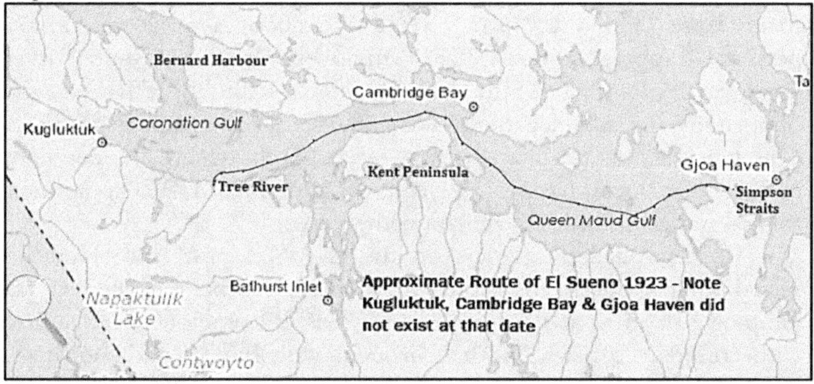

Eastward extension of the Fur Trade
From the Atlas of Canada – Toporama, marked-up by the author

For this most recent expedition, Pete Norberg was selected as leader. This was likely arranged in Winnipeg when he was on furlough during the winter of 1922. District Manager Hall had visited Winnipeg that winter and it is probable that Norberg and he had met with Angus Brabant. At the time, Norberg was one of the few local inhabitants who could communicate with the poorly-understood inhabitants of the central Arctic region.

Godsell, Hall and District Inspector Clarke had been present at the famous trial of the accused murderers at Herschel Island in July 1923. The trial, which ended with a guilty verdict for both, concluded with the departure of the judicial party by schooner to reach an upstream river steamer at Aklavik. Godsell and the HBC employees travelling to the Tree Island Post (the planned start of the expedition), awaited the arrival of the HBC supply ship *Lady Kindersley* from Vancouver at Herschel Island. She arrived on 3 August and, after discharging and transferring cargo, sailed to the east.

On board (as mentioned by Godsell in his books *Arctic Trader* and *They Got Their Man*) were Pete Norberg, Otto Torrington and HBC company accountant and replacement Tree River Post Manager R. C. MacGregor. Godsell made no mention of Henry Bjorn or of HBC District Inspector Clarke. That Clarke was aboard was confirmed by *Kindersley*'s radio officer Reginald Harold Fricker. Fricker also noted that Danish photographer Leo Hansen, who was scheduled to join the Knud Rasmussen 5th Thule Expedition at Kent Peninsula, was also on board.

In his book, Godsell mentions an animosity that had developed between himself and Clarke over Clarke's action at Herschel Island. Clarke had sold a large number of pelts from his personal trapping to an independent trader in violation of HBC policy. Godsell also noted that Clarke tended to turn a blind eye about a large amount of personal trapping done by HBC employees. In the western Arctic, employees often used their employment with the HBC as an opportunity to advance their own interests over company interests. This practice was peculiar to the western Arctic where the company had to hire local trappers instead of traditional HBC apprentice-trained traders in order to remain competitive.

After a rollicking voyage on the *Lady Kindersley* from Herschel Island with Godsell and other fur traders, Norberg arrived at the jumping off point at the Tree Island Post. By previous arrangement with company officials, he had brought with him an old motorized scow dubbed *The Hobo.* Together with *El Sueño*, the only vessel remaining at Tree River (though lacking an engine) the two were to be the means of extending the company's line of posts across Queen Maud Gulf to King William Island. The assistant for the voyage as reported by Godsell was to be Otto Torrington, who had travelled with Godsell from Herschel Island.

Their departure is described in Godsell's books, *Arctic Trader* and *They Got Their Man.*

> Just as midnight approached and the sun dipped momentarily below the horizon, Pete and his helper, Otto, shook hands, stepped on board "The Hobo" cranked up the engine and were away. Soon the *put, put, put,* of the motor was lost in the distance. Pete had left for the Unknown.

While this dramatic account lends colour to Godsell's book, it is doubtful that it happened in the manner described or that in fact Godsell was even present at the midnight departure. Two photographs by Leo Hansen from the Danish Arctic Institute depict the adventure at Tree Island Post and Godsell is not included in the group. A third photo shows the schooners *El Sueño* and *Fort McPherson* in the anchorage roadstead but the *Lady Kindersley* is not evident. Tellingly, Godsell, an ardent photographer himself with hundreds of photos, does not appear to have recorded this important event.

Photo 16-1

"Barge Unloaded at Herschel Island 1923" by Leo Hansen, photographer to Knud Rasmussen's 5th Thule Expedition. It is not known if this is *The Hobo*, but she would have been handled on/off *Lady Kindersley* in similar manner.
Danish Arctic Institute photograph ID 122347

Torrington was a former Edmonton taxi driver who later became well-known in the region as a trapper and efficient winter traveler. In the later days of the HBC motor schooner *Fort McPherson*, he was her engineer during the summer transportation season. Renowned Danish explorer Knud Rasmussen, who witnessed the arrival of *El Sueño* at King William Island on 23 September 1923, mentioned that accompanying Norberg was Henry Bjorn, an HBC employee of Danish origin. Either Godsell was mistaken, not actually present at the departure, or an exchange had been made along the way. The Company motor schooner *Fort McPherson* had been at Tree River to load supplies when the *Lady Kindersley* arrived. Her normal engineer was Rudolph Johnson but during the winter of 1923-1924 he assisted Clarke at the Kent River Post.

As previously mentioned, Otto Torrington later became the engineer on the vessel. It is likely he replaced Johnson so Bjorn had to be reassigned to the King William Island mission. Fred Jacobsen was likely the captain of the *Fort McPherson* at the time but probably exchanged with William Seymour sometime after. Seymour had been ice pilot for the *Lady Kindersley* for the trip around Point Barrow. Jacobsen, in accordance with HBC records, spent 1923 as manager of a new outpost at Cambridge Bay. There were very poor company records from this time so this theory is somewhat speculative. Also, because there was "bad blood" between Clarke (the local man in charge) and Godsell, Clarke may have simply refrained from informing Godsell of the substitutions.

Photo 16-2

Happy HBC adventurers at Tree River Post in 1923 (by Leo Hansen, photographer to Knud Rasmussen's 5th Thule Expedition.) Author's researched guess of those shown, left to right: Henry Bjorn, Pete Norberg, Otto Torrington, Rudolf Johnson, William Seymour, and Fred Jacobsen.
Danish Arctic Institute photograph ID 122484

Nearly a year after the departure, Godsell received a report from Norberg advising of the early outcome of the mission. Godsell's summary of it is quoted below:

> With fair winds they had sailed the *El Sueño* and towed *The Hobo.* When the wind or ice were bad they cranked up *The Hobo* engine and towed the *El Sueño.* On the southern shore of King William's Land they built their shack of sailcloth and lumber and covered it with snow blocks when winter came along. Afterwards Pete scoured the country with his dog-team. He visited Adelaide and Boothia Peninsulas and at these two places, and the mouth of Back's River,

> located altogether four hundred unknown [Inuit] with whom he had done a thriving trade. Knud Rasmussen, the Danish explorer, had passed through the Arctic that winter so he received one visitor to break the monotony of his isolation.

The report probably reached Godsell as a result of a winter trip by Bjorn. William Hoare, in the early winter of 1925 (while working on field wildlife research for the Canadian government), reported travelling the final part of a journey to Fort Norman, Northwest Territories, with Bjorn and his Inuit travelling partner. Bjorn informed him that their journey had started on King William Island in December 1924.

Photo 16-3

Canvas house HBC King William Land, September 1925.
This was the post established by Pete Norberg and Henry Bjorn in 1923.
Library and Archives Canada/81-1925 L.T.B (Lachlan Taylor Burwash)

The year of 1924 was a difficult one for the HBC as the *Lady Kindersley* was lost near Point Barrow, about 300 miles north of the Arctic Circle (see following map), and as a result there was an extreme lack of new goods for the trading posts. Personnel were scrambling to distribute available goods and few records of events were kept. The activities of *El Sueño* during this period are unknown, but it is unlikely that she remained idle. Norberg's inclinations would be to take his fur trading returns out and to resupply his trading goods. As recorded in HBC post records, Sergeant Fred A. Barnes of the RCMP detachment at Tree Island did make contact with Norberg on a patrol to King William Island in the winter of 1925. It is noted in the post record of 3

June 1925 that Norberg reported to Barnes that he had traded for 400-500 foxes but was not contemplating making a dog team trip out that spring.

Map 16-2

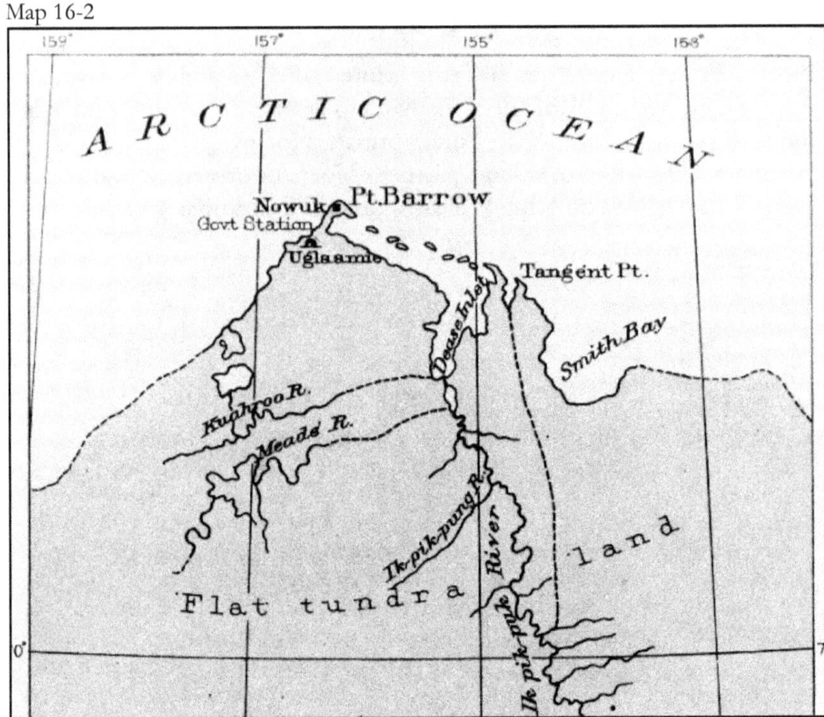

Point Barrow, northernmost point of Alaska, U.S., is situated on the Arctic Ocean. Naval History and Heritage Command photograph NH 75834

Barnes' contact with Norberg was made during a 1,357-mile winter patrol from 1 April to 3 June 1925 under horrific conditions. As reported in the RCMP Commissioners reports for 1925 and 1926, the sergeant investigated several murders in the area of King William Island as a consequence of the Canadian justice system extending into the lands and customs of the almost isolated peoples of the central Arctic. Of interest to the *El Sueño* history, one such murder involved an Inuit man (first known to authorities as Tekack but later as Toongnaak), who, shot another man in a dispute over a woman in early January 1921, long before the patrol. Barnes was unable to pursue the accused to a distant hunting location; but he did gather details of the case and announced he would return to make an arrest.

Subsequently *El Sueño* and Norberg returned to the Tree River Post on 20 September 1925 after stops at Cambridge Bay and Kent

Peninsula. Her entrance into Cambridge Bay on 30 August was too late for Norberg to meet the HBC supply ship *Baychimo*, or Fur Trade Commissioner Angus Brabant who was travelling aboard, having departed Cambridge Bay on August 22nd. Brabant must have been very interested in Norberg's venture as he had the *Baychimo* make a second visit to Tree River on August 25th to seek news about Norberg's return. As no note appears in the Tree River Post records of his fur trade, it is presumed these were left in the warehouse at Kent Peninsula.

Norberg arrived with Otto Torrington (presumably picked up at the Kent Peninsula Post) and surprisingly also brought along a large number of passengers from King William Island who also served as his crew. They were the accused murderer from King William Island along with five witnesses, three women and some children. To the surprise of those at Tree Island, the accused had voluntarily given himself up and was being transported with Pete's assistance to the police post there to be arrested, thus obviating a further patrol to King William Island by the police. After arrest at Tree River, and transportation west over the ice, the accused was convicted of a lesser charge of manslaughter and sentenced to a year of confinement on Herschel Island.

In the following photo in front of the Cambridge Bay Post building, Peter Norberg is on the left and "Lockie" Burwash (petting dog) on the right, with several members of the *Fort McPherson* crew. The rest including the accused, (second from left in the rear row) are the passengers carried by *El Sueño*.

Photo 16-4

Group at Cambridge Bay after boats arrived, 1925.
Library and Archives Canada/ ID 5274804 (Lachlan Taylor Burwash)

Well-known Canadian government investigator Major Lachlan ("Lockie") Taylor Burwash (who had disembarked from the *Lady Kindersley*) was residing in the vacant HBC company camp building at Cambridge when the *El Sueño* arrived in company with HBC's *Fort McPherson.* The *McPherson* was returning to Cambridge Bay to pick up another load of supplies after delivering a first one from Bernard Harbour to King William Island. Burwash was waiting for the *Fort McPherson* to pick him up for transport to King William Island. He photographed both vessels as well as other scenes around Cambridge, and later the post building at Simpson Strait on King William Island established by Norberg's mission. He and replacement HBC Post Manager William "Paddy" Gibson, as well of the crew of the *Fort McPherson*, resided at the post during the winter of 1925-1926.

In addition to the canvas residence house, the post contained a cache/store structure. It appears, from another of Burwash's photographs, that the base of this structure may have been the old scow *The Hobo* that Norberg and his partner used to bring their supplies and trading outfit to the location. The entire building was supported by, and rested on, old oil drums.

When *El Sueño* eventually arrived at Tree Island she was taken over from Norberg by HBC Post Manager Foster Rymer ("Ray") Ross. Ross immediately readied the vessel for a winter trading venture to the west in the Coppermine area (formerly Fort Hearne, and later renamed Kugluktuk) under employee Ambrose. The latter individual was a former CAE member thought to be the long-term HBC interpreter and trapper Ambrose Arnavigak. Sadly, he was reported, in *The Beaver* magazine of March 1936, to have died along with his wife of measles in 1935.

Reverted to free-trapper status, Pete Norberg sailed with the vessel to aid in navigation and the establishment of winter quarters. He intended to spend the winter trapping in an area about 40 miles west of Tree River but, because of weather delays, the vessel did not get away until 28 September when there was a favourable sailing wind. Interestingly, the prisoner and some of his party were entrusted to Pete's care pending their later transportation west for trial, initially to Herschel Island, and finally to Aklavik. This action speaks highly of the rapport he had developed with the peoples of the central Arctic and the respect he had developed with both the HBC and RCMP. Although he was not renowned for his writing or clerical abilities, his presence at the forefront of the march of traders into the area probably softened the highly impactful process and avoided conflicts because of miscommunication.

The departure was almost the last record of *El Sueño* found in HBC records. Based on interviews and personal communications by John MacFarlane in 1991 with both Sven Johansson and Scotty Gall, it appears the vessel was eventually sold to Pete Norberg who fitted her with an engine. Afterwards she was apparently passed to his son Johnny.

Frustratingly, the Norberg purchase of *El Sueño* cannot be confirmed. It is also possible, as mentioned in the 3 January 1933 issue of the *Vancouver Province*, this was one of the vessels wrecked by Pete: "Though a skilled navigator Norberg has wrecked about five schooners in Arctic waters and lived, of course to tell the stories."

An introduction to the Captain Gustav ("Gus") Foellmer album, kept by Ian Malcolm ("Jack") MacKinnon and now held by the Vancouver Maritime Museum, indicates that *El Sueño* was one of three HBC vessels lost in the Arctic along with schooners *Fort McPherson* and *Fort James*. MacKinnon was an HBC employee who served on the *Lady Kindersley* and was post manager at Cambridge Bay from 1927-1932. A photo of *El Sueño* grounded and angled against a shore in the album captioned "Schooner '*El Sueño*' Lost at Tree Island 1922" is either mislabeled or simply another one of the apparent losses she recovered from during her long life.

Photo 16-5

El Sueño grounded and heeled over to port.
Courtesy Vancouver Maritime Museum (from Captain Gustav Foellmer album)

Pete's history following the King William Island HBC venture is somewhat difficult to trace. The *Vancouver Province* of 15 October 1926 reports that he must have returned to the King William Island area where he discovered traces of the Franklin Expedition at Thunder Cove on the Adelaide Peninsula, ten miles across Simpson Strait from the island. The items consisted of a skull, fragments of navy cloth, a piece of shoe leather, and a piece of oak from a sled runner. The finds were eventually taken to Ottawa, and then to England, where they were identified as belonging to the lost Franklin ships.

Life was never boring in the northern regions as the 4 August 1927 *Edmonton Journal* story "Children with Viking Blood in Veins save Their Father's Boat" revealed. Pete, and a partner Dan J. Bromfield, with Pete's 16-year-old daughter Agnes and 14-year-old son Johnny were on the way to winter trapping in the remote Back River region when, during a huge storm, the children's vessel the *Sea-Lion* (which was under tow) was de-masted and separated from Pete and Bromfield who were on the powered vessel *Ujuk*. A frantic search effort was undertaken, ending in success when the two children were found two days later in Stapleton Bay. Owing to the lateness of the season, both vessels were forced to winter in the bay, where the children caught more than fifty white foxes.

The location of "Stapleton Bay" is a bit of mystery. In the context of the previous newspaper articles, it might be assumed that it was close to Thunder Cove (where the skull was recovered), but current maps do not make reference to such, although there are numerous, small, unnamed bays and inlets in the area. There is, however, a "Stapyton Bay" near Bernard Harbour, many miles to the west of Thunder Cove; its existence does not seem to seriously distract from the theory that the location of the shipwreck was on the Adelaide Peninsula.

Pete's family and Bromfield seem to have dedicated their winter activities, up until the winter of 1929, to trapping on the Adelaide Peninsula and Back River areas. Pete and Agnes came out to the "bright lights" during the winter of 1929-1930, when they spent time on Vancouver Island and acquired the motor boat *Cinderella*. In the summer of 1930, they made an epic voyage down the Mackenzie River and along the Arctic coast to Coppermine where Agnes was married to Slim Semmler. While they were away, as noted in Richard S. Finnie's book *Lure of the North*, Johnny Norberg spent the winter trapping with his future brother-in-law near Bernard Harbour, where both were involved in a fracas with a Russian trapper named Graubline.

It is not known where Pete spent his time following the wedding, but in early 1931 he made a trip to eastern Canada for vacation, leaving by air. His return from Fort McMurray to Coppermine, arranged by Patsy Klengenberg, was on Bill Spence's Fairchild float plane. Patsy was returning from Vancouver with a new partner, Jimmy Lythgoe, for his fur business. He had been in Vancouver to attend to his late father Christian Klengenberg's affairs. An "enigma of the Arctic," Christian had passed away while completing his autobiography. He was hated by some, feared by a few, but grudgingly respected by many for his survival skills and his loyalty to his family. His son was bringing back his ashes to be spread at his old home on Rymer Point and were reportedly contained in a tobacco can carried in the plane's cabin.

When the plane landed on 26 June, an impromptu gathering took place on the riverbank as the plane was being refueled. Whether there to pay last respects or merely from curiosity, it did represent a change of guard from the original tough characters that established the fur trade in the western Arctic to the newer ones as better transportation and communications were creeping in and permanent settlements were being established. Christian Klengenberg was gone and only Pete and Ambrose remained of the old generation. It had been twenty-six years since Klengenberg had first contacted the isolated Inuit people of Victoria Island.

Photo 16-6

Shown left to right are: Bill Spence, Richard Bonnycastle (HBC district manager who was in the Arctic struggling to restore the Company to financial viability), Revered J. H. Webster (Anglican minister based at Coppermine), Pete Norberg, Fred Barnes (former RCMP sergeant and HBC's Coppermine post manager) Ambrose Aranavigak (who accompanied Scotty Gall on his overland winter journey to Fairbanks in 1924), Jimmie Lythgoe and Patsy Klengenberg.
Library and Archives Canada/5275538 (Richard S. Finnie, 26 June 1932)

Photo 16-7

Bill Spence's Fairchild float plane taking off from Coppermine River.
Library and Archives Canada/5275538 (Richard S. Finnie, 26 June 1932)

AFTERMATH AND CONCLUSION

Further glimpses of the final fate of the *El Sueño* remain shrouded at the present time. One of the final photographs of her taken at Cambridge Bay reveal her original fine lines as those of a racing yacht despite the many years of hard labour in Arctic waters for, at times, indifferent owners. Her wheel, the racing tiller-helm replacement and presumably the one skilfully crafted and described by William Coffee, is evident on her cabin wall.

Pete Norberg died in 1933 in a canoe mishap while trying to shoot Bloody Falls, Nunavut. His body was never found. His extraordinary life and valuable exploits have now been documented in a film made by TV Ontario, "Edna's Bloodline," narrated by his granddaughter Edna Elias, the former Commissioner of Nunavut.

C. H. Clarke left the HBC in 1924. After a brief business venture in Vancouver, he returned to the Arctic as a principal with the newly formed Canalaska Fur Trading Company that was partly owned and closely associated with Captain Christian Theodore Pedersen. Canalaska competed with the HBC until Pedersen sold out to the HBC in 1939. It appears that former HBC employees Rudolph Johnson and Henry Bjorn joined this new company. In 1927 the trading post that Norberg had established at Simpson Strait was moved east to where Amundsen had wintered in 1903-1905 and where the rival Canalaska Company was setting up a competing post. These two trading posts evolved and became the permanent settlement Gjoa Haven (named for Amundsen's ship) in the heart of the Northwest Passage.

Photo 16-8

El Sueño at Cambridge Bay in 1925. The vessel behind is the HBC trading schooner *Fort MacPherson.* Note the ship's wheel mounted on the cabin.
Library and Archives Canada/MIKAN 3394078 (Lachlan Taylor Burwash)

From the date of *El Sueño*'s initial voyage many other fur trading vessels visited Gjoa Haven from the west. In 1928 Major Lachlan Taylor Burwash made a second wintering visit to King William Island, this time on the government schooner *Ptarmigan.* In 1929 a vessel of different origin wintered there. She was the HBC's schooner *Fort James* out of St. John's, Newfoundland. She had wintered at Oscar Bay north of Gjoa Haven in 1928-1929, her arrival marking a significant achievement for the Hudson's Bay Company, whose vessels had finally completed the navigation of the long-sought-after Northwest Passage. Indeed, considering that Company vessels had previously reached the Pacific Coast both by the Panama Canal and via Cape Horn, they had circumnavigated not only North America but all of America. Yet little fuss was made of the event; the venerable old company merely continued on exchanging their tea and rifle cartridges for fox pelts.

The *Fort McPherson* was the most frequent of the visitors. Her final voyage to the island was made in 1930 just before she was wrecked off the south coast of Victoria Island (today, part of Nunavut). Her master was David O. Morris, and her engineer, Otto Torrington. Like the schooner, it was also Torrington's last voyage in Arctic waters. After the wreck Otto attempted to return to the "bright lights" of the city but he had been in the north too long. Almost broke, he returned to the north to try to settle down at Port Radium on Great Bear Lake but even this compromise did not work for him. In his book *Lure of the North* Richard S. Finnie reported, "One day, not long ago, he was found in a cabin, dead, a gun beside him."

Many vessels have long and varied careers. *El Sueño* and her pioneering voyage across Queen Maud Gulf without an engine in uncharted waters stands as a magnificent piece of seamanship that extended settlements along the Northwest Passage. With this achievement she put the HBC out in front in the western Arctic fur trade and gave the company bragging rights to claim a first in the west-to-east navigation of the Northwest Passage. Her significance in helping to establish early Arctic trade cannot be overstated, especially in light of the fact she had been built to race. In the Arctic, she had realized another ribbon-worthy victory.

Photo 16-9

Vancouver Maritime Museum 2018 Northwest Passage Hall of Fame Award
Expedition Inductee:
Hudson's Bay Company Expedition to King William Island 1923-1925.
Presented to Gordon Norberg, grandson of Pete Norberg.
George Duddy collection

17

Arctic Trading Schooner *Anna Olga*, A Poulsbo Vessel

Photo 17-1

Schooner *Anna Olga*, constructed in 1912, with sails down, at sea.
Wikimedia Commons

As the Klondike and Alaska gold rushes waned, the pursuits of northern-looking adventurers and entrepreneurs turned to other tangible economic ventures and the means of accessing them. One such enterprise was the expansion of fur trade, which had begun across the wild, forested expanse of what is now Canada in the early seventeenth century, sustained by the trapping of beavers to satisfy the European demand for felt hats. In the early 1900s, as settlement spread north and west, the HBC, and rival free traders, intensified the northward push of the trade. Fur traders moved into the Arctic territories previously the domain of whalers, who had abandoned their posts as the whaling economy declined and, from 1912 to the early 1930s, the HBC established a series of trading posts in the Arctic.

In the first half of the twentieth century motor schooners were the prime tool that allowed the fur trade, and hence the practical Canadian boundary, to be carried across the Arctic Ocean. These hardy vessels were wooden, of various sizes, mast and sail plans, and filled an important role in the Arctic fur trade. They transported people, dogs, equipment and trading supplies, and the harvested fur. As well, fuel and building materials were brought to the area, the Arctic being mostly devoid of trees suitable for cabin-building and firewood collection.

One such motor schooner was the *Anna Olga.* American-built and owned, she later came under Canadian ownership and continued to ply deep waters until 1945 when aircraft and ice-strengthened steel-hulled vessels largely replaced wooden boats. During her long service, she touched the lives of many of Canada's western Arctic residents and sojourners in the early half of the twentieth century, as well as their neighbours in the United States' Pacific Northwest.

FAILED WHALING AND TRADING VENTURE

Anna Olga came to life in an American shipyard, financed and built in the small Puget Sound community of Poulsbo, in Washington State. Much of the early fur trapping in Canada's western Arctic region was conducted by Americans. Many were ex-whalers from the Beaufort Sea region, entering by way of the Alaskan coast, west of the Canadian boundary. As late as 1896 they maintained a wintering community at Herschel Island in the Yukon close to the international boundary.

Photo 17-2

Poulsbo, Washington, 1911.
Poulsbo Historical Society photograph

In 1912 the community of Poulsbo—located on the Kitsap Peninsula overlooking Liberty Bay, on the west side of Puget Sound—was populated mainly by Norwegian-Americans. (Today, Poulsbo is proudly called "Little Norway.") At the time it was the base of an Alaskan cod fishing and processing business. Captain Steen (sometimes spelled Stein) was of Norwegian birth and lived near Herschel Island with his Inuit wife and family and visited the community to convince George C. Teien and Nels Sonju—two partners in a cod fishing business—about the rich potential of fur trading in the Canadian Arctic.

Steen was much influenced by his encounter with Roald Amundsen during the winter of 1905-1906 when Amundsen had wintered his famous schooner *Gjoa* near Steen's home at King Point, Yukon, on completion of his celebrated voyage through previously unnavigated waters of the Northwest Passage. Teien and Sonju put up $1,500 each to match Steen's investment and the venture, known as Poulsbo Whaling and Trading Co., was created. A local shipbuilder Einar Nilsen was engaged and the vessel *Anna Olga* was built, outfitted, and finally registered, in the spring of 1912.

A four-man crew made the initial voyage to the Arctic with Captain Steen, Teien's 17-year-old son Clarence as cook, John Sundbiad from Minnesota who was a good friend of George Teien and served as engineer, and John Erland, an older yet very experienced Finnish sailor who was the mate. Lastly, Mr. Wagoner, who was supposed to be their pilot, turned out to be a fraud and was left ashore at Nome.

Stories of *Anna Olga*'s voyage to the Arctic, her use in trapping on the Mackenzie Delta during 1912-1913, her return to Teller, Alaska, after wintering on the northern coast in 1913-1914, along with the return of members of the crew with their furs to Seattle, is richly told in a journal article "Questing for Gold and Furs in Alaska" by Svene Arestad (*Norwegian-American Studies*, University of Minnesota Press 1962). Included is the story of George Teien and Nels Sonju's unsuccessful attempt to bring replenishment supplies to *Anna Olga* at Point Barrow in 1913.

Anna Olga's two-year Arctic fur trading venture should have been a financial as well as an operational success. However, it was not, owing to the failure of the crew to take advantage of a generous offer by Mr. Swanson of the trading schooner *Red Wing* while wintering on the coast, and the precipitated fur price collapse brought on by WWI, which left the partners with a small loss for all their efforts. The collapse was unknown to the crew and Swanson at the time the offer was made— such are the whims of fortune in the trading business.

The return of the *Anna Olga* in the summer of 1914 to Teller, Alaska, was nothing short of remarkable; the whole of the voyage being under sail, necessitated by the loss of her propeller before entering Clarence Lagoon in the Yukon. At Teller she was stored for future use or sale. Steen quit the venture and presumably returned to his home and family, while the remaining crewmembers returned to Seattle, with the fur, by commercial steamer.

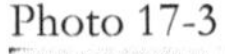
Photo 17-3

Ice shoved up on the beach at Clarence Lagoon, Yukon Territory, 2 July 1914.
Canadian Museum of History Archives photo by George H. Wilkins
uploaded to Wikimedia Commons

No trace has been found in the record about the fate of the schooner *Red Wing*, which had been forced to winter in 1913 with the *Anna Olga* in Clarence Lagoon because of impassable ice conditions to the west, blocking their passage to Point Barrow, where, by prearrangement, the relief supplies were supposed to land and be stored, but as previously noted, this had not been achieved by George Teien and Nels Sonju.

ANNA OLGA PURCHASED BY MARTIN ANDREASEN

The schooner *Anna Olga* was sold after 1914 to American Captain Martin Andreasen, a friend of Nels Sonju. In the U.S. Registration Record "M. Andersen" appeared as owner as late as June 1925. Andreasen was well familiar with *Anna Olga*, having encountered her in 1913 during his fur trading endeavours, and also knew her builder in Poulsbo.

Norwegian-born Martin Andreasen and his younger half-brother Ole are thought to have come to the Arctic aboard a whaling ship. Henry Larsen, of *St. Roch* fame, reported that Ole came from a village close to where he was born near Olso. The brothers had settled in the north Arctic coast area, becoming trappers and fur traders, and operated along the Alaskan and Canadian coasts and the Mackenzie Delta. (In 1942, Larsen as master of the *St. Roch* became one of the first persons to sail the famed Northwest Passage from west to east after starting the voyage in 1940.)

Martin Andreasen was convinced of the potential of Arctic fur trade by Roald Amundson in 1906, and following construction of the vessel *North Star* at Poulsbo in 1908, he took her to the Arctic coast and brought out a fortune in fox pelts. Andreasen is reported to have made a profit of $150,000 from the furs. No doubt Captain Steen's visit to Poulsbo, and spearheading of the establishment of the Poulsbo Whaling and Trading Co., was tempered by his almost certain knowledge of the success of the *North Star*.

Photo 17-4

Schooner *Anna Olga* owned by Martin Andreasen at Baillie Island, NWT.
Arctic Institute of North America, University of Calgary (Frances Gladys O'Kelly's online photo album for the maiden voyage of the *Lady Kindersley* in 1921)

The crew of the *Anna Olga* had encountered the Andreasen brothers at Clarence Lagoon on the Canadian side of the Yukon-Alaska border in the late summer of 1913. Here, where Martin Andreasen maintained a small trading post, they were forced to winter because of impassable ice conditions to the west, blocking their passage to Cape Barrow. Trapped with them was the Alaskan trading schooner *Red Wing*. Facing them along the Alaska coast was a group of ships striving to make Herschel Island before the summer shipping ended.

This group included Vilhjalmur Stefansson's ships of the Canadian Arctic Expedition (CAE): *Arctic*, *Mary Sachs* and the ill-fated *Karluk*; Captain Christian Pedersen's ill-fated trader *Elvira*; Captain Louis Lane's *Polar Bear*, and Captain Stephen F. Cottle's *Belvedere*—the last of the old steam whalers. The *Polar Bear* had several American adventurers and academics on board completing an Arctic cruise while the *Belvedere* was under contract to bring supplies to the expedition as well as to the Herschel Island settlement.

During the winter of 1913 two perilous overland transits—involving crossing the northern Alaskan mountains—were made by crewmembers escaping the ice-trapped fleet. The first was by the very adept and well-liked San Francisco-based trader Captain Christian Pedersen of the abandoned *Elvira,* and Captain Olaf Swenson a well-known Arctic trader and part owner of the *Belvedere.* Using hired Inuit guides and their dog teams, Pedersen and Swenson's mission was to carry news of the difficulties of their ships, the status of the CAE and the disappearance of the *Karluk,* and to arrange for relief supplies. They left Icy Reef on 21 October and reached Fairbanks nearly a month later on 15 November, covering an estimated 630 miles over rough terrain.

The second overland transit from the ice-locked ships was made by Captain Louis Lane who had "urgent business" in Seattle, and three crew members of the *Polar Bear.* A description of their ordeal is found in Will E. Hudson's aptly titled book, *Icy Hell.*

Photo 17-5

Wife Welcomes Castaway Seadog

Elvira's Chief Home From Arctic

Photo of the ice-gripped vessel *Elvira* in an article covering Pedersen's epic journey. *San Francisco Chronicle,* 22 December 1913 (Newspaper.com)

Anna Olga's arrival at the Lagoon coincided with that of the two Andreasen brothers who were on the schooner *North Star*, sporting a fine cargo of fur. Having expended their trading goods, the brothers were bound to Nome for replacements. Unable to proceed—and unlike Teien and Sonju—they sold their furs to Mr. Swanson on the trading schooner *Red Wing* for a good price (reported to be about $45 per skin) and obtained fresh supplies. Martin Andreasen returned east with the *North Star* to pick up more fur, assisted by a local Inuit as Ole elected to remain behind.

While at his nearby cabin, located west of the border in Alaska, Ole was visited by some of the Stefansson party. Shortly after, Ole joined the CAE 1913–1916, which famed explorer Vilhjalmur Stefansson organized, and was directed to explore the regions west of Parry Archipelago for the Government of Canada. Ole Andreasen and Storker Theodor Storkenson, together with Stefansson, completed a remarkable ice journey to the north, discovering a number of new islands.

Meanwhile, Martin Andreasen returned the *North Star* to the Lagoon for wintering after further trading to the east before freeze-up. He transported the new furs by sled to the *Elvira* where he sold them to Pedersen. They were subsequently lost when the *Elvira* was abandoned and sank. Martin Andreasen's prized season was not yet over. Stefansson showed up at the wintering site in early 1914 and purchased the *North Star* and all of the trading outfit for $13,000 (prior to purchase of *Anna Olga* by Andreasen).

The year 1919 marked Martin Andreasen and *Anna Olga*'s final involvement with the CAE. As reported by a 25 September 1919 Associated Press release, the last participants Martin Killin and Adelbert Gumaer left the Arctic on the *Anna Olga* bound for Nome. Martin Andreasen continued to use *Anna Olga* in his fur trade business until his death of a heart attack in the winter of 1922-1923. He had been successful in his fur trading and trapping endeavours to the very end, reflected in an excerpt from Sven Johansson and John MacFarlane's 1990 online Nauticapedia article "Captain Christian Theodore Pedersen and the Arctic Fur Trade" describing Pedersen's encounter of the *Anna Olga* in 1923:

> They then steamed into Amundsen Gulf where there was no sign of ice. Steaming toward Coronation Gulf, Pedersen sighted a small schooner in the harbour at Pierce Point. It was the *Anna Olga* with only the engineer, Pete Brandt aboard. The owner, Captain Martin Andreassen (sic), had died of a heart attack while in winter

> quarters at Coppermine. They had more than 1,600 white foxes [furs] on board.
> Hoping to profit from this unexpected turn of events Pedersen offered to help them get the *Anna Olga* to Baillie Island and then to Herschel Island. He hoped that the RCMP Inspector at Herschel Island would put the skins up for sale. Arriving at Baillie Island he saw the *Arctic* unloading all of the supplies for the RCMP buildings there instead of at Cambridge Bay. Inspector S. T. Wood was there and took the skins back to Herschel Island with him. Pedersen made a brief foray for bowhead whales in the area to the east of Baillie Island but soon started to head home. The *Arctic* had already left for San Francisco from Herschel Island. Inspector Wood asked the Hudson's Bay Company manager and Pedersen to bid on the fox skins. Pedersen bid $2,000 more than the HBC and was able to purchase the entire lot.

The last year that foreign-registered vessels, including those commanded by the well-liked and expert ice navigator Captain Christian Pedersen, were permitted to trade in the Canadian Arctic east of Herschel Island was 1923. RCMP Inspector Stuart Taylor Wood, who was well-respected and served at Herschel Island from 1919 to 1924, had the responsibility of enforcing this new order as well as myriad other duties, including dealing with estate matters relating to Andreasen's sudden passing, the disposition of his fur, schooner and other assets.

OLE ANDREASEN

Photo 17-6

Ole Andreasen at Herschel Island, Yukon Territory, August 1930.
Library and Archives Canada (Richard S. Finnie collection)

Ole Andreasen, the likely beneficiary of his brother's assets, was the third owner of the *Anna Olga*. Based on Sven Johansson's experience (a modern-day Arctic explorer and former master of the *North Star of Herschel Island*), formal registration and transfer of ownership of vessels in the Canadian Arctic was not enforced, obscuring owner histories. However, Andreasen's ownership appears confirmed by references in Bruce MacDonald's book *North Star of Herschel Island*, including one from an Inuit source:

> Yeah! When we get out to Qikiqtatruk (Herschel Island) with Ole Andreasen's boat named Ann Olga (sic). When we arrived Pedersen's big ship used to arrive.

It is known from Richard S. Finnie's book *Lure of the North*, and one of his photographs, that Ole travelled to Herschel Island in 1930 where Finnie managed to capture a photo of him.

Ole Andreasen and his Inuit wife Susanah, with an address of Atkinson Point, NWT, became naturalized Canadians on 2 March 1927. The *Anna Olga* remained on the US vessel registry with her home port in Seattle, Washington, in 1925 under ownership of M. Andersen (sic). However, in 1926 she was listed under "Vessels Sold to Aliens" (British). It is likely that the transfer occurred as a result of the settlement of Martin Andreasen's estate.

Photo 17-7

Fishing for char on the Yukon coast between Herschel Island and Shingle Point, circa 1930. The boats are the *Anna Olga* and the *Blue Fox*.
Library and Archives Canada/MIKAN 364912

Details of Ole Andreasen, his family, and his life as a trapper and fur trader at Shingle Point in the Yukon, and Atkinson Point and

Richardson Islands in the Northwest Territories (today Nunavut) are revealed in the article "The people of the CAE" under the banner, "The Story of the Canadian Arctic Expedition 1913-1918" (2003, Gray). Ole Andreasen's hallmark was generosity. He is said to have made a fortune in his fur trading business but gave most of it away without discrimination to natives or foreigners. From knowledge he acquired during the CAE, he encouraged and assisted local Inuit to travel to Banks Island to find superior trapping potential.

Throughout most of his trapping and trading career he worked with Captain Christian Pedersen. A lover of the isolation of the Arctic, Ole was a self-effacing personality who accomplished extraordinary things. His last adventure was as mate of the *St. Roch* when she made her historic east-to-west crossing of the Northwest Passage in 1944.

In the 1930s Ole Andreasen moved his family to Richardson Island near the south shore of Victoria Island in Coronation Gulf. Records held at NWT Archives in Yellowknife, document his fur trade work for Christian Pedersen from 1931 to 1935. It is not clear what his business arrangements were after Pedersen's Canalaska Company was sold to the Hudson's Bay Company in 1936.

Photo 17-8

Schooner Lady Richardson in winter quarters at Richardson Point 1943. Hudson's Bay Company Archives, Archives of Manitoba, L. A. Learmonth HBC collection files, HBCA 1987/363-E-393/7 (photographer L. A. Learmonth).

Based on photographs found in the Hudson's Bay Archives, Ole owned the schooner *Lady Richardson* in 1942. It is not known at this time whether this vessel was a replacement for the *Anna Olga.* Bruce MacDonald's book *North Star* provides a reference (at page 188) that in 1947, after Ole's death, the *Lady Richardson* was bound for King's Bay on

Victoria Island, in company with two other vessels, was wrecked and subsequently lost in a storm. One of the other vessels, the *Krochik*, was tossed on the shore and smashed. The other, the *Blue Fox*, survived but had her bow smashed in.

During the war years when Henry Larsen was looking for crew for the *St. Roch,* to make the now famous east-to-west Northwest Passage voyage, RCMP Commissioner Stuart Taylor Wood remembered his old western Arctic colleagues and recommended that Ole Andreasen and Rudolph Johnson be made special constables for the undertaking. Johnson was also a well-known personality. He had served as engineer on the Hudson's Bay Company vessel *Fort McPherson*. Both men were hired, flown to Halifax, Nova Scotia, to join the *St. Roch*, and completed the voyage to Victoria in 1944. Johnson served as second engineer and Ole as mate. Both received the Polar Medal—awarded to persons who render extraordinary services in the polar regions and Canada's North.

Arctic Polar Medal

Following Ole's passing, in Victoria on 8 December 1947, he received "full Mounted Police honours." It was a doubly important recognition for him considering thirty years previously he had been one of three ice travelers of the Stefansson party who had travelled far to the north to find new islands for Canada.

FRED L. "SLIM" AND AGNES SEMMLER

The last and presumably fourth owner of the *Anna Olga* was the well-known trader Fred L. "Slim" Semmler. He arrived in the Arctic via the Mackenzie River from a farm in Alberta and ended up trapping in the Coronation Gulf area where he met the fabled Arctic adventurer Pete Norberg. He and his mate, Henry Bjorn, had made Arctic history by setting off in the old, unpowered schooner *El Sueño* and a powered barge, *The Hobo*, establishing the first trading post on King William

Island for the Hudson's Bay Company in 1923. Slim also met Pete's son Johnny and his daughter Agnes whom he later married.

Richard S. Finnie, in his delightful book *Lure of the North* describes the wedding that was performed by Reverent J. H. Webster after the Hudson's Bay Company supply ship *Baychimo* arrived at Coppermine. The book includes a wedding photograph of the groom and bride and other members of the wedding party.

Retreating briefly in chronology, it is worth describing events preceding the wedding to understand Agnes's background. In accordance with an article by Donald Gillingham, "Pete Norberg of the Land of the White Fox and Black Day Light," published in the *Province* of 3 January 1932, Agnes and her brother Johnny were sent to the Anglican residential school at Hay River, NWT, where they stayed for ten years, visited by their father only once. Finally, he sent for them and they lived and trapped with him on the Arctic coast, where Agnes survived a shipwreck with Pete, her brother and Pete's trapping partner.

Photo 17-9

At left: Pete Norberg and daughter Agnes aboard *Cinderella* at Coppermine, 1930. NWT Archives photograph N-1979-003-0029_141. Photo at the right is from an article in *The Vancouver Daily Province*, 3 January 1932.

In the winter of 1929-1930 Agnes accompanied Pete to the "white lights" of the outside, visiting cities in Canada, though they spent most of their time in Vancouver. After the ice break-up in 1930, she and Pete sailed down the Mackenzie River system and along the Arctic coast in a 30-foot motorboat, the *Cinderella*. The boat, which had been purchased for a cruise around Vancouver Island, had instead been shipped to Waterways where Gillingham encountered them, for their epic voyage. The vessel eventually reached Coppermine, taking Agnes to her wedding with Semmler.

Pete drowned shortly after Slim and Agnes' marriage in 1930, while attempting to run Bloody Falls on the Coppermine River in a canoe—his body was never recovered.

From 1932 until the mid-1940s the Semmlers operated their popular main trading post at Cape Krusentern in the Coronation Gulf area. They moved their main business to the Tuktoyaktuk area (in the Northwest Territories) in 1945 and eventually to the new town of Inuvik on the Mackenzie Delta in 1956. Here, as in their other locations, they were well-regarded, and added to their fame for their exploits and community service in the Arctic. Agnes was greatly lauded, receiving in 1967 the National Council of Jewish Women award as the "Woman of the Century in the North." She was also the first woman Justice of the Peace and the first woman member of the government of the Northwest Territories.

Photo 17-10

Fred and Agnes Semmler Wedding Party. From L-R: Otto Torrington, Inuit bridesmaid and child, Pete Norberg, Richard Finnie, Agnes Norberg, Fred (Slim) Semmler and the Reverent J. H. Webster.
Library and Archives Canada/MIKAN 3607299 (Richard S. Finnie, 1930)

The HBC established Tuktoyaktuk, a port on the east side of the Mackenzie River Delta on the Beaufort Sea, for transfer of Arctic-bound freight from the Mackenzie River to Arctic supply vessels, after it abandoned ocean supply around Point Barrow. After so many years of providing critical support and services to the Arctic, a tragic end awaited the *Anna Olga*. She was wrecked on a reef near Tuktoyaktuk while delivering trading supplies to Slim's post.

Photo 17-11

Aerial view of Tuktoyaktuk, NWT, July 1946.
(HBC post is behind left spit at top of photo.)
NWT Archives, Kirk family fonds, N-2005-001-0136

While some reports indicate *Anna Olga* was lost in 1944, reports of other details—such as the state of the weather at time of the wreck—are not consistent, and Slim is quoted in the following newspaper account that it was in 1945. Regardless, he and his crew were rescued and part of the cargo was recovered by the schooner *North Star* under Captain Fred Carpenter (the second vessel of this name, subsequently renamed *North Star of Herchel Island*).

Grizzled, Old-Time Trapper In Arctic Always Ready To Discuss Old Days

INUVIK, N.W.T. (UPI) — At a time when it is difficult to find a grizzled, old-time trapper in the Arctic, Slim Semmler represents a real discovery for a southern schooled in romantic yarns of the North.

The streets of most communities in the Northwest Territories aren't really paved with adventure anymore — too many public servants have come here on their civilizing mission for that.

But a cache of the old North lies hidden on Inuvik's Main Street, in a modest wooden building bearing a sign reading:

L. F. Semmler, general merchant and raw fur dealer.

"Get the hell out, I'm closed" is likely to be your greeting if you walk through the door at lunch hour.

But if you don't want to buy a tin of condensed milk or a wolf pelt — but just want to talk about the old days — well there might be time for that.

Semmler forgets the exact year he set out for Canada. "It's so long ago I forget," he says, but the year 1919 sticks in his mind.

He homesteaded in Alberta, relieving the summer stump-pulling with winter fishing and trapping.

"An only Finlander there used to say that Alberta was a school — as soon as you learned to fish and trap and everything then you went North."

He earned his passage on a schooner heading north down the Mackenzie River by piloting the boat and helping to haul it across blocked passages.

Semmler's voyage ended many months later at Young Point on Coronation Gulf, deep in the frigid heart of the Northwest Territory.

"There wasn't a soul there," he says wistfully. "I stayed there 19 years."

He didn't see anybody for several months, but when he came out of the local trading post with the white fox pelts he had trapped during his first year, he met Agnes, now 60, the daughter of a white trapper and an Indian of the old Crow tribe.

They eventually married and had four children.

He summarizes thost 19 years cryptically: "They didn't do much for me. I made a lot of money trapping and trading — some years as much as $12,000 — but I stayed too long.

"I should have got out when the going was good."

The going got bad when he was caught in a hurricane at Tuktoyaktuk in 1945, losing a schooner and $52,000 worth of supplies he had been bringing into his frozen winterland.

It got worse when he left the supplies he managed to rescue with an unscupulous fellow who ran off with them. His losses totaled $100,000.

"If I wasn't broke after 19 years of work I was badly bent," he said.

Semmler's misfortunes were not over. Although he decided that it was time to move into the safer environment of the Mackenzie Delta, near where Inuvik is today, he tried to get another load of fox pelts out of his trap run.

"We tried to overhaul the boat in open sea and had got it done just as the storm hit, but the engineer had put the rods in wrong and she wouldn't go.

"There were waves higher than this house going by the cabin just like express trains. We hit the ice and I flew into the water and the next wave sucked me way up.

"The others were on the shore and I waved goodbye as it caught me, but God must not have wanted me to die just then because it put me down right on top of the ice cake."

The boat had been smashed to bits. It was fall in the Arctic and the snow was coming cold and wet.

But Semmler, his partner and the engineer walked 30 miles until "as luck would have it" they ran into an Indian family where they got "a few dry beans and some half-rotten Arctic char."

That was enough of the traplines. Semmler started a mink ranch in the delta and "did very good" with it until the government made him quit hunting whales to feed the mink.

In 1967 he came to Inuvik and set up a store in a tent.

"When they made roads in the days they didn't have much gravel and after they got into the permafrost everything became soupy mud.

"They'd drag this mud into the tent and we'd have to shovel it out every hour because it was up to our knees."

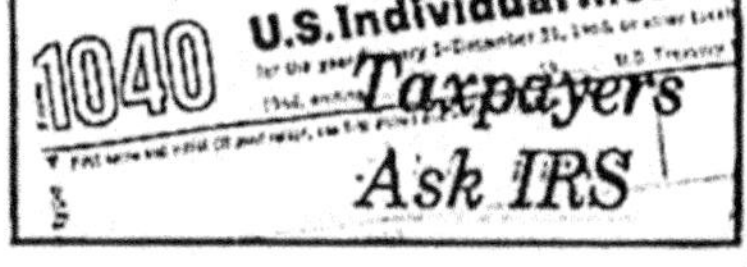

This column of questions and answers on federal tax matters is provided by the local office of the U. S. Internal Revenue Service and is published as a public service to taxpayers. The

reduced by $100 in the case of personal property, but can be deducted in full in the case of business property. For more information, write your IRS district office and ask for a

Escapee To Appear In Film

ATLANTA (UPI) — A convicted murderer who escaped from a South Carolina prison 17 years ago will be returning this fall.

Lewis Wiley won't be going back to serve time, however. He will be the star of a documentary film re-enacting his escape.

Wiley will trek part of the 60 miles he covered in his

The Greenville News (Greenville, South Carolina) 27 August 1972. Newspapers.com

CONCLUSION

The story of this vessel over a forty-year period provides a unique look at the life of Arctic dwellers, providing a common thread to tie together personalities and events that enabled change in the lives of the Inuit as well as immigrant inhabitants, influencing Arctic settlement and socio-economic status. The account of the *Anna Olga* connects innovative and risk-taking southern shipbuilders to significant and interesting Arctic characters who contributed to the modern development of the Arctic.

Based on the opportunities of the arctic fox trade that became available because of changing fashion trends, and recognized by Amundsen and those in the failing whaling industry, Arctic residents looked to southern shipbuilders for supplying the work-horse vessels that would permit the rapid development of this trade. Universally known in the Arctic as motor schooners—regardless of their actual rig—they were built and supplied from shipyards in Vancouver; Edmonton; Poulsbo, Washington; and as far south as San Francisco, California, to be delivered down the Mackenzie River system to the Arctic seas. Dozens of such vessels were eventually owned by prosperous Inuvialuit fur trappers in the Mackenzie Delta but initially, the uncharted shallow waters of the Mackenzie Delta discouraged this supply route. Instead, customers looked to more-reliable supply routes around Point Barrow by sea.

After *Anna Olga*'s initial voyage, Captain Christian Pedersen supplied many vessels, carried on the ships under his command, from builders in San Francisco, chiefly from the George W. Kneass Boat Builder firm. Later, when the HBC entered the Arctic fur trade after 1915, they did likewise with schooners and boats from Vancouver builders. Very few vessels made the entire journey, including the treacherous ice conditions of Point Barrow, under their own means.

The tenacity of the *Anna Olga* represents an outstanding example of superior construction by her builder, and the pluck and skill of those who sailed her.

Photo 17-12

Ole Andreasen (right) greeting Vilhjalmur Stefansson and his wife Evelyn shortly before his death in 1947. Glenbow Archives photograph NA-3457-12

18

Vancouver, Herschel Island, and the Mackenzie Delta

Photo 18-1

Power schooner *Ruby* loading at North Vancouver, 1914.
Vancouver Archives photograph AM54-54: BoP385

Propelled by the fur trade, the Port of Vancouver played a pivotal role in the establishment of Canada's presence and sovereignty in the western Arctic, which led to the founding of settlements along the Northwest Passage. The next chapters describe the hazardous voyages and key events of this enterprise over the span of nearly two decades from 1914-1933.

Except for a shipment made by Captain Christian Klengenberg in his schooner *Maid of Orleans* in 1926, the Hudson's Bay Company (HBC) was the only business to use Vancouver exclusively for Arctic supply. The HBC was a late-comer to the fur trade in the western Arctic, entering after 1913 when Fur Trade Commissioner Robert Hanley Hall realized the company was missing out on the valuable arctic fox trade. It soon became apparent that ocean transport around Alaska was cheaper and more effective than extending their existing Mackenzie River supply system through the twisting shallow maze of the Mackenzie Delta. Thus, Vancouver became the prime source of supply for this trade, with Pauline Cove on Herschel Island (just east of the Yukon-Alaska boundary) as the primary destination port. (See summary Appendix B: Vancouver-loaded Fur Trade Cargos.)

The HBC experimented with overland supply from Hudson Bay in 1928. However, ocean shipping continued until improvements were made to the Mackenzie River transportation, and the port of Tuktoyaktuk was established on the Arctic coast (near the eastern side of the Mackenzie Delta) in 1934. With this improvement, regular voyages from Vancouver were halted, and most shipments were made via the Mackenzie River system—with goods consigned to Tuktoyaktuk.

During this same period, Captain Christian Pedersen was the HBC's main competitor in the western Arctic. He was employed by H. Liebes and Co. of San Francisco until 1923 when he formed his own firm known as the Northern Trading Company. In 1936 this firm, and its Canadian subsidiary the Canalaska Company, were sold to the HBC and the assets—the fur trade posts and Pedersen's last Canadian-registered ship—were integrated into HBC operations.

THE NAUTICAL HIGHWAY TO HERSCHEL ISLAND AND CANADA'S ARCTIC

The route to reach Herschel Island in the western Arctic from the Port of Vancouver was a challenging 3,600-mile transit. Vessels departing Vancouver typically proceeded westward out the Juan de Fuca Strait to the Pacific then followed a great circle route to the Bering Sea via passage through the Aleutian Islands. After transiting the Unimak

Pass near Unalaska Island, ships passed through the Bering Strait to enter the Beaufort Sea (an outlying sea of the Arctic Ocean north of Canada and Alaska).

Map 18-1

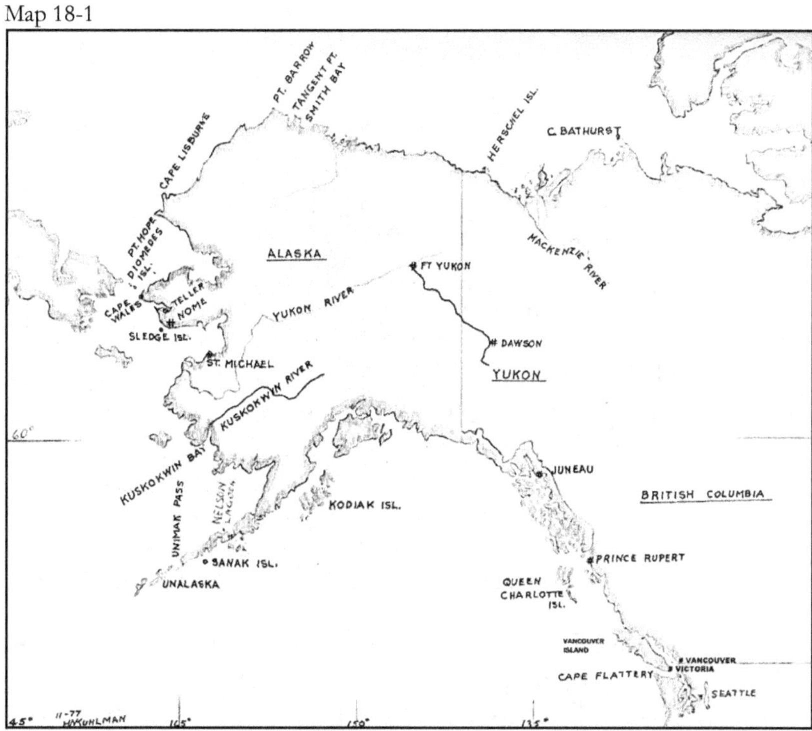

Western Canada and the Arctic. The new HBC Baillie Island Post at Cape Bathurst was the ultimate point in *Ruby*'s 1915 voyage.
From "Aux. Schooner Ruby - Arctic Supply Voyage" by Capt. Ed. Shields, courtesy of *The Sea Chest* (Vancouver, Victoria, and Vancouver Island labeled by author)

Alternatively, ships might travel via the Inside Passage waters to the north end of Vancouver Island or northwards to Prince Rupert before crossing the often storm-wracked Gulf of Alaska. The passage around Point Barrow was fraught with danger. It was difficult and uncertain due to the presence of pack ice most of the year. In the summer, the ice usually receded from the shoreline permitting a navigation window from mid-July to mid-September, which enabled experienced—and lucky—mariners to make their supply runs into Herschel Island and beyond. For ships assembling near Point Barrow to make the run, it was a great source of pride to be the first to reach Herschel Island. Pauline Cove on Herschel Island presented the only safe anchorage on the Arctic coast for large ships. The community was established circa 1890 by wintering-over whalers pursuing bowhead whales.

Photo 18-2

Fleet of Inuit schooners at Pauline Cove, Herschel Island, Arctic coast. Library and Archives Canada/R216/C-66708

A BRIEF HISTORY OF THE SETTLEMENT OF HERSCHEL ISLAND PRIOR TO 1913

There was a large Euro-American presence at Herschel Island, mostly San Francisco-based Americans, hunting bowhead whales for their oil and baleen. In 1893 the Pacific Steam Whaling Company (PSW Co.) constructed buildings on the island that remain today. The "community house" contained a recreation room, an office for the manager and storekeeper, as well as storage facilities. The adjacent "bone house" warehoused whaling products. On 1 February 1924, the building served a grim purpose, as a gallows in answer to the murders of an Inuit named Pugnana and those of Corporal William Andrew Doak of the RCMP and HBC Tree River Post Manager Otto Binder. There, the convicted culprits, after being tried in July 1923 received their punishment and were hung. Alikomiak together with Tatamigana on the first day of the trial had been found guilty of murdering Pugnana, while Alikomiak on the second day received an additional verdict for killing Doak and Binder. In 1893-1894, at the height of the whaling industry, the population on the island was estimated at 1,500 residents making it the largest settlement in the Yukon at that time. As whaling neared its end, due to a diminished population of the mammals and a collapse in demand for whale products, the PSW Co. buildings were lent to the Anglican Church from 1896-1906.

Lacking any formal Canadian presence, the residents of the island operated as a freewheeling frontier outpost under "whaler" law and justice as administered by the whaling captains present on the island. This practice began to change when the first non-native Canadian arrived in 1893. This was Reverend Isaac O. Stringer (later Bishop of the

Yukon) of the Anglican Church of Canada who came to minister to the whalers and evangelize the Inuvialuit who congregated on the island as followers of the whaling industry. In 1896 after a furlough to eastern Canada, Stringer returned with his new nursing-trained bride Sadie and assistant William D. Young, Sadie's uncle who had sold his farm to come with them to act as lay assistant. As the Mackenzie fur trade steamship service which started at Athabasca Landing on the Athabasca River, only extended as far as Fort McPherson south of the Mackenzie Delta, it was necessary for them to complete the final 400 miles of their circular odyssey through the delta and along the coast by open whaleboat, the usual conveyance for this type of journey in those days.

The couple spent five years in the area including four on the island from 1896 up to 1901 and finally returned south to San Francisco on a whaling ship with their two children who were both born in the area. What personal energy was not expended on religious and basic living duties was spent in caring for medical and social needs of the population of the island, and providing education for both natives and whalers alike. Working with whaling captains, they were able to ease many of the problems previously caused by excessive use of alcohol. These were remarkable gifts to the community. As documented in an article in the 9 July 1955 *MacLean*'s magazine by Sadie, the couple was invited to Windsor Castle by King George V and Queen Mary to share with them their remarkable work and experiences in the north.

Noting the rampant use of alcohol and abusive employment by the whalers of the local Inuvialuit (men as meat hunters, and women as clothes-making seamstresses), Stringer successfully helped to induce the Canadian government to establish a police presence on the island. In 1903 Northwest Mounted Police (NWMP) Inspector Francis J. Fitzgerald visited the island. The following year he and Constable Forbes Sutherland established a detachment on the island, housed in two sod huts, until better facilities could be found. In 1911 the police purchased all of the assets of the PSW Co. including the "community house" that had been on-loan to the Anglican Church.

As the NWMP had done on the southern border of the Yukon, at the Chilkoot and White Passes during the gold rush, a handful of dedicated policemen were able to bring about the orderly, and mostly peaceful, establishment of fur trading settlements in the Arctic using Herschel Island as the base and reaching eastern outposts with long-distance patrols. Their presence helped ensure Canada's sovereignty over a vast Arctic region.

To put the scarcity of the population and the geographic vastness of their task into perspective, it was reported in the June 1922 issue of

The Beaver magazine by RCMP Inspector Stuart Wood (the NWMP changed names to Royal NWMP in 1904 and to the more familiar Royal Canadian Mounted Police in February 1920) that along the 1,200-mile coastline from Herschel Island to the eastern end of Coronation Gulf, including King William Island, the native population consisted of just 1,364 people. This would be equivalent today of the student body of an average high school being distributed in small groups along the Trans-Canada Highway between Vancouver and a point just east of Regina, the capital of Saskatchewan, situated on Wascana Creek.

Canada North West Mounted Police and Royal Canadian Mounted Police badges

EVENTS GALVANIZE PUBLIC INTEREST IN ARCTIC

As the whaling industry was in its final death pangs in 1905, several events in the Herschel Island area drew public attention in the south to the Arctic and the its almost unknown citizens of its central area. The first was emergence of Roald Amundsen's party on his ship *Gjoa* from the east after completing the transit of previously unnavigated elements of the Northwest Passage. On 26 August Captain James McKenna of the US registered schooner *Charles Hansen* was first to spot and congratulate the *Gjoa* in the gulf that would later bear Amundsen's name. The party had spent two winters on King William Island undertaking scientific measurements and living amongst the Nechilli peoples. Amundsen brought with him enlarged knowledge of these people, such as their ways of survival, their customs and the animals on which they depended. As a result of his experience, Amundsen later encouraged several of his friends and countrymen to enter into Arctic fur trapping in Canada. These included Christian Sten, and Martin and Ole Andreasson. No doubt Amundsen's neighbour at King Point, where he wintered the *Gjoa* in 1905-1906, is the same Captain "Steen" who showed up in Poulsbo, Washington State in 1912 to arrange for the purchase of the *Anna Olga* (see Chapter 17).

Photo 18-3

Schooner *Gjoa* meeting with US whaler *Charles Hanson*, 26 August 1905.
Photo from *Roald Amundsen's the North West Passage: Being the Record of a Voyage of Exploration of the Ship* Gjoa *1903-1907; Volume 2*

The second event also involved an emergence of a vessel from the east; the reappearance of the US whaling schooner *Olga* also owned by Captain James McKenna. It had "disappeared" the previous fall while under the command of Christian Klengenberg on a whaling voyage from Herschel Island in company with McKenna's other vessel *Charles Hanson.* Klengenberg, a naturalized American citizen of Danish origin, had been instructed to keep the *Charles Hanson* in sight and to return to Herschel Island in the fall in spite of an arrangement Klengenberg claimed he had previously made with McKenna. This would have permitted him to sail east to investigate trading opportunities he conceived many years earlier.

Although the captain of the *Charles Hanson* managed to return as scheduled (*Nunanatsiaq News* 27 February 2009). Klengenberg had ended up far to the east at Penny Bay on Victoria Island. A variety of reasons accounted for this deviation from the planned voyage route; including alleged fog, east blowing storms, and crushing ice being blown in their intended path. Aboard the vessel, in addition to Klengenberg, were the following persons: his family, including his Inupiaq wife Gremmia from Alaska and four children, daughters Weena and Etna and sons Patsy and Jorgen (the latter was born on board); what turned out to be a mutinous crew of nine; and three Inuit families that had been taken aboard to assist with the whaling.

Penny Bay was a location strikingly similar to one that Klengenberg had mentioned to McKenna that he wished to visit after completion of whaling. There, during the winter when the ship was in winter quarters, he made contact with the almost unknown Copper Inuit of that region. Soon thereafter these people were loudly and erroneously touted to be a lost tribe of Blonde Eskimos who had Scandinavian blood flowing in their veins. Through trade with them, Klengenberg accumulated many artifacts and a fortune in fox pelts.

Contact with these people was of huge significance, exciting the interests of explorers like Stefansson and Doctor R. M. Andersen, and educational institutions. Unfortunately for Klengenberg, his discovery was largely overshadowed by the scandal of dead or missing crewmen from his ship. During the winter Klengenberg had shot and killed the ship's engineer Jackson Paul in what was later accepted by a court to be an act of self-defence, possibly because, three others of the crew, who were alleged to have been witnesses to the killing, either died or mysteriously disappeared.

Following *Olga*'s return to Herschel Island in 1906, Klengenberg was not prosecuted, as at the time all of the remaining crew backed his version of events (some later recanted saying they had been intimidated by threats). The whaling community however, was less forgiving; blackballed, Klengenberg could not even obtain passage on a whaling vessel for his family to his home in Alaska. He quickly beat a hasty retreat from Canadian territory, making a perilous voyage to Hope Bay in an open whale boat. He took with him on this voyage his stash of fur acquired on Victoria Island but was forced to hand over half of it to McKenna by US officials in Alaska where he was again subjected to vigorous examination, and again succeeded in avoiding prosecution.

Later in 1907, Klengenberg faced trial in a San Francisco court for the murder of Jackson Paul and was, once and for all, acquitted. Subsequently in 1910, he and his expanded family returned to the Canadian Arctic eventually ending up in the Coronation Gulf area. There, his family established an independent fur trading dynasty that provided stiff competition to both the HBC and the Canalaska companies until Klengenberg retired to a home in Vancouver in 1928, leaving the business to his children who quickly made alliances with the other traders. Klengenberg's version of these events and other reflections of life in the Arctic, published in his autobiography *Klengenberg of the Arctic*, makes for fascinating reading. Despite his dubious past and checkered reputation, his children were well-liked and respected in the North, as are their descendants even to this day.

Events such as these attracted the world's attention to the Arctic and related matters involving both economic exploitation and sovereignty. Soon thereafter interest in Arctic exploration, largely dormant since the Franklin searches (mid-1800), again came to the fore. In 1906, the year Amundsen completed his epic voyage from his wintering location at King Point near Herschel Island in Canada's Yukon Territory to Nome, Alaska, explorers like Stefansson were already present in the area. Even Canadians from Victoria became involved, such as key financiers of the Anglo-American Arctic Expedition whose ill-fated schooner, *Duchess of Bedford*, ended up a wreck on the north Alaska coast in 1906.

There followed the Stefansson-Anderson Expedition of 1908-1912 under the auspices of the American Museum of Natural History, New York. Canada finally woke to the realization they had a third ocean—the Arctic Ocean—as well as a vast Arctic region to exert sovereignty over. The Canadian Arctic Expedition, promoted by Stefansson and financed by the Canadian government, was launched in 1913, signalling a desire and interest to send its own personnel to examine this "new" frontier. People like Major Lachlan Burwash and William Hoare were tasked with surveying the land, taking note of the prolific wild life, establishing a presence in these vast regions, and also to make contact with the poorly known indigenous peoples already there. Fortunately, the fur trade, the Mounties and the missionaries were solidly established to help bridge these connections.

THE HUDSON'S BAY COMPANY ENTERS THE FUR TRADE IN THE WESTERN ARCTIC, 1912-1913

When the HBC finally established satellite trading posts in the Mackenzie Delta (at Aklavik and Kittzigazuit, Northwest Territories) in 1912, American traders had already been operating from ships and schooners east of Herschel Island. These individuals included: Fritz Wolki, brothers Martin and Ole Andreassen, Joseph F. Bernard, and Christian Klengenberg. By 1913 only a few traders still participated in the whaling industry. The luxuriant fur of the arctic fox (also referred to as the white fur fox) fuelled a new fashion craze and another economic boom on the heels of the previously wildly profitable whaling exports.

Prompted by suggestions from famed Arctic explorer Roald Amundsen and Klengenberg's experiences with the Copper [Inuit], Alaskan-based trappers (many of them former whalers) were engaged in the fur trade in Alaska and neighbouring Siberia, and began entering Canada in search of the highly valuable white fur of the arctic fox. Brief excitement was also generated by Vilhjalmur Stefansson with purchases and employment for the Canadian Arctic Expedition (CAE).

Map 18-2

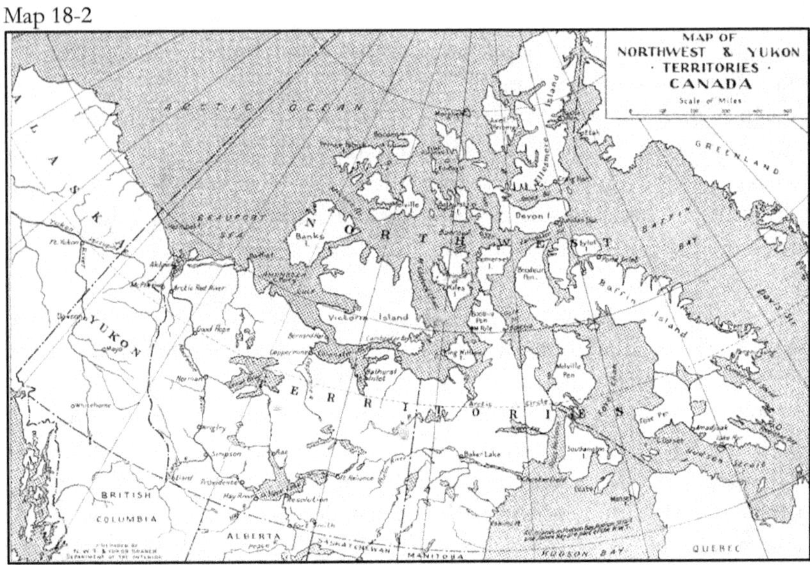

Northwest and Yukon Territories, Canada
From *Canada's Western Arctic Report on Investigations 1925-26, 1928-29 and 1930*

Prior to 1912, when the HBC first established satellite posts in the Mackenzie Delta, they confined the extent of their northern Mackenzie River trading to the fur bearing animals of the boreal forest regions. Although downriver Inuit sometimes ventured upstream for trade, the limit of the HBC's river-supplied network was, for the most part, the areas serviced by their trading post at Fort McPherson on the tributary Peel River, and the Arctic Red River Post on the main stem of the Mackenzie. Realizing they were missing out on valuable trade and would require ocean transport (to be competitive with the supply of trade goods, supplies and post building materials), the Company publicly announced in 1913 that they were entering the Arctic fur trade in a major reorganization and would establish new posts within the Arctic Circle with "vigorous aggression."

REVOLUTION IN FUR TRADE

Hudson's Bay Co. Starts Big Reorganization Scheme

Winnipeg, October 24.—A small advertisement in the columns of a Victoria newspaper has revealed a story of sweeping reorganization that will create an entirely new order in the development of the Hudson's Bay Company's fur trade in Northern Canada.

The advertisement calls for tenders for the building of two new auxiliary steamers, large enough for ocean travel, to be ready for launching early next spring. The information was given out that they were to be used on the Arctic Ocean, about 2,000 miles north of Winnipeg, principally around the delta of the MacKenzie River.

On October 5 the Hudson's Bay Company placed in commission its first permanent vessel, an eighty-tonner, to ply along the west coast of Hudson Bay. Now comes the news that plans are being consummated for a revolution of the fur trade in the north, and that the three new steamers are but an integral part of these plans. It was ascertained that the order has gone out for a new line of fur-trading posts across the extreme northern edge of Canada, within the Arctic Circle, and that the new policy of vigorous aggression will extend to all parts of the north, and include the interior forts.

HBC's expansion announcement in the 25 October 1913 *Montreal Gazette.* Only one of the two vessels mentioned was built, the 58-foot auxiliary schooner *Fort McPherson.*

Photo 18-4

Motor schooner *Fort McPherson* at King William Island, September 1925.
Library and Archives Canada/MIKAN 3394211 (Lachlan T. Burwash)

An article in the *Daily Colonist* on 8 November 1913 expressed that the city of Victoria was favoured to be the base of the western Arctic expansion and two ocean-capable vessels were to be built for the trade. However, things did not work out entirely that way and only one was constructed—perhaps because of the changing fur markets and shipbuilding priorities caused by the start of WWI. In any case, only one company-owned vessel was built: The 58-foot auxiliary schooner *Fort McPherson*, launched by Vancouver Shipyards in 1914. (The name painted on her stern by the builder was *Fort MacPherson* but references to her usually cite *Fort McPherson*, without the "a" in Mc.)

The *Fort McPherson* was designed to distribute cargo brought to the Arctic by larger ships and was the first Canadian-built and registered ship to enter the western Arctic to ultimately reach King William Island—one of the most remotely inhabited areas on the earth. During her working life, from 1914-1930, this sturdy and reliable schooner was an important tool of the Company in establishing western Arctic trading posts from Herschel Island and throughout the Northwest Passage.

These posts were the foundation of permanent settlements in the Arctic. Regularly supplied fur posts beyond the Arctic Circle extended almost entirely across Canada's Arctic oceans and by 1929, company ships had finally navigated the Northwest Passage, first transited by Amundsen in 1906. The location and in-service dates of posts serviced by the Vancouver-based supply ships from 1914-1932, may be found in Appendix C.

19

The Chartering Years, 1914-1920

Although the HBC's foray into the Arctic was led by the *Fort McPherson*, most materials destined for the HBC posts and police detachments in the early days were carried by American-chartered ships. Under the command of experienced "ice" captains, men who had previously been involved in the whaling trade, their cargos included building supplies, fuel, boats, living supplies and trading goods. Four such voyages were made in vessels owned by Captain J. E. Shields and Captain Louis Knaflick, both of Seattle. For several years prior to 1914 they had freighted into the Bering Sea area with their 78-foot power schooner *Bender Brothers.* After the 160-foot *Ruby* joined their fleet in 1914, she was chartered by the HBC to make the initial passage north to commence their Arctic expansion. Newspapers of the day, such as Vancouver's daily newspaper the *Province,* were keen to describe northern-bound adventures, which helpfully included the voyages of these two vessels.

Contrary to some reports, the *Fort McPherson* left first, on 13 June, a full month ahead of the *Ruby* (*Province* 14 July 1914). In accordance with the *Fort McPherson*'s log book, Captain Otto Bucholtz was in charge with a crew consisting of the following: engineer E. Miller; cook H. Simmons; three ordinary seamen, M. Larsen, Rudolph Jensen and Daneill Jones; and the ship's dog Laddie. Bucholtz's crew took her through the Inside Passage and around Alaska to a location south of Point Barrow where she was joined by *Ruby.* Bucholtz was an experienced sealing master from Victoria BC who had operated in northern Alaskan waters and caused notoriety precipitating an international incident in 1892 by defying arrest by US officials in a dispute about sealing rights (*Province* 22 November 1924). One of his sealing commands was the schooner *Casca* once owned by famed Scottish novelist Robert Louis Stevenson.

Ruby, under Captain Louis Knaflick, had taken aboard stores and fuel at Seattle, then proceeded to North Vancouver to load a huge cargo of goods including an astounding 135,000-board feet of lumber. The supplies were intended to satisfy the HBC's needs for three years. *Ruby* also carried supplies for the Royal Northwest Mounted Police (RNWMP) detachment at Herschel Island, and also for an independent trader at Baillie Island, her final destination.

Before *Ruby* sailed for the Arctic on 13 July, she was joined by Chris Harding, the HBC Mackenzie River fur trade manager, and his wife, as well as other HBC personnel who were to build and staff the new posts. It is interesting to note that the *Province*, reporting on the departure, noted about the venture:

> This is practically the first time that Vancouver has been a base of Arctic supply and opens up a new and expanding field to local merchants.

After rendezvousing, squeezing ice halted the progress of both ships twenty-five miles east of Point Barrow and damaged *Ruby* above the waterline. Only the intrepid Captain Pedersen made it through to Herschel Island that year. *Ruby* and *Fort McPherson* retreated to Teller, Alaska. *Ruby*'s cargo was put into storage ashore and she returned to Seattle for repairs and to pursue other cargos. Departing with her were Captain Bucholtz and three members of the *Fort McPherson*'s crew (*Alaska Daily Empire* of 15 October 1914). The *Fort McPherson* was put into winter quarters and the remainder of her crew weathered-over at Teller during the winter of 1914-1915 to oversee the vessel and the cargo ashore. These individuals were the Hardings, and two others, possibly Danes Heinrich ("Swogger") Hendrickson and Rudolph Johnson (who would later captain and be the engineer of the *Fort McPherson*). However, although a 25 January 1925 *Vancouver Province* links Hendrickson and Johnson with the *Fort McPherson* during this idle period, log book entries and newspaper accounts about returning crew members indicate these individuals should have been M. Larsen and Rudolph Jensen.

Ruby returned to Teller the next year, on 15 July 1915, captained by Stephen F. Cottle, a more experienced ice master. An article in the December 1977 issue of *The Sea Chest* by Captain Ed Shields, "Aux. Schooner *Ruby* - Arctic Supply Voyage," describes the voyage. (Ed Shields is the son of Captain J. E. Shields.) Upon arrival she discharged her cargo to the schooner *Bender Brothers*, before reloading the stored cargo. After Chris Harding and his wife boarded on 23 July, *Ruby* completed the passage to Herschel Island. She arrived there on 14 August, moored alongside the beach near *Fort McPherson* and discharged the materials for constructing the new post at Herschel Island.

A log book does not appear to have been kept for *Fort McPherson* during her voyage in 1915, so it is not clear who was in command. It is known that she travelled in company with another schooner, the *Gladiator*, owned by well- known Arctic pioneer trapper and trader Fritz Wolkie. Stefansson, who purchased this vessel from Wolkie at Herschel Island, indicates that John Hadley, a former CAE member and survivor of the loss of the expedition's ship *Karluck*, travelled with *Fort McPherson* to Herschel Island as "ice-pilot." There, Stefansson promptly re-hired Hadley for his expedition.

Photo 19-1

Power schooner *Ruby* at Herschel Island and flying the American flag, August 1915. The building is the RNWMP Post—the former Pacific Steam Whaling Company "community house."
Library and Archives Canada/MIKAN 4100500

On 18 August, *Fort McPherson* pulled alongside *Ruby* and materials for forwarding to the new post at Baillie Island were transferred to her. Ten days later, *Ruby* proceeded on the 28th to Baillie Island to discharge the balance of her cargo, for a trader reported to be "Wilkie" (likely Fritz Wolki). From this point *Ruby* returned westward picking up cargo from other American traders in Alaska destined for Seattle.

During the return voyage to Seattle, *Ruby* encountered a succession of gales that damaged her sails, then, on nearing the entrance to the Juan de Fuca Strait, her motor failed completely and she had to be towed into Port Angeles by the tug *Snohomish*. She arrived home under tow on 2 November 1915.

An article in the 28 April 1917 edition of the *Province* indicated that the HBC dispatched some freight aboard *Ruby* for the Company in 1916, but that she never reached Herschel Island. It is doubtful that much support was required, as the southern party from the Canadian Arctic Expedition had departed the Arctic that summer and left behind lots of surplus supplies. The same article elaborated that the HBC contracted with H. Liebes and Co. for transport of materials in 1917, to be carried by the power schooner *Herman* (Captain Pedersen) from Vancouver to Herschel Island. An article in the *San Francisco Examiner* of 20 September 1917, informed readers of the return of the *Herman* following her delivery of supplies to Herschel Island. Pertaining to Liebes' own trading, it said that *Herman* was prevented from proceeding eastward into Coronation Gulf because of adverse ice conditions.

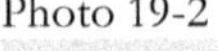
Photo 19-2

H. Liebes and Co. power schooner *Herman*. Under Captain C. T. Pedersen, she made many successful trading and whaling voyages in the Alaskan and the Canadian Arctic. Glenbow Archives photograph PA-3886-33-1

From 1918 through 1920, the HBC again turned to Captains J. E. Shields and Louis Knaflick's firm in Seattle for their Arctic supply freighting. In 1918 and 1919, Captain S. T. L. Whitlam and the *Bender Brothers* was able to get supplies from Vancouver through to Herschel Island and return fur to Victoria's Ogden Point docks in spite of difficult ice conditions. Aboard the *Ruby* in 1920, he made a record voyage, reaching as far as Baillie Island with supplies loaded at Victoria for the HBC and RCMP outposts. The cargo included building supplies for the establishment of new facilities on the Kent Peninsula. Laden with two tons of fur, *Ruby*'s return to Victoria on September 24th marked the last use of the Seattle-based power schooners on this route.

Photo 19-3

Power schooner *Bender Brothers* unloading at Herschel Island, 1919. Schooner on the right is thought to be from Fort McPherson (possibly the *Tilyak*), with the filming crew for the HBC movie *The Romance of the Fur Trade Country*, on board.
Hudson's Bay Company Archives, Archives of Manitoba. Arthur M. Irvine fonds, 2012/1/214 Schooner *Bender Bros.* Herschel Island, between 1919-1920

20

The *Lady Kindersley* Years, and Supply Voyages 1921-1924

Photo 20-1

Lady Kindersley berthed at Evans & Coleman dock in Vancouver.
Vancouver Archives photograph AM 1535 - CVA99-3364

As economies recovered from the austerity of World War I and the world entered the roaring twenties, fur markets recovered and the HBC was finally able to pursue its dream of acquiring its own supply vessel for the western Arctic trade. *Lady Kindersley,* a 187-foot power schooner, was already under construction for use in the 1921 season. Named in honour of the HBC governor's wife and boasting both wind and auxiliary power—three masts and a two-cycle semi-diesel engine—she was launched in Vancouver on 26 March 1921. Her sponsor, Frances Gladys O'Kelly, wife of HBC Manager Tom P. O'Kelly, broke a champagne bottle across her bow. Under Captain Gustav ("Gus") Foellmer, *Lady Kindersley* made three successful voyages to the Arctic.

THE 1921 VOYAGE

Married couple Frances and Tom O'Kelly sailed on the *Lady Kindersley* during her maiden voyage. The voyage was through the Inside Passage to Prince Rupert, and then past the Aleutian Islands, calling at Akutan, Nome, and Teller before finally rounding Point Barrow and reaching Herschel Island on 9 August. After unloading there, she proceeded on to the Baillie Island Post at Cape Bathurst, then onward through Dolphin and Union Strait to Bernard Harbour, a first for a supply ship of her size. Her final destination was the tiny settlement of Tree River, midway in Coronation Gulf, where both the HBC and the RCMP had established outposts in the protected anchorage near the river's mouth.

Photo 20-2

Crew of *Lady Kindersley* in the early 1920s with Captain Gus Foellmer seated at centre. Vancouver Archives photograph CVA - 3362

Details of the many adventures and firsts of the voyage, including the ship's miraculous escape from the pack ice midway between Herschel Island and Point Barrow on their homeward journey, can be found in an amazing journal and photographic album that Frances kept. These documents, including a typed transcription of her handwritten text, are available online from the Arctic Institute of North America and hosted by the University of Calgary. The journal offers a gripping account of her impressions of the native people and animal populations encountered, the challenges of the environment, the inadequacies of the ship despite innovative repairs, and all other aspects of the voyage—that proudly set out, but limped home—albeit with a fortune of Arctic fur. Frances left a fascinating record that will be illuminating to anyone who cares to peruse it.

Photo 20-3

HBC pioneer post at Tree River with *Lady Kindersley* in roadstead, 1921. Tom O'Kelly (in blanket coat) takes a photo of his wife, Inuit residents and Post Manager Otto Binder. Structures left to right: post hut, meat/cache store (on stilts) and fur press. University of Calgary Arctic Institute of North America photograph (Frances Gladys O'Kelly album)

Notable passengers carried on *Lady Kindersley*'s outbound voyage included Miss Roberts (the intended bride of Gabriel Elton Merritt, who was the Anglican missionary at Bernard Harbour), Reverend Geddes, HBC District Inspector C. H. Clarke, and RCMP Inspector Wood. The wedding took place in the salon of Lady Kindersley while the vessel was at Bernard Harbour with Reverend Geddes officiating and Frances as the matron-of-honour. Inspector Wood gave the bride away and Pete Norberg, C. H. Clarke and Tom O'Kelly served as witnesses. Also on board was Corporal Doak, who was tragically murdered, along with HBC Tree River Post Manager Otto Binder, in 1922.

Norberg later piloted *Lady Kindersley* to her final destination at Tree River with his own vessel the schooner *El Sueño* under tow. Homeward-bound, *Lady Kindersley* carried Harold Noice—known as "the youngest Arctic explorer"—on the first leg of his return trip to Seattle. He was a former CAE member who was returning from a remarkable but lonely, single-handed expedition to the Kent Peninsula and Victoria Island. During this endeavour, he mapped the eastern shore of Victoria Island and collected numerous historical artifacts representing the area's earliest civilization.

Noice was photographed in 1916 with other members of the CAE Northern Party. Led by Vilhjalmur Stefansson, the mission of the Northern Party was to explore north of Alaska and the Canadian mainland, and beyond the known islands of the western Arctic.

Photo 20-4

Members of CAE Northern Party by flash light: (back row, from left) Lorne Knight, Charles Thomsen, Aarnout Castel, Harold Noice, (front row) Martin Killin, and Captain Pierre (Peter) Bernard, at Kellett Base, Banks Island, NWT, 1 January 1916. Canadian Museum of Civilization photograph GHW 51098 uploaded to Wikimedia Commons

THE 1922 VOYAGE

Captain Gus Foellmer, wary of ice conditions experienced between Point Barrow and Herschel Island during a voyage that year which resulted in a late arrival at the island on 30 August, proceeded no further with *Lady Kindersley*. He hastily dumped all the carefully stowed supplies needed for eastern posts and reversed course to beat a retreat westward to clear Point Barrow. This action created a supply problem for eastern posts as the only company vessel available at the time for forwarding desperately needed supplies was the motor schooner *Fort McPherson*.

In the Mackenzie Delta, the RCMP moved its Fort McPherson Post to Aklavik, which also replaced Herschel Island as its administration centre for the Arctic. Coincidentally, the new river steamer *Distributor* extended her service to the new settlement, which had previously terminated at Fort McPherson.

THE 1923 VOYAGE

In this year, *Lady Kindersley* was able to repeat her journey as far east as Tree River. Captain O'Kelly, this time without his wife, was again senior HBC management representative on the voyage. It was a very tumultuous year in the Arctic. There were problems with supply distribution, and the gathering of fur returns that had not yet been accomplished because of the failure of the eastward leg of the supply voyage of 1922. This was eased somewhat by the arrival of the new motor schooner *Aklavik*, which had been transported down the Mackenzie River for Arctic service. Additionally, there was the troubling matter of the double murders, the subsequent trial, and justice by hanging.

Photo 20-5

Motor schooner *Aklavik* possibly at Cambridge Bay, loaded with supplies and likely alongside RCMP vessel *St. Roch.* Cargo handling involved long hours of intensive labour in the short shipping season.
Lorenz Learmonth fonds, Nunavut Archives, N-1987-033-0404

Another matter that undoubtedly led to tension with HBC staff was the arrival of Phillip Godsell, a special inspector for HBC Fur Trade Commissioner Angus Brabant, who was tasked with inspection of the Company's Arctic operations and business practices (that would eventually shake up their operations and lead to staff replacements). He joined *Lady Kindersley* at Herschel Island and travelled with her to Tree River. Finally, although apparently not publicized at the time, there was the matter of executing a further eastward expansion of the Company's trade to Victoria and King William islands. As was discussed in Chapter 16, this was the expedition lead by Pete Norberg on the schooner *El Sueño* that made the first-ever west-to-east crossing of Queen Maud Gulf.

As reported in the *Province* newspaper of 11 October 1923, *Lady Kindersley* had arrived at Prince Rupert the previous day. Here she landed a sailor suffering head and internal injuries from an accident aboard ship. On the inbound leg the ship carried Leo Hansen (a Danish photographer) to Tree River on his way to join Knud Rasmussen's expedition at Kent Peninsula. Outbound, she had conveyed missionary Gabriel Elton Merritt and his wife and a newborn son, Edward. Other passengers on that leg included Bessie and Teddy Jacobsen (children of HBC employee Fred Jacobsen on their way to schooling in Vancouver under Captain Gus Foellmer's care) and Constable J. H. Bonsour from Tree River. The ship, also carrying a large cargo of fur, arrived safely in Vancouver on 18 October 1923, after logging over 12,000 miles.

An interesting independent account of the voyage by the ship's radio operator Reginald Harold Fricker may be found at page 44 of his book *The Ramblings of a 'Matelot.'* Fricker describes the failure of the American power schooner *Arctic* (owned by H. Liebes and Co. of San Francisco), contracted by the Canadian government to take building supplies into the Canadian Arctic to establish a new RCMP detachment at Cambridge Bay. Instead, she landed them at Baillie Island, owing to propeller damage sustained earlier at Point Barrow, which prevented her from proceeding. The police used the building supplies to establish a "temporary" detachment at Baillie Island while *Lady Kindersley* earned a windfall in forwarding the remaining supplies to the RCMP detachment at Tree River.

THE 1924 VOYAGE

A surprising start to a fateful 1924 season was made during the winter of 1923-1924. In response to a telegram sent to Fort Yukon in Alaska, Inspector Godsell and District Manager Herbert Hall set out to report to Fur Trade Commissioner Angus Brabant at HBC headquarters in

Winnipeg. The telegram had been brought to Herschel by RCMP Sergeant Thorne, the sad bearer of news of the confirmation and the date for the hanging sentence. HBC employees elected to follow basically the same route over the mountains to Fairbanks that the Klengenbergs had used in 1923 (referenced later in this chapter). They arrived in Winnipeg on 19 February 1924.

Unfortunately for Hall, who was popular in the Arctic and excelled in the field of winter travel and in establishing new posts, it was the end of his career with the HBC. His business practices—mainly over-stocking of inappropriate goods and over-extending credit revealed by Godsell's investigations—lead to an "early retirement" and his replacement by Tom O'Kelly. O'Kelly had been the senior HBC official on Godsell's eastward inspection voyage on the *Lady Kindersley* in 1923, although Godsell conveniently omitted this fact in popular books he published long after the event. As reported by HBC Manager Richard H. G. Bonnycastle (a subsequent district manager mentioned later) the replacement choice was very unpopular with post managers and O'Kelly's tenure only lasted a little over a year.

In August 1924, HBC officials, members of the RCMP detachment, and dozens of local trappers and traders on Herschel Island, awaited the arrival of *Lady Kindersley* bringing their annual supplies. Joining them were four members of the Canadian Corps of Signals who had journeyed down the Mackenzie River to install a powerful radio station on the island, the materials and radio set carried north aboard the *Lady Kindersley*. At long last the Arctic would have instant and reliable communications with the outside world.

Royal Canadian Corps of Signals
Cap badge

The much-anticipated arrival did not come to pass, however. Transiting near Point Barrow, the *Lady Kindersley* became trapped in the pack ice. On 31 August, after weeks stuck in the ice, despite repeated attempts to free the ship, Captain Gus Foellmer was forced to order the ship abandoned and arrange to transport the crew to safety. The ships purser, Percy Patmore, had already managed to land near Point Barrow and organized land-based rescue efforts with the help of the crew of the US Government vessel *Boxer*, under the command of the HBC's old friend Captain S. T. L. Whitlam. The *Lady Kindersley*'s crew travelled over the ice and, with the aid of canoes and an umiak (a type of open skin-hulled boat in use by the Inuit), reached the safety of the *Boxer*.

Shortly afterwards HBC's steel steamship *Baychimo*, which had been rapidly dispatched from Vancouver, arrived and was able to embark the *Lady Kindersley* survivors from the *Boxer* and transport them back to Vancouver. *Baychimo* had only just arrived at Vancouver from England via the Suez Canal before being sent to aid in the rescue. Prior to leaving the Arctic waters, she patrolled the edge of the ice for several days, hoping to find and secure the *Lady Kindersley* to save at least part of her valuable cargo but all was lost—including the prized radio equipment.

The *Lady Kindersley* was not the only vessel lost at Point Barrow that season. The H. Liebes and Company vessel *Arctic* was abandoned on 10 August, after being crushed in the ice. Only two vessels reached Herschel Island that summer, both of them American: Captain Klengenberg's *Maid of Orleans* and Captain Pedersen's *Nanuk*.

Photo 20-6

Captain Pedersen's schooner *Nanuk* at San Francisco, 1925. She provided relief when *Lady Kindersley* was trapped in the ice and eventually lost. Saltwater People Historical Society photograph

Further compounding supply issues, the year 1924 was significant, in that Canadian coastwise navigation rules—forbidding trade by foreign vessels—were evoked in the Arctic. No doubt this was done with some persuasion by the HBC. It is evident in Godsell's report that the HBC was concerned by competition from American traders and were aware of Klengenberg's voyage and trading plans in March 1924. These came about following the disastrous preceding year of 1923.

Referring to the loss of supplies carried by the *Lady Kindersley*, Heather Robertson stated (in her biography of HBC Manager Richard H. G. Bonnycastle, *A Gentleman Adventurer: The Arctic Diaries of Richard Bonnycastle*):

> Unimpressed by the Company's failure to fulfil its obligations to its [Inuit] trappers, the police at Herschel Island were unsympathetic when the Company had Charlie Klengenberg banned from the Arctic coast because he was not a Canadian citizen.

In 1923 Klengenberg and his family, located at Rymer Point, were in desperate straits because of the failure of H. Liebes and Company to deliver contracted and prepaid supplies and trading goods to them. He, together with his two sons, escaped the clutches of HBC's Arctic fur pricing by a hazardous winter trip over the mountains to Fairbanks, taking with him sample furs from those stored in a RCMP warehouse at Herschel Island. After Fairbanks, they travelled by railway to Seward, and then by steamer to Seattle. On arrival they sold the Arctic-stored fur based on their samples and used the huge proceeds to purchase the motor schooner *Maid of Orleans*, hire a crew, and equip the ship with supplies, not only for his family but also for a large trading outfit.

It would have been a brilliant move, but the implementation of the trading ban caught Klengenberg by surprise when his vessel arrived at Herschel Island in August. He was forced to winter there and suffered for a time as the main suspect in the overboard loss of RCMP Constable Ian MacDonald, while heading east by transit on Klengenberg's ship, until it was deemed the man had likely accidentally slipped on the icy deck and fell into the Arctic waters. Death would have come swiftly with little chance of calling for help—or even being heard.

Fortunately, Captain Christian Pedersen and his ship *Nanuk* were on hand to mitigate the 1924 situation, which relief action seems to have been precipitated by Canadian officials in reaction to *Lady Kindersley*'s predicament and the looming dire privations if she failed to reach her destination. Although Canadian newspaper stories failed to mention *Nanuk*'s participation and arrival at Herschel Island, Californian ones certainly did. The *Santa Ana Register*, in its 10 October 1924 edition, quoted Pedersen's glowing account of supply relief and that the vessel had penetrated far into banned Canadian waters to do so.

Thirty Stops In North

"We made thirty stops east of Herschel island, after arrangements with the Canadian government had been made, and landed supplies of provisions for the mounted police, hunters and trappers," Captain Pedersen said. "Arrangements to this end were made by wireless.

From the *Santa Ana Register*, 10 October 1924, under the headline "Mercy Ship in Port with Rich Cargo of Furs."

The annual reports of the RCMP, usually full of Arctic information, do not seem to mention this vital service provided by Captain Pedersen to relieve pending disaster. Certainly, there is great contrast to the welcome given to Captain Pedersen and the "arrangements with the Canadian government," and the outright ban levelled on Captain Klengenberg with the restrictions placed on him being able to manage any kind of trade.

The loss of the *Lady Kindersley* late in the season left the HBC struggling to supply its far stretching line of posts. The new post at Cambridge Bay had to be closed because of lack of fuel but others received some supplies through use of the Company vessels *Fort McPherson* and *Aklavik*, as well as by conscripted native schooners.

After freeze-up, a group of Company officials were forced to make a frigid dog team trek over the mountains to Fairbanks, Alaska, to gain telegraphic access to communicate with the Company and to make the railroad connection in order to travel back to Vancouver. Most proceeded on the railway but E. J. "Scotty" Gall, an HBC apprentice, and Ambrose Arnavigak a former member of Stefansson's CAE, returned to Herschel with cash, vital supplies, fur trading prices, and Company instructions to enable trading to continue.

Despite setbacks and outright disaster, trade and progress in the north continued. Nothing remained static; not the ice, not the landscape, and certainly not the determined people who populated areas that were slowly growing into established settlements through the delivery of trade goods and steadying routes of supply.

21

The *Baychimo* Years, and Supply Voyages 1925-1931

Godsell's inspection report (see Chapter 20), published in March 1924, included a recommendation that the *Lady Kindersley* be replaced by a fully powered vessel (as opposed to an auxiliary-powered one) to take advantage of the limited time given for Arctic navigation east of Herschel Island. The sad happenstance of the loss of *Lady Kindersley* and the availability of the *Baychimo* for the 1925 season provided an early satisfaction of this recommendation.

Photo 21-1

Captain Sydney A. Cornwell, Herschel Island, 1930.
Library and Archives Canada/MIKAN 3388944 (Richard S. Finnie)

The replacement under the command of Captain Sydney A. Cornwell was the *Baychimo*. She was a 230-foot, steel-hulled steamer, built in Gothenburg, Sweden, in 1915 and purchased by the HBC in

1920, registered with London as her homeport. Originally employed in the Company's eastern Arctic trade, she had been used from 1922 to 1924 in a new fur trading venture the Company started in Kamchatka, Siberia. (As shown on the below map, the Kamchatka Peninsula, in far eastern Russia, lies between the Sea of Okhotsk on the west and the Pacific Ocean and Bering Sea on the east.) Her subsequent summer employment for western Arctic service was timely, as relations with the Soviet government had broken down and the much-needed permissions for this trade were not forthcoming.

Map 21-1

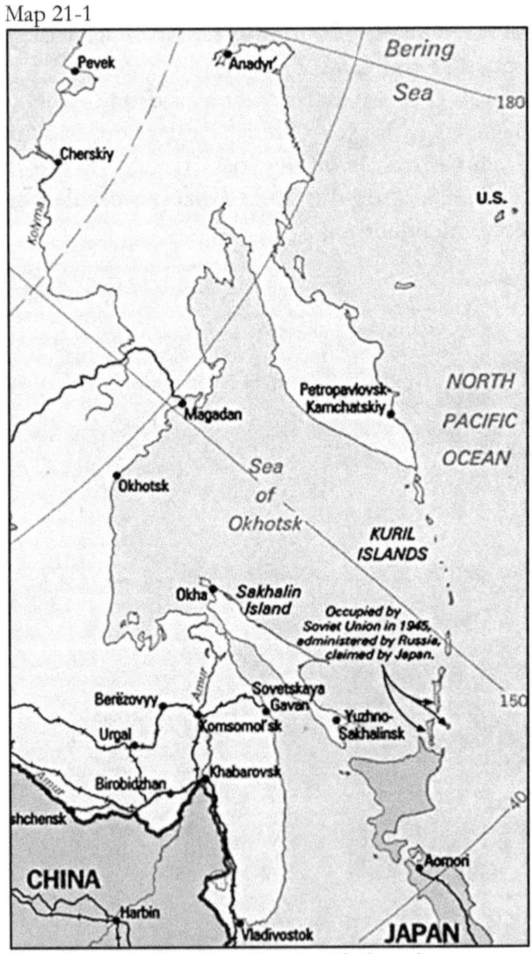

Petropavlovsk, Kamchatskiy, identified on the map,
is the largest city on the Kamchatka Peninsula in Siberia.
https://maps.lib.utexas.edu/maps/commonwealth/russia.94.jpg

Baychimo was the largest and first steel vessel to enter the treacherous "ice infested" waters of the western Arctic. Many "beach scoffers" predicted failure of a steel hull in such conditions. Although owned by the HBC, she was registered in London and, as such, was operated primarily as a "British" ship with a "British" crew. When cargoes could be found, winters were spent transporting them to and from Britain—usually ending up at Ardrossan, a port in Ayrshire on the Clyde coast of Scotland, for necessary maintenance.

Photo 21-2

The steamship SS *Baychimo* at dock, Vancouver.
City of Vancouver Archives photograph AM 1506-53-2, CVA-447-1987

As documented in Anthony Dalton's well-researched and readable book *Baychimo: Arctic Ghost Ship*, she completed seven outbound voyages from Vancouver but only six return ones. In 1931, she became trapped in the ice, was abandoned, and the derelict vessel became a "ghost ship." Prior to this tragedy, *Baychimo* courageously delivered cargoes and personnel to the western Arctic through the notoriously shallow and poorly charted waters, while often facing violent summer storms and fog. She bounced between—and over—shallow reefs, threading her way through ice flows to bring sustenance to the Arctic and to take out the valuable fur returns. Her crew became very efficient at temporarily "lightening" ship and "heaving-off," through the use of her powerful steam winches and heavy anchors, to free her when she grounded.

In the process, however, she suffered dents and damage to her hull, and the inevitable loss of propeller blades—which brought work to Vancouver and other shipyards. The eastern limit of her voyages was usually Cambridge Bay, on Victoria Island, although in 1928 she went as far as Flagstaff Island to the southwest, also located in what is today, Nunavut. In her time, tiny flimsy buildings ashore were replaced by more substantial weather-tight structures and trading posts were established southward into Bathurst Inlet.

THE 1925 VOYAGE

Baychimo's initial voyage in 1925 was a very busy one, particularly since Arctic posts had received inadequate supply in 1924 because of the loss of the *Lady Kindersley*. This marked the first time that a large supply ship ever reached Cambridge Bay. The post building there initially consisted only of a vacant hut and served as an outpost for the Kent Peninsula Post. *Baychimo* left supplies beside the building to be forwarded to King William Island by the *Fort McPherson*, which had not yet returned from her first trip to that island. That summer *Baychimo* carried many prominent passengers, intent on getting first-hand information on the Arctic. They included HBC Fur Trade Commissioner Angus Brabant, Inspector Hugh Conn and Marine Superintendent Captain George E. Mack.

During an HBC company interview of Scotty Gall, he indicated that Captain Mack had been involved in sounding a channel into Tuktoyaktuk, so it seems clear that the Company was already looking at alternatives to the Point Barrow route at that time. Also on board, were replacement HBC staff. They included Ray Ross for the Tree River Post, Canadian government investigator Major Lachlan Burwash bound for King William Island, and former Anglican missionary William Hoare for Tree River, to start wildlife investigations for the government.

Baychimo's eastern trip through Coronation Gulf, Dolphin and Union Strait, and Amundsen Gulf, and return to Herschel Island, seems to have been made without serious incident. However, from there, it proved to be the one in which she had the greatest difficulty in exiting the Canadian Arctic. With preparation already in hand for wintering at Herschel Island, she was able—at the last possible moment—to escape. As final freeze-up was occurring, she arrived at Point Barrow on 2 October, four full weeks later than planned.

After returning to Vancouver, *Baychimo* journeyed to Britain via the Panama Canal with a grain cargo for Devonport, a port city in southwest England. Afterwards she proceeded to Ardrossan, her usual Scottish base, for repairs and discharge of the crew.

Other important events were taking place that year: At Aklavik, the Royal Canadian Corps of Signals opened the Arctic's first radio station, the one originally planned for Herschel Island. The All Saints Anglican Hospital was built and a Roman Catholic mission and hospital was also established. The HBC facility became a full post and was moved across the river to the main part of the settlement.

THE 1926 VOYAGE

The annual voyage to the Arctic in 1926, which reached Cambridge Bay, was made without serious difficulties. At Tree River *Baychimo* was successful in freeing a sister Company ship, the auxiliary schooner *Baymaud*, from a grounding that had held her captive for several days. Once again at the end of the season, *Baychimo* returned to Britain with a lumber cargo. The annual report of the RCMP noted the establishment of a new detachment at Bernard Harbour and the relocation of the Tree River detachment to Cambridge Bay. It is reported that the HBC carried supplies for the RCMP that summer and it is evident *Baychimo* and other HBC vessels must have been used for the establishment and relocation of the detachments.

THE 1927 VOYAGE

The 1927 RCMP report reinforced the one for 1926, that new police detachments were established at both Bernard Harbour and Cambridge Bay, the latter mainly with materials from the post at Tree River, which had been closed. Ian MacKinnon became the HBC post manager at Cambridge Bay in 1927 where new buildings were being erected. The location became the key fur trade centre in the central Arctic under a new government policy that centralized competing posts away from animal migration routes. The closing, and transfer of, the Kent Peninsula Post to Cambridge Bay and the establishment of a post in Bathurst Inlet in 1927 ensured a busy year for *Baychimo.*

Important cargo delivered to the eastern expanding fur trade included new distribution schooners—*Polar Bear* that unloaded at Tree Island, and *Blue Fox* that probably unloaded at Cambridge Bay—a new Anglican mission house for Cambridge Bay, a new eight-ton engine for the venerable *Fort McPherson* (also at Cambridge Bay), and material for a new post in Bathurst Inlet that was to be established by HBC Chief Inspector Hugh Conn. Conn travelled on the ship that year in connection with his inspection duties of Arctic posts.

The *Polar Bear* and *Blue Fox* were likely the two 41-foot centerboard schooners reported to have been constructed by Eriksen Shipyard in North Vancouver for the HBC, and shipped as deck cargo (as reported in the May 1927 issue of *Harbour and Shipping* magazine.) Anecdotally, they appear to have not been registered, at least not in the Vancouver registry. Their function was likely to assist in local distribution as the *Baymaud* was to be retired from active service. *Baymaud* was tied-up at

Cambridge Bay to serve as a floating warehouse and workshop prior to the departure of most of her crew (wireless operator and carpenter remained) on the *Baychimo* on her return trip that year.

Photo 21-3

L-R: Donald C. McKechnie (with pipe), Consolidated Mining Company geologist; unknown Inuit woman; Otto Torrington, skipper of small Hudson's Bay Company schooner; Ray Ross, manager of Hudson's Bay Company post at Tree River; unknown Inuit woman; unknown Inuit man, 1927.
Glenbow Archives NA-1258-87

Conn also had an additional assignment following establishment of the new post. That winter he was to reconnoitre a possible trade route from the western Arctic through to Wager Inlet on Hudson Bay (inlet above Rankin Inlet on following map). An article in the *Province* of 20 July 1927 announced that Consolidated Mining and Smelting Co. geologist Donald C. McKechnie would sail on the *Baychimo* and meet Conn at Herschel Island and "...travel with him by canoe and dog train across the hinterland of Canada as far as Hudson Bay."

To facilitate the mission, *Baychimo* brought Hugh Conn's special eight-sled-dog team from Vancouver for the expedition. It is not clear if McKechnie completed the trip but Conn certainly did. Bishop Isaac Stringer and his wife travelled with the ship from the Mackenzie Delta to Cambridge Bay, where he oversaw the erection of the new mission house for the community, observed the new police detachment and the hoisting of the new engine into the *Fort McPherson*.

After *Baychimo* left Cambridge Bay on her homeward journey, a new post was finally established in Bathurst Inlet to Conn's satisfaction after one false start. While Captain Sydney A. Cornwell and some other crew members returned to Britain for the winter, several officers stayed with the ship at Esquimalt, where major repairs were undertaken at the Yarrows shipyard.

Map 21-2

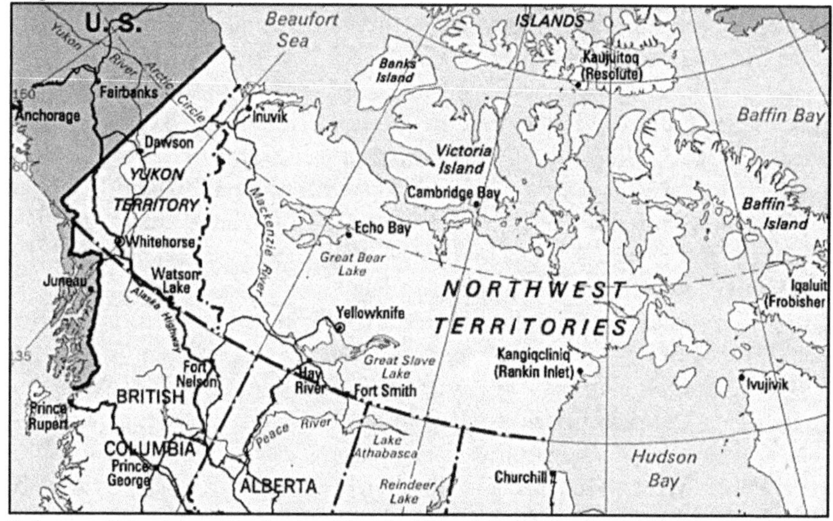

Yukon and Northwest Territories, Herschel Island lies 470 miles NE of Banks Island. https://maps.lib.utexas.edu/maps/americas/canada_pol97.jpg

THE 1928 VOYAGE

After his marathon winter trip, Inspector Conn returned to the Arctic in 1928 to continue his investigation into the sorry financial state of Company affairs that persisted after Godsell's earlier 1925 inspection. He travelled down the Mackenzie River accompanied by Richard Henry Gardyn Bonnycastle, who was a recent Oxford University graduate and joined the Company seeking adventure, and who would accompany Conn on his travels to HBC posts on the *Baychimo* that summer. Bonnycastle started that year as an accountant and would become the district manager for the western Arctic in 1929, a position he held until 1933.

When *Baychimo* reached the mouth of the Coppermine River, Bonnycastle noted in his journal that a new store surrounded by tents had been erected marking the establishment of a new permanent community that he referred to as Fort Hearne (often confused with the neighbouring post of Cape Krusenstern, closed in 1929). It was later known simply as Coppermine before its present name Kugluktuk came into prominence. At Wilmont Island (Nunavut) he noted they left off "the trapper-trader Patsy Klengenberg and Ikey Bolt with their outfit."

(Patsy was the son of Christian Klengenberg, introduced earlier in Chapter 16.)

The implication that "their outfit" had been transported by the HBC reflected the increasing cooperation between the HBC and the Klengenberg fur trade family after Christian Klengenberg's retirement and the sale of his schooner *Old Maid No. 2* to the Company in 1928. The relationship previously had been—to say the least—very competitive. It couldn't have hurt relations any when *Baychimo*'s crew rescued Patsy Klengenberg and Ikey Bolt and a small child when their vessel, the *Doctor Rymer*, shipwrecked on a small island west of Wilmont Island. They had been the victims of a huge storm that had delayed the *Baychimo* at Cambridge Bay, and was responsible for wrecking several schooners at Baillie Island.

Baychimo carried building materials to complete the consolidation of HBC posts in the Coronation Gulf in accordance with new government regulations. The materials included those necessary for expanding the warehouse at Cambridge Bay. After leaving that post she traveled 120 miles southeast to Flagstaff Island near the mouth of the Perry River. This marked the farthest eastward destination she would ever reach. Here, as recorded by the Ottawa-based government official Hon. Francis ("Frank") Robert Oliver in an article published in the 2 March 1929 edition of the *Calgary Herald*, she anchored and some of her crew discharged freight for the new King William Post onto the *Fort McPherson.*

Photo 21-4

Hudson's Bay Company post at Cambridge Bay, Victoria Island circa 1930.
Library and Archives Canada/MIKAN 3327746

Much to Conn's chagrin, the government forced the removal of his company's recently installed Perry River Post, and other *Baychimo* crewmembers travelled ten miles by launch to complete the disassembly and abandonment. Before making a final visit to Baillie Island, where storm damage was previously noted, *Baychimo* called at the five-year-old Fort Harmon at the head of Albert Sound and took down and brought aboard all the post buildings. She then proceeded to the north mouth of the sound—a body of water adjacent to southwestern Victoria Island—where they were re-erected at the new post of Walker Bay, which later came to be known as Fort Collinson.

Other significant events of the year included a return of government investigator Major Lachlan Burwash, who travelled along the Arctic coast in the government schooner *Ptarmigan* before wintering at Gjoa Haven on King William Island. Later when the sea had frozen, he visited the HBC motor schooner *Fort James* which had entered the western Arctic from St. John's, Newfoundland, and was wintering at Oscar Bay on the Boothia Peninsula east of King William Island. *Fort James*' visit was part of the practical attempts being made to find a better means of supplying the fur trade in the central Arctic and to evaluate fur trapping possibilities east of King William Island (described long after the event in an article in the September 1936 issue of *The Beaver* by W. E. Brown). Included in this fascinating account is the eastern schooner's visit and a mention of a trial tractor-expedition from Wager Inlet on Hudson Bay. The year also marked the entrance of the RCMP-owned *St. Roch* into Arctic service.

Baychimo experienced little difficulty in returning to Vancouver from Herschel Island that fall. She was able to obtain a wheat cargo and proceeded to Britain for the winter.

THE 1929 VOYAGE

Baychimo's business was expanded in 1929, as a mining prospecting boom had sprung up in the Arctic. It was centered around the new community of Coppermine and in Bathurst Inlet. At Coppermine, building supplies were landed for completion of fur trading facilities, mission buildings for both the Anglican and Roman Catholic churches, the construction of a medical clinic, and huts for the exploration companies. At Burnside River on Bathurst Inlet, materials were landed to build a base for Dominion Explorers. Winter provisions, fur trading outfits, coal and liquid fuels, including a huge amount of aviation fuel for caches in the district, made up record cargos that were brought-in and distributed by HBC ships that season.

The rapid mineral investigation program that ensued over a vast and inaccessible area was only possible by the use of bush planes, which had never been used in this area before. Winter conditions posed no obstacle as ski-equipped aircraft could land on the frozen tundra. In summer, float-equipped planes could land on the innumerable lakes of the region, rapidly taking prospectors and supplies to potential areas of mineralization. The prospecting companies included North American

Mineral Exploration Company (NAME), Dominion Explorers and the Consolidated Mining and Smelting Company.

Baychimo's cargo for NAME even included a set of floats for one of its aircraft, allowing it to be changed from winter to summer flying in the Arctic avoiding the time-consuming diversion to a southern base to perform the conversion. Dominion Explorers chartered the HBC schooner *Polar Bear* to support its operation in Bathurst Inlet that year.

Photo 21-5

Gas-powered schooner *Polar Bear* twenty miles north of Burnside River, Bathurst Inlet, 23 September 1929.
Library and Archives Canada/MIKAN 3393549 (Lachlan T. Burwash)

On 31 August, only five days after *Baychimo* sailed eastwards, HBC Coppermine Post Manager Barnes noted in his journal the first arrival of aircraft in the western Arctic. They consisted of two NAME aircraft, each with three occupants. He also wryly reported that the celebration of the important event took a terrible hit on his permit (annual allowance of alcohol—usually 12 bottles). Later that year two aircraft belonging to Dominion Explorers, carrying the MacAlpine Party, who were attempting a pioneering flight from Hudson Bay to Bathurst Inlet, became lost and had to land near Dease Point in Coronation Gulf after they ran out of fuel. Their crews and passengers, consisting of eight persons in total, eventually turned up at Cambridge Bay after safely crossing Coronation Gulf with the help of local Inuit after freeze-up. In the meantime, their disappearance precipitated the Arctic's first major air search, at the time reported to have cost the staggering sum of nearly $400,000.

Another significant event in 1929 was the arrival of the HBC motor schooner *Fort James* at Gjoa Haven on 28 August. The vessel, which had left St John's in 1928 and wintered at Oscar Bay on the Boothia Peninsula, had duplicated Amundsen's journey to this remote location through Lancaster and Peel Sounds. *Fort James*' accomplishment finally marked HBC's long dreamed-of conquest of the Northwest Passage by their vessels. That year the *Baychimo* made the western segment from Vancouver arriving at Cambridge Bay in late August. The *Fort McPherson*, which had waited 14 valuable days at Cambridge Bay for the *Fort James* to bring out the King William Island fur returns for shipment on the *Baychimo*, finally, in desperation, made a dash to obtain the fur, arriving at Gjoa Haven on 23 August. After leaving supplies for *Fort James*, she quickly returned to Cambridge Bay so that the valuable cargo could be shipped out on the *Baychimo* on the 1st of September.

The *Fort James*, following her arrival at Gjoa Haven on 28 August, and after picking up the supplies left for her, made a "bluff attempt" to reach Cambridge Bay. The "bluff attempt" description was recorded in the diary of Cecil E. Bradbury, senior HBC fur trader on the vessel, and represented the crew's frustration with their captain whose main objective seems to have been the avoidance of another winter in the Arctic. Fearing the loom of ice, her captain retreated and proceeded to attempt a homeward voyage to Newfoundland. When this too met in failure, because of blocking ice, *Fort James* returned to Gjoa Haven, arriving on 21 September, only seven hours after the *Fort McPherson* had departed from her second trip to the King William Island after bringing in the "winter trade outfit" referring to the trading supplies for the season.

Photo 21-6

Cecil E. Bradbury and crew of the schooner *Fort James*.
Cecily Hinton collection

A more detailed account of *Fort James*' achievements, failings and the heroic efforts of Cecil Bradley, HBC King William trader Jack Livingstone, and a 13-year-old Inuit boy to avert the starving pangs of the crew is given in Appendix D.

The 21 September date was a missed opportunity to acknowledge a truly marvellous achievement. The headline that begged to go out on the occasion of the *Fort James*' arrival at one of the most remote places on the inhabited earth was that two Canadian-built and registered vessels, one from each coast, had finally achieved the Northwest Passage and furthermore, that the three vessels working together had achieved it in just two years.

Instead, the cautious, closed-mouthed Company hesitated, perhaps hoping for the more complete result of the *Fort James*' arrival at Cambridge Bay (her intended destination), or even better, her return to her home in St John's. In the delay, the epic accomplishment was further eclipsed by headlines reporting on the missing MacAlpine party.

An erroneous story of the accomplishment, supplied by an unknown source did appear in the *Calgary Herald* on 25 October 1929, announcing fur brought back by the *Fort James* had been delivered to London. The article was accompanied by a fanciful map showing *Fort James*' route through Bellot Strait to the Gulf of Boothia and then by Fury and Hecla Strait to Foxe Basin in Hudson Bay.

The Company-based version of events finally appeared in the *Montreal Gazette* of 7 November 1929, sharing a headline with news of the survival of the MacAlpine expedition.

N.W. PASSAGE IS FINALLY FORCED

Three Hudson's Bay Company Ships Accomplish Purpose After 259 Years

WITHIN ARCTIC CIRCLE

Amundsen Navigated Route in 1903-1905 in Gjoa—McAlpine Party Assisted by Trick of Destiny

Headline from *Montreal Gazette*, 7 November 1929.

Some years after the event, HBC District Manager W. E. Brown (as recorded in the September 1936 *Beaver* article previously mentioned), made this remark about the publicity given the event:

> The feat was the bridging of the Northwest Passage, and, being given little publicity at the time, the event passed almost unnoticed.

As a final comment on this rather bizarre story, it is utterly amazing that *Fort James'* captain, upon reaching Gjoa Haven, refused to proceed on to Cambridge Bay where his winter supplies were waiting for him; this given that *Fort McPherson* had left only hours before his arrival and had an easy return voyage. A plausible explanation was that Captain A. W. Bush was under orders to position his vessel, with its powerful radio sets, at this location to assist in the MacAlpine party search, but this does not seem to have been communicated to the crew and no mention seems to have been made of such in the literature. As it turned out, the news of the party's recovery *was* relayed over *Fort James'* radio set, and the crew, short on supplies, passed a very uncomfortable winter.

Another important event for the people of the Arctic that year was the opening of a residential school by the Anglican Church for Inuit and other children using the HBC's old post facilities at Shingle Point. This action had been suggested by native leaders from the Mackenzie Delta and the western Arctic, to enable their children to obtain education closer to their homes. Short of sending their children by ship to Vancouver, as mentioned for the Jacobsen children, the nearest option was the residential school at Hay River that served primarily Dene children. (In Canada, the Dene, which means "the people" in their own language, include the Denesoline (Chipewyan), Tlicho (Dogrib) and Dinjii Zhuh (Gwich'in). The Dene are also known as Athabascan, Athabaskan, Athapascan or Athapaskan peoples.)

Baychimo seems to have had little trouble in following her itinerary in 1929 including landing materials for Dominion Explorers in Bathurst Inlet. She arrived back in Vancouver on 25 September. Travelling aboard were Christian Klengenberg's daughter Etna and her husband Ikey Bolt. Etna was in Vancouver to stay with her father while recovering from pleurisy (a condition that causes painful breathing). *Baychimo* spent the winter under "orders" as no winter cargo appears to have been found for her.

1930 VOYAGE

Ikey and Etna Bolt returned to their home via the *Baychimo* on her inbound journey. At Herschel Island she picked up a number of passengers including, Reverend J. H. Webster and special Arctic investigator Richard Finnie.

Although the 1930 voyage north was successfully completed by *Baychimo*, it was also a disappointing one. She had been cleared to try for the Northwest Passage if conditions proved favourable. Indeed, at least pertaining to ice conditions, the *Fort James* had been able to return to the east without incident from the Company's post on King William Island. However early in the season, the ice gods of Point Barrow threw a wrench in these plans. During the annual race around this headland, which was "won" by the RCMP's schooner *St. Roch*, *Baychimo* lost several propeller blades which caused her to limp through the remainder of the voyage.

The risk to continue through the passage in such condition, where there was no support for hundreds of miles, was far too great and Captain Cornwell reluctantly returned by the usual route. With that one decision, *Baychimo* lost her single opportunity of gaining the laurels of being the first ship through the passage west-to-east in a single season, the first ship to circumnavigate North America, and the first ship to circumnavigate the world through the Northwest Passage. That year, even in her dilapidated condition, she was successful in heaving *St. Roch* off a reef near Cambridge Bay.

Observers stated that without *Baychimo*'s assistance, the grounding would have ended the police ship's career. Demonstrated time and again in the stories from the Arctic: survival and success rendered down to a matter of timing and outright sheer luck. That *Baychimo* could have taken these Arctic "firsts" instead of *St. Roch*'s crew, who ultimately claimed these honours, is yet another example of the role that chance plays in that harsh and unforgiving environment.

The final chapter of the *Fort James'* Northwest Passage saga played out in 1930. As recorded in Bradbury's personal diary on 5 August 1930, the *Fort McPherson*, 4,800 miles from her building yard in Vancouver, pulled alongside the *Fort James*, 3,500 miles from hers in Shelburne, Nova Scotia, and transferred supplies needed for the *Fort James'* homeward journey. She left on 7 August and arrived, without serious incident, at St. John's on 12 September 1930, completing the first ever east-to-west crossing of this section of the Northwest Passage; and if the other ships involved were included, the first ever east-to-west crossing of the Passage.

These are the words of Henry Lyall Ross Smyth, *Fort James'* young radio operator, historian and photographer, in an essay he wrote for his studies at McGill University in Montreal, Québec (part of the collection of the Library and Archives Canada):

> September 12th 1930, we arrived St John's, Newfoundland, having safely completed a voyage to the Western Arctic, during this expedition we met ships entering the Arctic from the Pacific

Ocean, thus linking the Pacific with the Atlantic through the Northwest Passage, which had been the goal of mariners.

Again, and particularly disappointing for the employees who were responsible for the accomplishment, the staunch old Company's press announcement was muted, if such existed, and this long-sought goal remained unheralded. Perhaps it was too much for the present managers to confront the ancient dreams of their ancestors with the thought that the Company's greatest achievement with respect to the Northwest Passage was in the wrong direction. In contemplation it would be fun to contrast the thought of what publicity may have ensued, if one of the several twentieth century adventures, bent on the west-to-east passage, had pulled it off first. What if it had been Stefansson? As events played out, he was only able to hold what *Fort James* had achieved as a forgotten dream!

Fort McPherson was not so lucky in reaching a home in 1930. On 3 October, after her third trip to King William Island, the indefatigable vessel was wrecked in a gale on her way to winter quarters at Bernard Harbour off Richardson Island in Coronation Gulf. Fortunately, there was no loss of life and only a little of cargo. The crew, including Captain David O. Morris and Engineer Otto Torrington, were rescued. Fittingly, the location of her remains lies only about one hundred miles to the east of those of her Arctic companion *Fort James*, when crushed in the ice and lost in 1937.

Photo 21-7

Schooners *Fort James* being crushed in ice and *St. Roch*, which got free.
P377-163 Alaska State Library – Ted Pedersen Photo Collection

A significant visitor to the Arctic in 1930 was Richard Finnie. That year, he travelled with Major Lachlan Burwash on parts of the government investigator's third trip to that region. Finnie was on special assignment, with typewriter and both still- and movie-cameras, to document Arctic conditions. Finnie's travels on the *Baychimo*, other Arctic vessels, on aircraft, and by dog team, together with his descriptions of events and characters, are delightfully narrated in his book *Lure of the North*. For his Arctic adventures he took up residence at Coppermine in the same building housing the radio station that was installed soon after his arrival.

Later, Finnie was a huge help to a selfless Arctic hero, Dr Russel Martin, a young Scot, who had come to Coppermine the previous year to operate the first medical station in the western Arctic. In 1929, the year that the medical station had been opened by Dr. Martin, convicted murderer Uluksuk (or Uloqsaq) had been returned to the community on the *Baychimo* after serving his sentence. Tragically for the community, Uluksuk was badly infected with tuberculosis and an epidemic soon spread throughout the community and adjoining countryside. When Martin travelled to Ottawa to beg for desperately needed help in dealing with the epidemic, he was told his services were no longer required. He was forced to return to Scotland. Finnie's photographic work was used in the National Film Board movie *Coppermine* that documented the short but heroic work of Dr. Martin in trying to combat the spread of this terrible disease.

The RCMP made a change in an Arctic detachment that year. Because of storm damage sustained in 1928 and 1929 Baillie Island was gradually being washed away, jeopardizing their facilities. As a result, they closed their detachment at that location on 6 August and relocated it to Pearce Point where there was a safe harbour for small ships. As for the *Baychimo*, Captain Cornwell and officers stayed in Vancouver over the winter 1930-1931 as the ship needed work on her stern.

THE 1931 VOYAGE

In 1931, because of the ice conditions experienced on the inbound journey to Herschel Island, it was decided that *Baychimo* would only proceed to Coppermine. The decision was made after consultations between Captain Cornwell and Fur Trade Commissioner Ralph Parsons, District Manager Richard H. G. Bonnycastle and other Company officials who awaited the ship at Herschel Island. But shortly after leaving Herschel, due to persisting poor ice conditions, Captain Cornwell had second thoughts and came to the conclusion he should return to Herschel Island, land all his cargo, and immediately head to

Point Barrow. However, he was convinced by Parsons that they should stick to their plan, "Egged him on without taking any responsibility" as Bonnycastle put it, and they pressed on to Coppermine. As events played out, he should have followed his own intuitions.

On her homeward voyage, loaded with fur and other freight and carrying HBC employees, *Baychimo*'s service to the fur trade came to an end. Although she had run the 400-mile gauntlet from Herschel Island and made it past Point Barrow, she found it impossible to proceed south. The strange tale of her fate is told in detail in Dalton's book, *Baychimo: Arctic Ghost Ship.* In brief, she was held in the ice without hope of release. The crew and passengers transferred ashore, ingeniously building a winter structure out of hatch covers, hold-lining lumber and canvas. *Baychimo* broke free of her anchorage in an overnight storm, to become a "ghost ship" and was reportedly sighted for many years after abandonment, and even on occasion boarded by local residents. Naturally, these interlopers took advantage of the situation and, recovered most of her "free" fur cargo. The Arctic holds her secrets firmly; *Baychimo*'s final fate remains unknown.

Having the use of radio provided for rapid rescue for passengers and some members of her crew. After quickly obtaining permission from the head office, District Manager Richard H. G. Bonnycastle organized an airlift by local bush pilots for the evacuation. Lucky passengers and crew members, partially selected by lottery, were flown by wheel-equipped aircraft from a frozen lagoon located near their make-shift wintering location to Nome, Alaska. At Nome they were able to board the last steamer of the season to Seattle.

The American passenger ship SS *Victoria* reached Seattle on 2 November. Carrying the annual fur trade records, Bonnycastle and his accountant J. O. Kimpton, were back to Company headquarters in Winnipeg on 5 November to report the calamity to management. In March 1932, the remaining 14 members of the crew who had stayed behind at the winter enclosure, including Captain Cornwell, were finally evacuated by air and by steamer. At this point all hope of locating and boarding the missing vessel had been lost. Bonnycastle's article published in the March 1936 issue of *The Beaver* provides further details of the ordeal.

OTHER SHIPS IN THE *BAYCHIMO* YEARS, 1925-1931

During the *Baychimo*-era the HBC sent two other ships to trade in the Arctic. The first was the auxiliary schooner *Baymaud*, formerly owned by Norwegian explorer Roald Amundsen as the *Maud*. Amundsen had the *Maud* built in 1917 for his expedition to drift over the Arctic Ocean as the *Fram* had done, but further north and possibly over the North Pole. The HBC's fur trade commissioner authorized her purchase after Amundsen's "Arctic drift" experiment went bankrupt. The vessel had already completed the Northeast Passage, and finally after a further three years without further progress, popped out of the ice near Nome. In 1926 after purchase and Canadian registration, the HBC sent the *Baymaud* north with a fur trade cargo under Captain Gus Foellmer. It was intended that she be used for local transport and, when *Baychimo* was present, to act as "pilot" vessel.

Scotty Gall, a veteran of the Arctic (who readers will meet in the next chapter), strongly pronounced her unsuitable. Not only did Gall complain that her confined holds, laced with ice pressure bracing, impeded stowage and removal of cargo, she required a full engine room crew for operation. Underpowered, she could only sustain 5 knots, barely enough to maintain steerage and headway against Arctic currents. Considered "stellar" in some accounts, the words of experienced Arctic ice-masters say it best; Scotty Gall referred to her simply as "a lemon" which succinctly summed up her unworthiness for Arctic duty.

Baymaud was used in the summers of 1926 and 1927 to establish new posts at Ellice River and Perry River, and to move buildings from the Kent Peninsula to Cambridge Bay. In the fall of 1927 her crew, with the exception of her radio operator Terry Crisp and her carpenter, took passage for Vancouver on the *Baychimo* after she was tied up opposite the Company post at Cambridge Bay for the intended use as a floating warehouse and machine shop.

Photo 21-8

Auxiliary schooner *Baymaud* grounded at Cambridge Bay.
NWT Archives photograph (Archibald Fleming fonds/ N-1979-050-0348)

This stationary assignment, to serve as a building, also did not work out for *Baymaud*, as she began leaking badly through her propeller shaft stuffing gland and required constant pumping to keep her afloat. Eventually she was heaved up on the shore, listing, to become one of Cambridge Bay's chief landmarks. (Recently, ownership of the vessel has been passed to a Norwegian historical group who have raised her and returned her to Norway. It is ironic that having completed the Northeast Passage, she retained enough life to complete the Northwest one, albeit in reverse and buoyed on a float behind a tug.)

While not particularly successful for freight transportation, the *Baymaud* did possess a powerful radio transmitter-receiver set that provided the Company with direct and instant communication to the Arctic, providing a tremendous benefit. (Before *Baymaud* was stationed in the central Arctic and aircraft made their introduction about the same time, only limited contact for distant posts was possible. Some received mail only twice a year, either by the annual supply ship or by a once-a-winter dog team delivery.) In 1929, her radio was used in providing communications during the aerial search, and eventual recovery, of the lost MacAlpine expedition as well as in the planning and delivery of relief supplies to HBC's eastern schooner *Fort James* that was wintering at Gjoa Haven on King William Island.

The second vessel to figure prominently was the power schooner *Old Maid No. 2*, which HBC Fur Trade Commissioner Charles H. French had personally purchased from Captain Christian Klengenberg in 1928, when Klengenberg retired from the Arctic. French later resold her to the HBC. Under Klengenberg, the vessel had made two trips to the Arctic. The first was under American registry as the *Maid of Orleans* from 1924-1925 when she was forced to winter at Herschel Island, and the second voyage while under Canadian registry as *Old Maid No. 2* in 1926.

During the winter of 1924-1925 Klengenberg is reported to have made another awe-inspiring trip over the mountains. Also, that year, he was able, after applying for naturalization, to sort out his problems with Ottawa and obtain the release of his ship and goods to continue trading in the Arctic. Later, after returning with his ship to the Pacific coast in the fall of 1925, he was successful in winning compensation in a San Francisco court against H. Liebes and Co. for their failure to deliver the goods he had previously ordered.

Under HBC ownership, *Old Maid No. 2* made two trips to the Arctic: in 1929 under sealing Captain W. H. Gillen and again in 1930 under F. L. Coe, former mate of the *Baychimo*.

Notorious from her early years as a "south pacific slave trader," and under Klengenberg's command in 1924 during the mysterious disappearance of RCMP Constable Ian MacDonald, *Old Maid* continued her infamy in 1929 when Captain Gillen was found dead floating amongst pilings near her berth in North Vancouver. Gillen, an experienced navigator, had piloted both Canalaska's new motor schooner the *Nigalik* (in 1926) and the RCMP's *St. Roch* (in 1928) to the Arctic. In 1931, HBC sold *Old Maid No. 2* to Paul Pane of San Francisco who used her in the rum-running trade.

Photo 21-9

Power schooner *Old Maid No. 2* unloading in the Arctic.
Vancouver Archives photograph BoP552

THE FINAL YEARS, 1932-1933

After *Baychimo*'s demise, two further attempts were made to supply the Arctic fur trade from Vancouver. The first was successful but the second was not. In 1932 the Company arranged a bare-boat rental of the 149-foot Danish motor vessel *Karise* from the Seattle-based fur trading company Swenson Fur and Trading Company to undertake the Arctic voyage. She was originally built in Thuro, Denmark, in 1918 as the *Svendorgsund* for ice service. She was purchased in 1930 by Swenson in Copenhagen to replace their lost vessel *Elsif* and renamed *Karise*. The vessel had seen service by Swenson in their Siberian trade.

Karise's voyage to the Canadian Arctic was made under Captain John Murray, an experienced HBC master from the Company's eastern Arctic trade, whose command prior to retirement had been the *Nascopie*. The first officer for *Karise*'s voyage was R. J. Summers who had served on the *Baychimo*. In spite of a broken-down compressor and the resultant lack of compressed air for starting the engine, the ship successfully completed a voyage to Coppermine and Fort Collinson before returning to Vancouver on 25 September. She brought back seven HBC officials including District Manager Richard H. G. Bonnycastle, who was finally able to complete the North Pacific voyage without interruption, and versatile company carpenter George McLeod who completed several tasks in the Arctic including the repair of the *Aklavik*. The chartered vessel was returned to her Seattle owners on 27 September 1932 and her master and mate returned to their homes in England.

Photo 21-10

Danish-registered motor vessel *Karise* at dock Vancouver, 1932.
Vancouver Maritime Museum photograph 7675

Karise was sold to Soviet interests in 1933 and renamed the *Soyuzpushina.* In 1934, she was the first vessel to leave the United States under the Soviet hammer and sickle flag, taking a cargo of salt from San Francisco to Vladivostok.

The well-known, Vancouver-based wooden freighter *Anyox*, under Captain B. D. Johnston, was chartered to make the 1933 Arctic voyage with a huge supply cargo intended for both the HBC and the RCMP. Under the supervision of HBC's Percy Patmore and R. J. Summers as first officer, she sailed from Vancouver on 6 July. It was a very difficult ice year, and when encountering the pack ice near Point Barrow, she damaged her bow and began leaking so badly she was in danger of sinking. The flow was stemmed somewhat when her crew were able to put a temporary timber and canvas patch in place.

Photo 21-11

Wooden freighter *Anyox*, engaged for the 1933 Arctic supply voyage.
Vancouver Archives photograph AM 1535-CVA99-4354 (Stuart Thomson)

They were assisted in the later stages of these temporary repairs by the crew of the United States Coast Guard cutter *Northland*, whose crew came to her aid in response to her distress calls, arriving on 28 July. After the cutter had cut a path in the ice, and assisted her out of the entrapment, it was determined that in her then-damaged condition, she could not continue the voyage. She was forced to turn south to Unalaska where further repairs were affected so she could safely return to Vancouver. She arrived there on 24 August while the USCG *Northland* returned to her base at Nome. Meanwhile the indomitable Captain Pedersen, whose ship the *Patterson* had been trapped in the ice slightly north of *Anyox*, succeeded in blasting himself free with dynamite.

Mindful of the loss of the *Lady Kindersley* and the huge difficulties in Arctic supply that ensued in 1924, as well as the increased supply needs of 1933, HBC's transportation system went into emergency mode. In spite of challenges occasioned by high water on the Mackenzie River (that damaged warehouses and dock facilities, including the loss of wood piles that fired their river steamers), they were able to respond effectively. Unlike previous emergencies, in 1933 they had modern radio communications that enabled them to plan and execute the delivery of replacement supplies and arrange for forwarding them all over the western Arctic.

Photo 21-12

Loading [Inuit] schooner from SS *Distributor* at Aklavik, 31 August 1933. Hudson's Bay Company Archives, Archives of Manitoba. Hudson's Bay House Library photograph collection subject files, 1987/363-E-393/44

The first part of the response played-out with the arrival of the Company's river steamer *Distributor* at Aklavik on 31 August, pushing a huge barge loaded with 700 tons of goods. The remaining problem of further forwarding goods before freeze-up, for a company nearly devoid of distribution vessels, was solved by the cooperation and mobilization of dozens of local concerned citizens (in an action akin to the miraculous evacuation of Dunkirk that would occur a few years later in the early stages of World War II.)

Waiting at Aklavik was a fleet of dozens of motor schooners chartered by the Company for the purpose of distributing the supplies. They were those owned by the prosperous Inuit and white trappers engaged in the fur trade. Some, like the *Anna Olga*, had been brought to the Arctic under their own power (bound for Fort Collinson) while others had been brought in as deck cargo on supply ships, but many of them, like the *Sea Queen* (she was headed for Baillie Island) had been constructed by Edmonton boatbuilders, transported to Waterways by rail and then sailed down the Slave and Mackenzie rivers to the Arctic.

The vessels quickly loaded from the barge and dispersed throughout the area. Some took supplies to the school at Shingle Point, while about twenty hurried to Herschel Island where the *St. Roch* was waiting to take on some of their loads for an unscheduled trip to Cambridge Bay. A few of the larger vessels ventured as far as Fort Collinson in the Coronation Gulf and one even farther to Bathurst Inlet to resupply fur trading posts. From this grand effort, the Arctic had been supplied but 1933 also marked the last year for any further attempts to supply out of Vancouver.

AFTERMATH

Photo 21-13

Schooner *Fort James*, at the new port of Tuktoyaktuk, seaworthy and ready for action. Hudson's Bay Company Archives photograph 1987/363-F-85/126 (R. N. Hourde, 1936.)

In 1934 HBC abandoned the ocean supply route and switched to its Mackenzie River system. With a reliable railhead at Waterways, substantial improvements at Smith Portage, and the introduction of powerful diesel, low-draft tugs like the *Pelly Lake* that could traverse the Mackenzie Delta, this alternative became competitive and compelling. Of greater importance, it avoided the risks of the Point Barrow route. Accordingly, the long-anticipated new port of Tuktoyaktuk was finally established. It was located a few miles east of the eastern side of the Mackenzie Delta, where cargo from the river system could be received and forwarded by Arctic distribution vessels. A new distribution vessel, *Margaret A.*, was acquired and the HBC schooner *Fort James* was transferred from the east coast via the Panama Canal, to assist *Aklavik* in the onward distribution along the Arctic coast.

After 1925, the HBC moved its headquarters from Herschel Island to Aklavik when radio communications were established. However, they continued to maintain a store at Herschel Island until 1937. Eventually all its facilities were removed, and no evidence of their presence exists today. Captain Pedersen's last voyage to Herschel Island was made on the *Patterson* in 1935. In 1936 he had all supplies for his Canalaska division shipped by the HBC down the Mackenzie River. In 1937 all his remaining assets, including his store and warehouse on Herschel Island, and trading posts at Cambridge Bay, Bathurst Inlet, and Gjoa Haven, and the venerable motor schooner *Nigalik*, were sold to the HBC and integrated into their system.

The RCMP which had transferred its sub-district headquarters to Aklavik in 1931, maintained a presence on Herschel Island until permanently closed in 1964. Their buildings, including the infamous "bone house," remain at Herschel Island as part of Herschel Island—Qikiqtaruk Territorial Park operated by the Yukon Territory.

Photo 21-14

Recent aerial view of Herschel Island. At the left are Captain Pedersen's store, bonded warehouse, and RCMP warehouse. In the centre are former RCMP buildings, including officer quarters, barracks/recreational building and the "bone house." HikeBikeTravel.com photograph

Although the HBC ended up with a dominant near-monopoly position in the western Arctic trade at the end of the Vancouver supply period, the venture from a profit-perspective, appears to have been far from successful, based on documents left behind by Philip Godsell and Richard Bonnycastle. In an interview of Scotty Gall conducted by Richard Valpy of the Northwest Territories Archives (after Gall's retirement), Gall remarked to Valpy, that he felt that the Company did not turn consistent profits from its western Arctic trade until after World War II when a welfare system for northern residents was introduced.

CONCLUSION

The port of Vancouver has for years had a close connection to the western Arctic and its related Northwest Passage. Anyone who has visited the Vancouver Maritime Museum, and strolled the decks of the preserved dry-berthed *St. Roch*, cannot escape this fact. However, what is less apparent, is that this connection goes back much earlier than the *St. Roch*'s arrival in the Arctic in 1928.

Following in the wake of whalers and other fur traders, the HBC established itself at Herschel Island in 1915, then reached eastward through the ice-plagued Dolphin and Union Strait into the central Arctic in the Coronation Gulf and Queen Maud Gulf areas, gradually expanding, and ultimately dominating, the trade. Police detachments and missionary posts, and even a medical station, followed the establishment of fur trading posts that in turn, enabled the foundation of permanent settlements along the liveable portion of the Northwest Passage.

The supply of this enterprise from Vancouver, from 1914 until 1932, utilizing an array of charter and Company-owned ships, stands as a remarkable achievement of logistics, seamanship, and luck. In spite of the loss of two Vancouver supply ships, and the venerable *Fort McPherson*, no lives were lost.

As a final thought, the author likes to contemplate the motor schooner *Fort James* on the 1930 homeward bound transit to St. John's, Newfoundland on her epic journey from Gjoa Haven through Peel Sound, under an anxious Captain A. W. Bush. Her engine, fuelled with diesel from a Vancouver dealer and her crew, fed with meals cooked using BC coal, were not embarked on another expedition to find the remains of John Franklin and his ships HMS *Erebus* and *Terror*. Instead, she had come to this most remote of locations to find a possible alternative commercial supply route and to seek out the lucrative fur of the arctic fox.

As she hurried on her way, making the first-ever east-to-west crossing of the final segment of the Northwest Passage, her crew no doubt enjoyed many hot cups of coffee. Likely it was HBC-brand, whitened with Pacific-brand condensed milk and sweetened with Rogers-brand sugar, both iconic Vancouver-based companies. The feat of two Canadian-built vessels, the *Fort McPherson* pulling alongside the

Fort James to deliver supplies, is surely an epic watershed moment in Canadian Arctic history.

A masterful painting of this event, by acclaimed Canadian artist John Horton, is the cover art for the book. Assisting him in his work was the photograph shown on the following page. Recently located by the author, the fact that it does not appear to have been publicized at any earlier date remains an unfathomable mystery.

Photo 21-15

Painting *Meeting at Gjoa Haven* by John Horton, depicts the historic meeting on 8 August 1930 of the motor schooners *Fort McPherson* and *Fort James* at Gjoa Haven in the central Arctic, after transits from the eastern and western reaches.

Photo 21-16

Motor schooners *Fort McPherson* and *Fort James* at Gjoa Haven, 8 August 1930.
Library and Archives Canada/PA-203025 (Henry Lyall Ross Smyth)

22

Pioneer Arctic Mariner, Trader and Explorer

Photo 22-1

"Scotty" Gall in his garden – a screenshot from the film Coppermine 1993. Photo copyright 1992 National Film Board of Canada (with permission to the author)

In February 2013 a plaque commemorating Ernest James "Scotty" Gall was placed on the wall of the causeway of Victoria BC's Inner Harbour. It can be found in the Explorers Walk section of this unique project, intended to honour local ships and navigators of note.

Photo 22-2

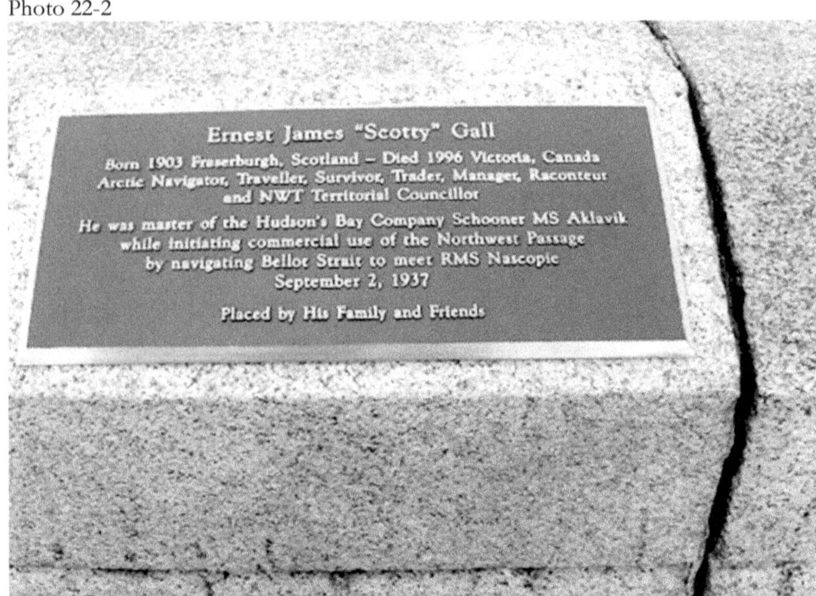

Scotty Gall Commemorative Plaque placed by Iain Cameron (Scotty's great-nephew) on behalf of the family, and the author, on behalf of Scotty's friends.
Courtesy of Achinback Foundry

The plaques are owned by and are under the administrative control of the Victoria Harbour Commission. A description of the proposed honoree, and their accomplishments, are required to be submitted for the approval of each plaque. For this plaque the sponsors stated:

> A plaque is proposed to honour and educate passers–by in Victoria's Inner Harbour concerning a long-term area resident who made significant contributions to Canada's Arctic navigation and settlement and northern development: Almost forgotten, the mortal remains of Ernest James "Scotty" Gall lay beneath the turf on a pleasant slope at an unmarked location in the Royal Oak Burial Park. For thirty years after his retirement, Victoria was home to this remarkable but self-effacing Arctic navigator, traveller, survivor, trader, manager and elected North West Territory councillor. In 1996 it became his final "harbour."
>
> During retirement many noteworthy writers, film makers, relatives of associates, archivists and historians came to his home to learn of his adventures, contacts with famous Arctic personalities and to share his firsthand knowledge of the fur trade, navigation and establishment of settlements in the Western Arctic. The most well-

known of these was author Peter C. Newman, who used material obtained from his interviews in his book *Merchant Princes*.

In his early career with the Hudson's Bay Company, Scotty travelled many thousands of miles both by motor schooner and by dog sled. The motor schooner was the tool that allowed Canada's last frontier to be settled and the long–sought Northwest Passage to be finally used for trade. He became a master in piloting these vessels through the shallow rock and ice infested waters through the school of 'hard knocks' and by listening to native advice.

His most famous accomplishment was the first successful west to east navigation of the treacherous Bellot Strait between the Boothia Peninsula and Somerset Island in 1937 (five years before the *St Roch*). The meeting and the exchange of cargoes between his schooner, the *Aklavik*, and the Hudson's Bay Company eastern supply ship, the RMS *Nascopie*, at the eastern end of the strait at Fort Ross was celebrated as the first commercial use of the Northwest Passage. Scotty continued on to Halifax with the *Nascopie*, being its first passenger from the Western Arctic, and thence to a planned furlough in Scotland.

Sadly, he travelled alone with his greatest triumph quashed. His beautiful and beloved wife Anna had died at the controls of *Aklavik*'s diesel engine while awaiting transfer of supplies at Cambridge Bay. He had met his wife Anna (nee Fagerstrom) at Nome, Alaska in 1931 on another of his adventures after being evacuated from the Hudson's Bay Company supply ship SS *Baychimo*. The ship became trapped in the ice near Barrow, was abandoned and later became the famous "ghost ship" of the Arctic.

HBC FUR TRADE APPRENTICE

An adventurous youth, probably a bit of a misfit, Scotty was unable to find satisfying employment in his native Scotland in 1923. He applied to be, and was accepted as, a fur trade apprentice with the Hudson's Bay Company. Out of the 21 apprentices engaged in Scotland that year only he, and a Donald Forbes Watt, were sent to Western Canada. His first posting was to the old whaling settlement on Herschel Island, an important destination at that time as most supplies for western Arctic settlements arrived by ships rounding Alaska from Vancouver. It was the only safe harbour for many miles on the northern coast. The western Arctic, unlike southern Canada, was settled from west to east. Settlement during this challenging time was occurring before air travel and two-way radio communication had been established in the area.

Travelling by train from Québec City, and after visiting HBC headquaters in Winnipeg, where he met senior officials and renewed his expended travelling funds, he continued to Waterways, Alberta. At Waterways his first task was to assist shipbuilder George Askew to complete the assembly and launching of the HBC's new 58-foot motor schooner *Aklavik*, a vessel he would be intimately associated with over the next years. After entering the river the vessel was taken in tow by the motor boat *Liard River*, which Askew had just launched. Both then proceeded down the Athabasca River to Fort Fitzgerald where they were hauled over the 16-mile Smith Portage to Fort Smith. At Fort Smith, Scotty assisted in the installation of *Aklavik*'s engine.

Scotty arrived at Herschel Island after helping with her navigation down the Mackenzie River system. The distance from Fort Smith was over 1,200 miles. He soon came into contact with many famous Arctic characters of the time. The first he encountered was Pete Norberg who had come over the mountains to Fort Simpson from the Yukon to help pilot the *Aklavik* through the lower reaches of the Mackenzie. Norberg went east later that year to establish the first trading post on King William Island.

Photo 22-3

The *Aklavik* being towed by the Lamson and Hubbard tractors at Smith Portage on her way to the Arctic Ocean. (The figure on the deck of the *Aklavik* may be Scotty Gall.) Courtesy of the Brabant collection

At Herschel Island, Scotty met other personalities including the independent fur trader Charles Klinkenberg (later Klengenberg), his sons, and the Hudson's Bay Inspector Phillip Godsell. He also encountered and travelled with Knud Rasmussen, the famous Danish explorer and scientist, who Scotty reported had honed the art of high-speed dog team travel and Arctic anthropological research. Rasmussen used a retinue of paid assistants to set up camp sites and food caches and a native female interpreter companion to help gather information. Scotty's eyes were further opened to the "wild west" when he had to deal with a Company trader at an outpost near the Alaska border who was involved with home-brewed liquor. After it was found that half the post's trade goods could not be accounted for, it was determined that the missing goods, along with the trader's native interpreter, had been bartered to the Alaskans.

Photo 22-4

Inuit dog sled on an ice floe, May-June 1884.
National Archives photograph #USN 900765

Scotty's early years in the Arctic fur trade involved a lot of travel. In the short navigation season from July to October he was busy with motor schooners transporting supplies, trade goods, building materials and fuel to an expanding chain of fur trading settlements. He also helped to set up and construct buildings. In the winter he travelled by dog sled with the Inuit, visiting posts from the Alaskan border to King William Island, delivering mail and helping the post managers sort out their accounts and records.

Map 22-1

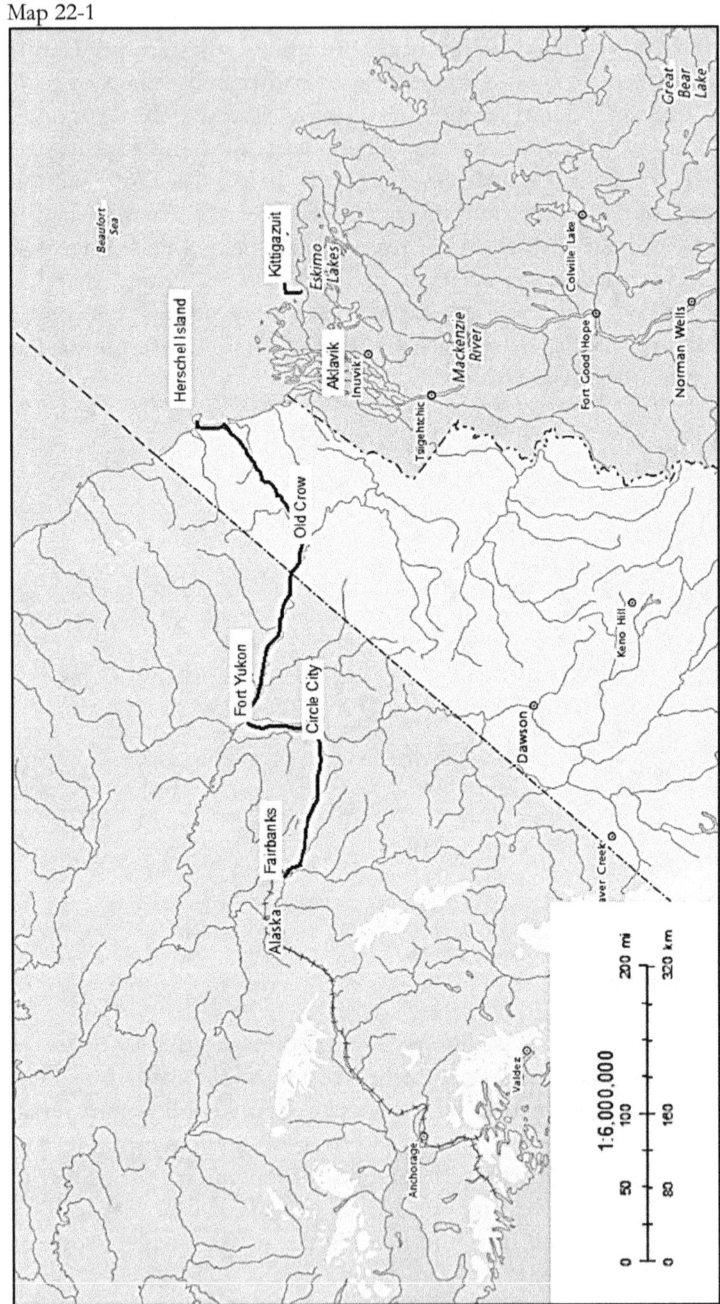

Winter Journey by HBC Party - Herschel Island to Fairbanks, 1924
From the Atlas of Canada – Toporama, marked-up by Iain Cameron

In the summer of 1924, the inhabitants of the western Arctic found themselves in a desperate situation. The Hudson's Bay Company's supply ship *Lady Kindersley* had been crushed in the ice and foundered off Point Barrow, Alaska. Urgently needed supplies, including cash for trading, and a radio transmitting and receiving set scheduled for installation at Herschel Island, did not arrive. In consequence Scotty was sent by dog sled from Herschel Island across the mountains to Fairbanks, Alaska, where there was telegraphic service, banks, supply depots and a railroad connection to the south. His mission was to obtain emergency instructions, fur prices, radio receiver parts, replacement dogs and presumably cash.

Their party on the outward journey of about 560 miles included three Company employees who were escaping the Arctic by the Alaska Railroad and the Alaska Steamship Company's service to Seattle. The return journey was made by Scotty and his companion Ambrose (believed to be Ambrose Aganygak who formerly worked for the Canadian Arctic Expedition), with the assistance of a Gwitchin guide whom they enlisted at Old Crow, Yukon. Scotty's winter travel in 1924-25, including a subsequent trip to Bernard Harbour with a return to Kittigazuit (which was the wintering location of the *Aklavik* near the mouth of the Mackenzie River), totaled over 2,600 miles. A transcript of a diary kept by Gall of the trip from Herschel Island to Fairbanks, Alaska, plus a map showing the approximate route is found on Iain Cameron's blog site (http://iain-cameron.blogspot.com/). The original copy of Scotty's diary was given to Iain in 2011 by his cousin and Scotty's niece, Patricia Gibson.

Although the trip from Herschel Island over the mountains in the depths of winter was not unprecedented, even for Company employees, it was still a remarkable achievement. Northerners, who particularly understand the challenges and hazards of such travel, hold those who accomplish such journeys in high regard. This is illustrated in remarks made in a speech by Alaskan Congressional Delegate Frank Waskey in a tribute after-dinner speech to Roald Amundsen in 1906 as reported by the *Nome Nugget*:

> ...what appealed to Alaska in Amundsen was not, perhaps his clever and lucky feat in taking the *Gjoa* through the northwest passage, nor even his determination of the position of the north magnetic pole, great as these performances would be in the eyes of the outside world, but the long and successful mush, he had made from Herschel's (sic) Island to Eagle alongside the Porcupine River.

Waskey was referring to a trip, similar to Gall's, that Amundsen and a partially incapacitated whaler named Captain William ("Billy") Mogg, had made over the 9,000-foot Ogilvie Mountains from Herschel Island. The trip was made with the assistance of several Inuit men who accompanied them as far as Fort Yukon on the Yukon River. They set out on 24 October 1905 and arrived at Eagle, Alaska, 500-miles distant, in early 1906 having endured -60°F temperatures along the way. At Eagle there was a telegraph station from which Amundsen announced to the world his successful transit of the Northwest Passage.

Photo 22-5

Fort Egbert and the town of Eagle, Alaska, 1914.
University of Washington: Special Collections photograph 842 uploaded to Wikimedia Commons

SURVIVAL OF THE CREW OF THE *EMMA JANE*

In 1927, Scotty Gall, newly assigned master of the 42-foot, two-masted schooner *Emma Jane*, was shipwrecked along with a young Scottish sailor Ian "Jock" Christie, and his Inuit assistants Ovilook and Ovilook's wife Canyiyuk, on a coastal island in Queen Maud Gulf. The HBC had charged Gall with taking advantage of the vessel's shallow draft to investigate the most favourable passage through the Gulf. He was then to continue east and deliver supplies to the King William Island post (previously established by Pete Norberg and Henry Bjorn, when their small vessel was wrecked.) Their resourceful survival, as related by Scotty to former district manager Dudley Copland, is recorded in a stirring account "The Wreck of the *Emma Jane*," published in the summer 1970 issue of *The Beaver* magazine.

The *Emma Jane* left Cambridge Bay on 16 September (with crew, six dogs, a sled and bundles of dried fish for dogfood as well as the supplies and freight), but was only able to make five knots owing to unfavourable winds, and little assistance from her small, labouring auxiliary engine. Nonetheless, the schooner managed to pass through a maze of islands by evening and enter the open waters of the Gulf. Scotty had intended to spend the night hove-to under sail, but with shoals in every direction, and the wind freshening, he decided to seek shelter in the lee of one of the coastal islands. Near midnight, after a lull, the wind began blowing even harder, *Emma Jane*'s anchor started dragging, and she was set hard aground.

During one attempt to free the vessel, Scotty and Ovilook used *Emma Jane*'s sponson canoe to move her anchor farther away in an effort to kedge her off the beach into deeper water. Unfortunately, Ovilook tipped them both out of the canoe while trying to redeploy the anchor. Scotty surfaced in the cold water and grabbed for the canoe but on seeing his companion thrashing and unable to swim, he grabbed for Ovilook instead. He employed a lifesaving stroke and began towing Ovilook toward the *Emma Jane*. Scotty reached the boat exhausted and with severe cramps, and while he had saved both their lives, the precious canoe was lost.

Subsequent efforts to get the beach-gripped schooner clear were successful. However, an even stronger wind, along with rising swell and waves, drove the *Emma Jane* onto a reef, snapped her mainmast and filled the vessel with water.

She was hard aground on a reef within hailing distance of a long point of land jutting out from a nearby island, but how to reach it with no canoe? Fortunately, there were three skids on deck intended to be used to haul the schooner out that autumn. Young Ian Christie lashed himself to one of the skids after it was put over the side and with a tending line leading back to the shipwreck, he was able to drift to the island. With a man ashore, everything salvageable on the vessel was passed to the beach until nothing was left and the remaining survivors made the shore.

Before Scotty departed, he dove underwater to recover from under his bunk a case of Irish whiskey consigned to Paddy Gibson on King William Island.

Survival of the vessel's crew would only be possible through teamwork which required the blended skills of two cultures. Ashore on the snow-covered island, using only native rocks, and salvaged mast booms and main sail, they rigged a shelter against the elements. However, it was apparent that heavier clothing, footwear, and mittens were required to survive imminent cold weather. They had a bale of deerskins as well as sinew (vessel cargo), but no needle for stitching. By chance Scotty found a needle in his artigee (Inuit style fur parka inner layer) apparently left there by a seamstress, but unusable, being broken off at the eye.

Scotty had saved Ovilook, and he and Canyiyuk were now the salvation of the entire, small shipwrecked party. Ovilook fashioned a bow and shaft, and obtained sinew to use as a bowstring to wrap around the shaft, to create a rudimentary drill. Canyiyuk obtained tiny chips of flint on the beach which could be used as cutting points. It took about three days of effort, but Ovilook was able to drill a new hole in the needle which was then used to fashion clothing.

Salvaged and foraged food available on the one-mile circumference island included a gull shot with a contrived bow and arrow, and a sacrificed dog, sustaining them until the water around the island finally froze. This allowed the survivors to mush off carrying a homemade skiff on their sled as a life-boat over the weak ice pulled by four dogs. The skiff was fabricated from wood salvaged from the deckhouse of the *Emma Jane,* and covered with paint-coated canvas. Their island was one of the outermost of the coastal fringe, some distance into the Queen Maud Gulf, so they would have to reach the mainland shore for rescue. They first attempted to paddle four miles to an adjacent island but failed after only one mile when they bogged down in slushy ice.

When the sea froze, they tried again and were finally able to progress, abandoned their skiff, and marched east. It was bitterly cold, and progress painstakingly slow, owing to their poor physical condition and weakness of the dogs, but sheer will prevailed. After a few days they reached Perry River where sign of life revived them: smoke could be seen rising from some buildings ahead and a small schooner was frozen in the ice. Drawing closer, the dwellings proved to be the new post of the Canalaska Trading Company and the motor vessel *Nigalik* with C. H. Clarke in charge.

The wreck of the *Emma Jane* is just one example of the stamina and fortitude required by those who ventured north. Despite their incredible survival, Scotty later remarked, "I left my first command a very tired and despondent young man."

SCOTTY SAVED A SECOND TIME BY OWN EFFORTS

Jock Christie's time in the Arctic was not long-lived, it ended in 1929, when as an employee of the Canalaska Company, he froze to death after falling into a creek in a spring blizzard in Bathurst Inlet. Shortly afterwards Scotty saved himself from a similar fate by applying a technique he had learned from his native companions. While trapping in the same area, he too broke through thin ice. He rolled in the snow letting his soaked clothes freeze and then quickly knocked the ice off of them. The difference between surviving or succumbing often came down to a matter of applying local knowledge and that had to be acquired from a willingness to learn from those who knew the area best—the Inuit—and also, a great degree of luck.

Scotty finished his apprenticeship in the fall of 1928 and returned to Scotland for a holiday but not without another survival adventure. While travelling south, he was nearly drowned helping to lay out a winching cable for the *Distributor* to ascend the rapids in the Ramparts section of the Mackenzie River in the low water conditions that prevailed that year.

DEPRESSION-ERA CANCELLED DREAMS AND AN ARCTIC LOVE STORY

In 1929 Scotty again sailed for Canada, this time arriving at Halifax on 1 March aboard the S.S. *Antonia* with a Canadian passport, to take employment with the Northern Aerial Minerals Exploration Company, based in Toronto, Ontario. This was a new firm which hoped to revolutionize mineral exploration employing aircraft to access very remote areas. Aircraft on floats in the summer or skis in winter could transport prospectors, geologists, supplies and equipment rapidly into remote sites—immensely increasing the scope of a season's investigation.

Scotty had dreams of a flying career by becoming a bush pilot. That summer he was sent back to the Arctic to prepare for the introduction of aircraft in the Coppermine area where a mineral-staking boom was in progress. In addition to helping with the servicing of the aircraft, he worked in the field assisting geological staff in claim-staking, and with winter transportation of personnel and supplies working with a dog team. Unfortunately, his aviation dreams were dashed when he was discharged in the fall of 1930 after the stock market collapse and the onset of the Great Depression. He stayed in the area supporting himself by working at odd jobs and by trapping.

His fortunes were reversed in the Spring of 1931 when it was discovered that his old vessel the *Aklavik* had partially sunk at her over-winter berth at Bernard Harbour. Richard Bonnycastle, the HBC district manager, hired Scotty to recover the vessel. Scotty's success with the venture resulted in salvage of both the vessel and his career with the Company, and led to continued employment with it until his retirement in 1966.

When he was rehired, an arrangement for passage for Scotty from the Arctic to Vancouver on the Company's supply ship *Baychimo* was made. He wished to see the Canadian west coast. The plan was that he would reside in Vancouver on retainer during the winter before rejoining the *Aklavik* the following summer. The voyage south proved to be another survival adventure for Scotty; surprisingly, it also resulted in his marriage. *Baychimo* became trapped in the ice after rounding Cape Barrow and was eventually abandoned by her crew, all of them forced into temporary quarters that they constructed ashore from pieces salvaged from the ship. Subsequently, with unobserved overnight ice movements, *Baychimo* drifted away and disappeared. For the crew then ashore, it must have left them with a sense of thankful salvation and desperate abandonment.

Photo 22-6

Scotty Gall and wife Anna at Jenny Lind Island, Nunavut.
NWT Archives photograph (Jack Wood's Family/N-1988-041: 0057)

Bonnycastle, together with Scotty and several other passengers and Company officials, were evacuated by air to Nome, Alaska, to take passage to Seattle on the Alaska Steamship Company's steamer *Victoria.* While in Nome, Scotty was smitten by a beautiful young lady he met there, Anna Fagerstrom. It was fortuitous she was also intending travel on the *Victoria.* Anna, born in the nearby Golovin Village, was the artistic and educated daughter of Charles Fagerstrom, a Swedish born miner and gas boat engineer, and Susan Kowak. Scotty and Anna were married in Whatcom County in Washington State on 6 January 1932.

In the spring of 1932, after working at odd jobs in Vancouver, Scotty returned to the Arctic, with Anna, to crew on the *Aklavik*. After repairs were completed under the supervision of a shipwright, he became her engineer, and later, her master. He and Anna spent more than five happy years working and living in the Coronation Gulf area, fur trading in the winters and running the *Aklavik* in the summer navigation season. During two winters of this period, they lived aboard the vessel.

Photo 22-7

Aklavik in winter berth in Bathurst Inlet. In autumn 1936 the Galls, with apprentice Jack Wood, had attempted a late season delivery of supplies to Perry River Post but were turned back by ice conditions. They attempted to reach the Bathurst Inlet Post to warehouse the goods but could not reach it either.
NWT Archives photograph (Jack Wood's Family/N-1988-041: 0112 Winter quarters.)

23

Conquest of the Northwest Passage at Bellot Strait

Photo 23-1

Illustration of the Bellot Strait, 1 January 1881.
McClintock, Francis (January 1881). *Fate of Sir John Franklin: The Voyage of the Fox in the Arctic Seas in Search of Franklin and His Companions*

The most significant navigational achievement of Scotty Gall's career was the first successful navigation of the Bellot Strait in 1937. As the navigation involved the transportation of fur and trade goods between the western and eastern Arctic, it also constituted the first commercial use of the Northwest Passage—an unrealized dream of the Hudson's Bay Company for hundreds of years.

Bellot Strait in Nunavut, about twenty miles in length, separates Somerset Island to the north from the Boothia Peninsula to the south. As shown by Map 23-1 on page 201, Fort Ross is located on its north shore, near the eastern entrance to the strait. A first attempt at the navigation of Bellot Strait was made by lost Franklin expedition-seeker Captain Leopold McClintock in 1858. On 6 September 1858 after six starts of pushing his vessel *Fox* westward, he managed to reach the western entrance of the strait; but ice blocked the way and it was impossible to break through.

An opportunity for the navigation of the strait by a Hudson's Bay Company vessel arose before 1937 but it was not part of their plans at that time. In 1928 their eastern Arctic vessel *Fort James* made an exploratory voyage from St. John's Newfoundland to the westside of the Boothia Peninsula and King William Island area. The *Fort James* followed Amundsen's route through Peel Sound into, and then out of, the area. The vessel wintered at Oscar Bay on the Boothia Peninsula during its first year in the area.

In 1929 after trying to reach her objective at Cambridge Bay, the *Fort James* turned back and attempted to return to the east but was not able to find passage owing to blocking ice conditions that existed near Oscar Bay, her previous wintering location. As a consequence, the *Fort James* wintered at Gjoa Haven on King William Island during the second year. Both the Hudson's Bay and the rival Canalaska companies maintained fur trading posts at Gjoa Haven, supplied by vessels from the west. As is described in Chapter 21, for the Hudson's Bay Company, the arrival of the *Fort James* at Gjoa Haven meant that Company vessels had finally navigated the full length of the long sought Northwest Passage.

Although the *Fort James* passed the western entrance of Bellot Strait on her entry in 1928, and on her departure in 1930, it is clear from records made by her on-board radio operator Henry Lyall Ross Smyth and senior fur trader Cecil E. Bradbury that she never entered or navigated through Bellot Strait. Further, she did not carry any fur trade returns from the western Arctic to the east other than those that had been trapped by her crew when wintering.

District Manager Dudley Copland paid a visit to the Galls in the early spring of 1937 by dog sled when they were wintering on the *Aklavik* in Bathurst Inlet. The idea of a voyage through Bellot Strait was hatched between the Galls and Copland when he informed them of the pending establishment of Fort Ross near its eastern entrance. The plan, sponsored by Copland and approved by Company management, was to link up a trading voyage by the *Aklavik*, forwarding fur returns from King William Island from the west, to a rendezvous with the Company's eastern supply vessel RMS *Nascopie* at Fort Ross.

Map 23-1

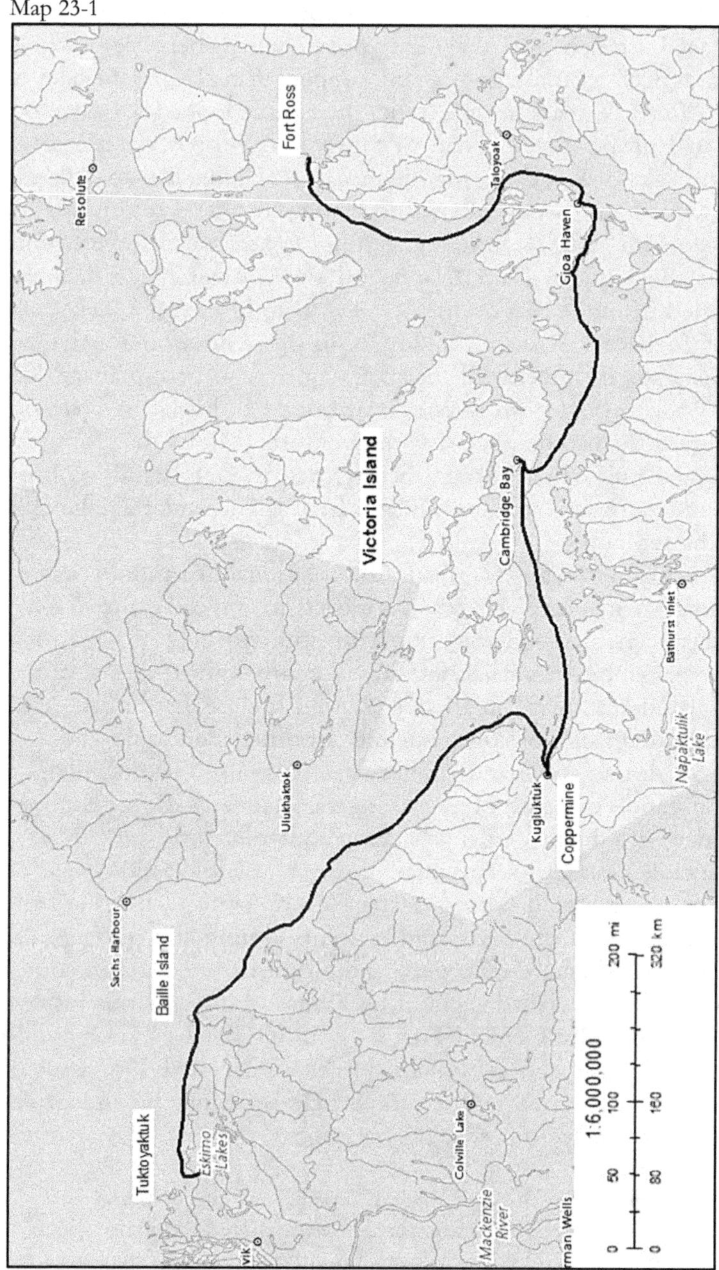

Passage of *Audrey B.* from Tuktoyaktuk to Cambridge Bay, and *Aklavik* from Cambridge Bay to Fort Ross
From the Atlas of Canada – Toporama, marked up by Iain Cameron

Nascopie was tasked with bringing supplies and building materials for the establishment of the new post; which her crew would construct, as well as trade goods and supplies for *Aklavik* to take to the west. After five years in the Arctic, the couple looked forward to a furlough in Europe—even a trip to Paris. If the trip was successful, they would take passage on the *Nascopie* to Halifax for an Atlantic crossing, while Patsy Klengenberg and his family would return west to Gjoa Haven with *Aklavik*, bringing supplies to serve as reserve trading outfits for the King William Island and Perry River posts that had been shipped from the east on the *Nascopie* from Montreal, Québec.

Chief Inspector William "Paddy" Gibson, who would arrive on the *Nascopie*, was to travel with them, taking over as post manager for the King William Post from Lorenz Learmonth. In his book *Coplalook*, Copland summed up the plans for the venture: "All of the Company men involved knew their Arctic history: Scotty Gall, Paddy Gibson and Lorenz Learmonth of King William Island. The undertaking could not be in better hands."

A principal advocate for Fort Ross, Lorenz Learmonth was to become its first manager. He was supposed to travel on the *Aklavik* but had his own plans. He set out with apprentice D. G. Sturrock, some native helpers, a whaleboat, an outboard motor, and a canoe, and completed his own remarkable journey to the new post. After completing a coastal passage up the Boothia Peninsula, he and Sturrock made an overland traverse across its tip, including a frightening canoe crossing of the eastern entrance of Bellot Strait to Depot Bay where the new post was being constructed.

Meanwhile, *Aklavik*'s passage through Bellot Strait was an internationally celebrated success. After suffering and recovering from a near fatal engine failure in rapid currents during the passage, the vessel linked up and exchanged cargo with the *Nascopie* on 2 September 1937. A detailed account by Richard Finnie of this historic event and the establishment of Fort Ross in his article, "Trading into the North West Passage," is contained in the December 1937 issue of *The Beaver.* The final paragraph of the article sums up the end of the endeavour with this historic wireless message:

> Gjoa Haven, King William Island (Special to the *Nascopie* by private wireless) – The schooner *Aklavik* arrived here on the fourteenth of September, thus completing the successful freighting of goods via the North West Passage. Chief Inspector W[illiam] Gibson sends his regards to all passengers on board the *Nascopie* and wishes them the best of luck.

Photo 23-2

Ernest James "Scotty" Gall of the *Aklavik* shaking hands with Captain Thomas Smellie of the RMS *Nascopie* after crossing the Northwest Passage on 3 September 1937. Mr. Downes, a passenger on the *Nascopie*, took the photograph.
NWT Archives photograph (Lorenz Learmonth/N-1989-020:0001)

A photo essay in the March 1939 issue of the *Beaver* about Fort Ross by photographer Lorene Squire complements Finnie's article. Squire visited the post while on assignment for the Company documenting *Nascopie*'s 1938 Arctic voyage.

It is noted that Patsy Klengenberg, popular Arctic fur trader and trapper, and his family (consisting of his wife Ann, two teenage daughters Amy and Dora Kelly, and adopted son Donald Ayalik), made up the majority of the *Aklavik*'s crew, and played a significant role in the achievement. They came prepared with winter camping gear, sleds, traps and dogs ready to spend the winter in the new lands, thus providing *Aklavik* with a "life boat" in the event she came to grief on the voyage. This also afforded an opportunity for Patsy to later test the new lands for its fur potential. At Fort Ross he took over as the skipper of the *Aklavik* on its return voyage and safely piloted the vessel back to Gjoa Haven.

Photo 23-3

Patsy Klengenberg and family, possibly his wife and daughter, at Fort Ross, 31 August 1938.
Library and Archives Canada/R685, R216

Photo 23-4

Grave of Anna Gall (nee Fagerstrom) at Cambridge Bay.
The inscription on the gravestone reads "ANNE GALL DIED AUGUST 16 1937"
Photo from collection of Helen Tologanak, enhanced by Iain Cameron

A nearly identical photo to the one above showing Gall and Captain Smellie, by reporter Lindsay Hoben and later editor of the *Milwaukee Journal* appeared with his article about the accomplishment in that paper on 11 September 1937. Hoben was one of the press and radio reporters that travelled on *Nascopie* that was on hand to record the event. Sadly, the triumph of the event turned out also to be a tragedy; Anna Gall died, apparently of a heart attack, while starting the diesel engine at Cambridge Bay. She was hastily buried and the grieving Scotty had to go on without her. He left immediately after the burial, with John R. Ford and Patsy Klengenberg and his family, for the Company's post at Gjoa Haven on King William Island to deliver supplies, pick up fur returns and take on a native pilot, Tommy Norkow.

Returning to Scotland alone, Scotty received a letter from HBC fur trade commissioner Ralph Parsons dated 18 October 1937 containing the following congratulatory statement: "This was a most historic occasion, and the important part you played in it reflects much credit on your navigation and mechanical ability." One can only wonder at such a bittersweet commemoration.

On 26 June 1938 Parsons sent a second letter to him via the western Arctic district office. It stated, "It is not often in the present day that such voyages are undertaken, and I think your effort deserves to rank with those of the great explorers." The letter enclosed a cheque and asked Scotty to accept "the souvenir I am sending you, as an indication of the Company's pride in your accomplishment." The souvenir turned out to be a silver cigar box engraved, "Presented to E. J. Gall, by the Fur Trade Commissioner, Hudson's Bay Company, To Commemorate His Negotiation of, The North-West Passage, September 2, 1937."

Photo 23-5

Silver cigar box presented to Scotty Gall by the HBC Fur Trade Commissioner.
Photo from John MacFarlane collection

The inscription reproduced here, followed by image of handwritten original, was found on a front leaf of a book, *Hudson's Bay Company, A Brief History*, published by the Company in 1934.

> From Scotty Gall
>
> To Mrs. J. E. McCuen,
>
> Two thirds of the way from east to west up Bellot Sts on the Aklavik on Sept. 6th, 1937 being the anniversary of McClintock's passage through the straits on Sept. 6th 1856.

The book, given to the author by his friend Chris Gardner, had been purchased in a used book store in Merrickville, Ontario. Mrs. McCuen was the wife of prominent Montreal cancer researcher Dr. J. E. McCuen. Both were on the RMS *Nascopie* in 1937; he on a northern research project while she was one of the first paying female tourists carried by the vessel.

Book inscription by Scotty Gall.
George Duddy collection

On 6 September 1937 Scotty made a final voyage as skipper of *Aklavik*, taking her through Bellot Strait to test a new propeller, shaft and reduction gears that had been fabricated by *Nascopie*'s mechanical staff. He took along government and company officials to view the fabled passage. It was the 79th anniversary of McClintock's final attempt to navigate this same passage. (The year of McClintock's passage was actually 1858.) It is apparent, despite the errors in the inscription, that not only were these Arctic navigators *making* history, they were more than aware of those who had trekked here before them.

HBC MANAGER AND NWT GOVERNMENT MEMBER

While in Scotland, Scotty reconnected with Isobel MacDonald whom he had known before coming to Canada. They were married in 1938 before Scotty returned to Canada on 14 May from Greenock to Montreal on the *Duchess of Atholl* to take employment as second mate of the HBC river steamer *Mackenzie River*. Isobel did not join Scotty in Canada until the summer of 1939.

While working on the river steamer, Scotty fell ill and had to take time off. The December 1938 issue of *The Beaver* indicated that he was recalled from Aklavik (settlement) after a full recovery, to manage the Rocher River Post near Yellowknife. Scotty's final seafaring duty in the Arctic was to act as pilot on the Company's new Arctic supply vessel, the motor schooner *Fort Ross*, on her first trip to King William Island in 1939 (see *The Beaver* magazine, September 1939 issue). Based on notes found in Jack Wood family fonds of the NWT Archives, it is thought that many of Scotty's ideas were reflected in the design of the new vessel.

The motor schooner MV *Fort Ross*, 127-foot replacement for the lost *Fort James*, was launched in Nova Scotia in 1938. After a passage through the Panama Canal and up the West Coast, she loaded a full cargo of Arctic supplies at Vancouver and proceeded to Tuktoyaktuk after rounding the Alaskan Peninsula. In accordance with a report in the December 1938 issue of *The Beaver* magazine, from there she distributed supplies as far east as Coppermine and Wilmot Island (Patsy Klengenberg's trading post), before going into winter quarters at Bernard Harbour. The vessel was owned by the HBC until 1951 when it was sold. Most of her service was in the western Arctic, except it is known during World War II she operated in the eastern Arctic (the vessel's wartime service remains unclear at the present time).

In accordance with the book *Fort Ross the Ship in the Shadow* by Roger McAfee, the ship was designed by W. J. Roue the designer of the *Blue Nose* the famous fishing schooner that is still portrayed on Canada's currency on its dime and was built in the same Shelbourne, Nova Scotia, shipyard that built the *Fort James*. The book contains many photographs and details of the building of the *Fort Ross*.

Photo 23-6

HBC motor schooner *Fort Ross*, circa 1940.
Vancouver Maritime Museum, Item HNOS-40-03

During the Second World War, Scotty served as post manager at Cambridge Bay. Isobel, who had been trained as a radio operator, made their daily transmission of weather forecasts as part of the war effort.

Photo 23-7

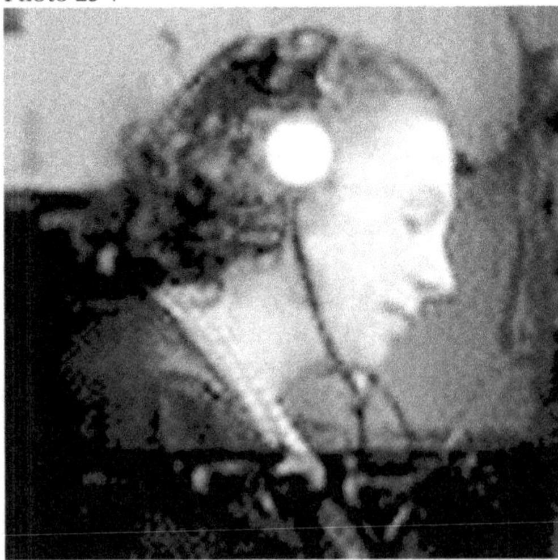

Isobel Gall wearing radio head phones at Cambridge Bay.
Photo copyright to the National Film Board of Canada (with permission to the author)

Scotty endured a second tragic event at Cambridge Bay in 1946. The *Aklavik* had been purchased by Patsy Klengenberg, who used it for freighting for the HBC. Early on the morning of 3 September, a fire and explosion occurred in the engine room. Patsy's adopted son Donald Ayalik was severely burned attempting to enter the engine room to save his father whom he presumed to be trapped inside. Undaunted, he faced the dangerous situation determined to help Patsy, but on the third try, and suffering from severe burns, had to give up. Scotty, along with many others ashore, was awoken by the explosion and rushed to the *Aklavik* to render aid. On board he found Donald, and was able to take him back to the settlement for assistance. Donald was flown by Norseman aircraft to Yellowknife for treatment.

The *Aklavik* burned to the waterline and subsequently sank; Patsy's body was found several days later. He had apparently drowned while attempting to swim to shore. The story of this sad event is told in an article "Boy Hero" by J. H. Webster published in the June 1947 issue of *The Beaver*. The location of the sunken vessel remains well known in Cambridge Bay in 2021.

In 1949 the Galls left the fur trade and the western Arctic. They worked at Waterways, Alberta, for two years, managing freight-forwarding for the Mackenzie River, and then moved to Yellowknife where Scotty managed the HBC stores in both the old and new towns. Here they became part of a community that was in a state of transition from a mining and mineral exploration outpost to the new capital of the Northwest Territories.

Photo 23-8

Scotty Gall at his desk in Yellowknife, Northwest Territory.
NWT Archives photograph (Henry Busse/N-1979-052: 6889)

Scotty took retirement on 30 November 1966 after spending almost 43 years in the Canadian Arctic. Scotty became a member of the Northwest Territorial Council in 1958; he served as an appointed member, and then from 1959 to 1964, after winning a by–election, as the elected member for the Mackenzie North District. He fought for employment opportunities and fuel subsidies for residents, and worked on plans for the eventual division of the Northwest Territories into a smaller one retaining the original name and the new, Nunavut. He understood the reasoning behind, but generally opposed, the centralization of indigenous peoples in communities within the region.

RETIREMENT

In the summer edition of the 1968 *Mocassin Telegraph*, the HBC staff magazine, it was announced that Scotty, fellow pensioner George Porter, and HBC serving store manager Henry Voisey, had all been awarded the Canada Centennial Medal. The announcement indicated "All three men received their medal for their outstanding contribution to the welfare of the [Inuit] people, and as pioneers in the development of the Canadian north."

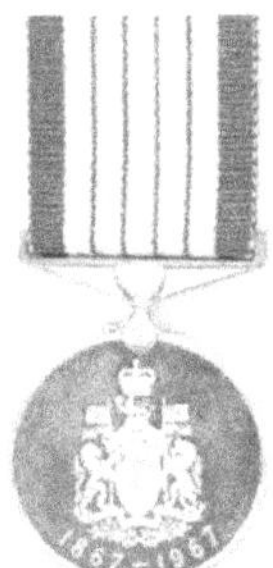

Canadian Centennial Medal

Scotty spent his retirement years in a comfortable home in Saanich, a rural suburb of Victoria. He was able to share its pleasant location, close to the sea and near the University of Victoria's Gordon Head campus, with Isobel until 1983 when she passed away. Scotty occupied his time on long walks with his dog and helped out at a local swimming pool. Not surprisingly, he attended regular meetings of the Arctic Club in Victoria. The club was an informal organization of Arctic veterans who met in a local restaurant for fellowship and discussion.

Many interviewers came to visit him in Victoria to record his reminiscences of Arctic events and characters which he related in a down–to–earth style. Some of these are recorded in Peter Newman's book *Merchant Princes*, and also Mark Dickerson's Arctic Profiles series for the Arctic Institute of North America. In spite of Scotty's popularity as a source for Arctic history, he was one to prefer contemplating the future more than reflecting on the past, even in his elder years.

His friend Jack ("Woody") Wood, who apparently was much more heritage-conscious, tuned-in to the worthiness of Scotty's Arctic exploits. Wood collected many of Scotty's documents. Combining them with his own material, and over 900 photographs, he donated the compilation to the Prince of Wales Archives in Yellowknife as the Jack Wood family fonds. Some of the photos are of Scotty and Anna, others are of *Aklavik*. It was also Woody who was responsible for the donation of the historic Thomas Harold Beament painting depicting the meeting of the *Nascopie* and *Aklavik* to the Maritime Museum of British Columbia.

Photo 23-9

Scotty Gall plaque celebration reception at the British Columbia Maritime Museum on 7 June 2013, with Scotty's great-nephew Iain Cameron (left) and author George Duddy (right), standing in front of the Thomas Harold Beament painting of the *Aklavik* and *Nascopie* at Fort Ross in 1937.
Iain Cameron collection

There is also a rich store of audio recordings that can be purchased from the Prince of Wales Northern Heritage Centre. In addition to helping fill in the details of the history of a man intimately involved in the settlement of Canada's last frontier, they reveal aspects of his character, philosophy and passions that do not fully come across from the written record. Excerpts from the CBC's "The Days Before Yesterday" series, available from the archives, can be heard online, in Scotty's own voice. It is remarkable to hear the stories told by the man himself, and recorded for all posterity. (The author reviewed three: The first by Les MacLaughlin of the CBC [N-1998-30: 0126], the second by the Prince of Wales Centre archivist Richard Valpy [N-1998-040: 001] and the third by Ian Christie [N-1994-034: 0032].)

Ian Christie had come to Scotty's home to try to learn more about the sad demise of his uncle, Ian "Jock" Christie, who had survived the wreck of the *Emma Jane* with Scotty but subsequently perished in the Bathurst Inlet area.

Another important source of Scotty's recollections is the HBC Archives collection of interviews that it conducted with significant retired employees, held in the Manitoba Archives. The author has gained much insight into life in the fur trade by listening particularly to those for his colleagues and friends, Post Manager Foster Rymer "Ray" Ross and Lorenz Learmonth, and of course those for Scotty Gall himself. Those for Gall are held under accession numbers: HB 1984/15, HB 1984/053 and HB 1984/068. The latter two accession interviews were conducted by Peter Neuman or on his behalf in connection with the writing of his book *Merchant Princes*, part of his well-known three book series on the history of the HBC. Scotty is featured and is frequently quoted, adding colour and insight to *Merchant Princes*. It was the author's first acquaintance with the main character of this chapter.

What emerges from these interviews is an image of a very humble, straight-forward person who enjoyed the simple life and independence he found in the North. Scotty respected the native peoples and was deeply conscious of the effect that European settlement had on them. At the end of one interview, Scotty was asked if there was anything else he wished to add. The inclusion of an event Scotty emphatically wanted recorded is a fitting way to end this account.

In the spring of 1937, before the trip to Fort Ross, Scotty, Anna and Woody were completing delivery of supplies to the Perry River Post. Proceeding in fog about one hour from the post, they heard, but could not see, what sounded like a very large aircraft flying at low altitude overhead. It seemed to be dangerously close to the ground.

When they arrived at the post, the post manager and the natives present confirmed that they had heard the same thing.

Scotty reported his observations to the authorities but no aircraft were supposed to be in the area. At the time of their report none of those on the *Aklavik* or at Perry River Post were aware that the Russian aviation pioneer Sigismund Levanevsky, with five companions on board, were attempting a pioneering polar flight from Moscow to Fairbanks in a four-engine, bomber–type aircraft. As described in an article in the *Whitehorse Daily Star* on 20 August 1937, the aircraft failed to arrive at its destination, and in spite of extensive searches, no traces of it or its crew were ever found. The case of the missing Russian airmen remains as one of the enduring mysteries of the western Arctic.

Scotty Gall was a witness to the changing Arctic ways; while he benefitted from the adventure of a lifetime, he was also a contributor, as he attempted to improve conditions and establish good policy for the Arctic region and the people who lived there—not only those who adopted the North as their homeland, but also for those who had settled and thrived there over many thousands of years beforehand.

Photo 23-10

2017 Northwest Passage Hall of Fame award exhibit at the Vancouver Maritime Museum. Winners in categories: Ship *St. Roch*; Individual Robert Hadley (*St. Roch* radio operator); Expedition Ernest Gall (HBC *Aklavik*)
Iain Cameron collection

24

Audrey B. Employment as a Rum Runner

Photo 24-1

Hudson's Bay Company Archives, Archives of Manitoba, *Audrey B.*, showing "swordfish" bow, at Tuktoyaktuk, departing the Arctic, 1939, HBCA 1987/363–A33/1

The Canadian power yacht *Audrey B.* was built in Nova Scotia in 1928, and immediately began her working life as a rum runner, work that lasted until the end of Prohibition in 1933. Prohibition in the United States was a nationwide constitutional ban, begun in 1920, on the production, import, transport, and sale of alcoholic beverages.

During her interesting service, which lasted until the early 1960s, she did valuable work for a variety of owners, sailing in all of Canada's major oceans. In retirement, after her voyaging days were over, she provided a floating home for a family in North Vancouver. It was the vessel's remarkable success in the Arctic, in an environment completely unsuited to her design and construction, however, that warrants special attention. In particular, it was her achievement in forwarding supplies during a very difficult ice year that allowed Captain Scotty Gall to complete the first-ever navigation of Bellot Strait of the Northwest Passage in 1937.

EAST COAST RUM RUNNING

Audrey B. was a vessel designed specifically for the rum running trade. A book by Geoff and Dorothy Robinson, *It Came by the Boat Load* (1984), reported she was designed by James S. Gardner and built in Liverpool, Nova Scotia, side-by-side with her identical sister the *Eleonor Joan.* Both vessels were named after the daughters of the vessels' agent, W. A. Shaw of Halifax, Nova Scotia. The yachts or power cruisers (by traditional definition) were 109.5-feet long, 20.5-feet wide and 8.5-feet in hull height, with a design similar to that of a World War I submarine chaser. Powered by two 180hp Fairbanks-Morse diesel engines, to drive twin screws, they were fast and their low banana-like profile made them difficult to detect.

About one hundred of these purpose-built vessels were constructed in Nova Scotia. As reported by the Robinsons, *Audrey B.* and nearly a dozen other Nova Scotia-registered vessels were thought to be part of a shadowy, American criminal organization based in Newark, New Jersey, that was referred to as the "Banana Fleet." The organization was well financed, provided bonuses for successful landings, and provided legal help, bail and bond money for seized crews and vessels. It was also thought to have been adept at arranging "pay-offs" for officials who could aid its operations.

The vessels had Canadian registrations and were based in Liverpool, Nova Scotia, for maintenance and repair but ran their liquor into the northern United States from the French Islands of St Pierre and Miquelon, uniquely situated in the Gulf of Saint Lawrence. (These islands are part of a self-governing territorial overseas collectivity of France in the northwestern Atlantic, near the Canadian province of Newfoundland and Labrador.) W. A. Shaw arranged for the recruiting and paying of crews from Liverpool.

An article in the *New York Times* of 27 December 1930 reported that the *Audrey B.* was seized off Long Island while landing liquor by the US Coast Guard (USCG). Her steering gear was damaged as a result of shells fired into her stern by a pursuing cutter. This action enabled the USCG to take the vessel, 2,800 cases of liquor and her 10-man Nova Scotia crew under Captain Robert J. Mosher into custody. The article stated the vessel was of British registry and owned by Water Transports Ltd. of Halifax, Nova Scotia. It further valued the vessel at $100,000.

Subsequent to her seizure, Transport Canada records indicate she was owned by the Nova Scotia firm Yarmouth Shipping Company Ltd. It is noted that seized vessels were often auctioned off and put back to work in the liquor trade but in her case, she was released after posting a bond. Correspondence between Canada's Charge d'Affaires to the United States and Canada's Secretary of State in Ottawa (obtained from Archives Canada files) indicated that the vessel was released after posting a $6,250 bond and the crew released on bail.

Subsequently in May 1931, Captain Robert Mosher and the Chief Engineer Joseph Pierce each received a 45-day jail sentence and four others of the crew were handed $200 fines for being in possession of liquor. Simultaneous with the crew sentencing, an order was filed decreeing the forfeiture of the liquor and the vessel. It was reported that the liquor was going to be destroyed. Because the vessel had already been released and presumably had left the jurisdiction, judgement was rendered against the bond and thus *Audrey B.* was able to keep her "British Registry."

The huge incongruity between the previously reported $100,000 value of the vessel and the $6,250 bond is noted. An article in the *New York Times* of 6 June 1931 describes a similar forfeiture of a $14,000 bond, a day earlier on 5 June, against the seizure of the *Eleonor Joan.* This vessel was seized in the same location as the *Audrey B.* on 27 December 1930. The article indicates that the bond was "posted to insure the presence in the jurisdiction" so it looks like the owners of both managed to get off fairly lightly in the court system.

The Robinsons tell an interesting anecdote about Joseph Pierce the engineer. Apparently, he had volunteered to be one of two individuals who had to serve jail sentences in connection with the seizure. In addition to receiving full pay while being on bail awaiting trial, he received eleven hundred dollars for serving the sentence before retiring from rum running. Presumably this treatment must have also applied to Captain Mosher, so caught or not, crime seems to have paid well in this instance.

TO THE WEST COAST AND MORE RUM RUNNING

The *Audrey B.* came to the Pacific Coast via the Panama Canal with a new crew under Captain Dennis Westhaver, not surprisingly with a cargo of liquor loaded at Bermuda and destined for the west coast trade, accomplished before any of the hearings and trials commenced. Westhaver had a previous rum running history and had been captured as a master of a rum runner off of New York and deported to Canada.

For the remaining two prohibition years, the *Audrey B.* operated on the Pacific Coast. Transport Canada records indicate, that although she operated out of Vancouver, her registry remained with Yarmouth Shipping Company, Yarmouth, Nova Scotia.

Ruth Greene's book, *Personality Ships of British Columbia* (1969), lists the *Audrey B.* as one of the "smaller rum-runners." Fraser Miles published his expository on the history of rum running on the west coast, *Slow Boat on Rum Row* (1992), providing details of how the rum running industry worked there and of the vessels involved, similar to what the Robinsons had provided for the east coast chronicles. The insight provided by his personal experience and records finally broke through the rum runners self-imposed veil of silence embodied in the brethren's motto "Don't never tell nothin' to nobody no how." His book includes a photograph of the *Audrey B.* and notes that she was one of the last vessels to return to port in January 1934 after prohibition finished.

Photo 24-2

Audrey B. in spring 1933, with her hold full to its 2,500-case capacity, and two large deck loads.
Courtesy of Jim Miles (son of the late Fraser Miles)

Canada's Department of Marine and Fisheries, Mercantile Marine Shipping Office, Vancouver, BC, records (now residing in the British Columbia Archives in Victoria) state that the *Audrey B.* operated on the west coast and made voyages toward "rum row" (Ensenada, Mexico) in 1931, 1932 and 1933. It is interesting to note the size of crews used for rum running in comparison with those used for Arctic navigation. The Mercantile records of *Audrey B.*'s first voyage from Vancouver leaving on 7 October 1931 indicate that a seven-man crew was in service, under Master D. Forrest of Cardiff, Wales. The crew consisted of, in addition to Forrest, a mate, a chief engineer, a second engineer, two able seamen, and a cook. It is evident from these records that most of the crew had served on other rum runners. For example, Forrest and the chief engineer previously served on the *Chief Skugaid.* The *Chief* is claimed to be the oldest local rum runner still afloat as of 2021.

25

Arctic and Subsequent Service

Audrey B.'s Arctic operations began in 1935 with a voyage from Vancouver through the Bering Strait and around Alaska to Coppermine, NWT. She was employed in the Arctic Ocean as far east as Perry River (east of Cambridge Bay) from 1935 to 1938 and made a return voyage to Vancouver in 1939.

In 1935 the vessel's registration was changed to Vancouver with her ownership listed as William Storr, Coppermine, NWT. It was Storr, together with his trapping partners William ("Slim") Purcell and Arthur Watson, who operated the vessel as an Arctic freighting and fur trading vessel.

Little detail is known about the voyage from Vancouver to the Arctic in 1935. It is assumed that Storr, who was reported to have had some navigation experience in the Royal Navy, was part of the initial voyage; but this is not recorded. What is known is based on interviews of Purcell and Watson by Vancouver newspapers and *Harbour and Shipping* magazine after the vessel returned to Vancouver in 1939. From these interviews it was revealed that the vessel departed from Vancouver on 23 July 1935 and arrived at Coppermine on 5 September, that she carried 5,000 gallons of fuel (sufficient for both the initial and the return journey), and that there was no difficulty with ice at Point Barrow.

Masters of self effacement and understatement, the partners provided little scope for the writers to further expand the scant details of their adventure. They spoke of their Arctic experience in terms such as "Nothing much to tell you," (*Vancouver Sun*, 25 September 1939) and "We traded and trapped, drove our dog teams here and there, but had no experiences worthy of note." (The *Vancouver Daily Province*, 25 September 1939). Perhaps having endured World War I trenches, there was nothing else that could impress this pair (it is reported they served together in the Argonne). They did offer the following description of the construction of the vessel and its engines to *Harbour and Shipping* magazine, published in the October 1939 issue.

> She is planked with oak below the waterline and fir above, over steam bent oak frames, with an occasional sawn frame for extra

> stiffening: while the power plant consists of twin 180 h.p. 6-cylinder Fairbanks Morse-Diesel engines, which Mr. Watson says proved satisfactory, having no major overhaul for four years.

They also stated they never used their non-ice-strengthened vessel to butt through ice but learned to take advantage of her speed to nip through leads in ice flows when they opened up.

Fortunately, on the return journey the partners carried a French adventurer as a passenger, the Vicomte Gontran de Montage de Poncins, who recognized and described the partners' achievements. De Poncins was portrayed in the March 1940 issue of *The Beaver* as "an adventurous young Frenchman whose home is a chateau in the Loire country, and who specializes in photography and ethnology." His experiences later became the subject of the book *Kabloona*, published in 1942 (well-known in its time).

A far better idea of the difficulties faced on Arctic voyages than those provided to the newspaper reporters is found in the description of the return voyage in 1939 in de Poncins' book *The Ghost Voyage out of Eskimo Land*, published by Doubleday and Company Inc. in 1954. Judging by this book, both voyages must have been truly remarkable achievements given the comparatively frail design of the ship, the general difficulties in navigation in a very remote region, and the hazardous ice conditions faced on the long path around Alaska that often stopped, hindered and crushed much stouter vessels. A reported lack of training of the partners in navigation and marine engineering, and their propensity for under-crewing, added to the difficulties that had to be overcome.

The partners were well known in the Coronation Gulf area of the western Arctic as trappers, traders, and operators of small schooners before they purchased the *Audrey B.* Storr previously owned the small, motor schooner *Eagle* (see photo in Chapter 26 when later owned by Johnny Norberg), while Purcell and Watson's vessel, the *Sea Wolf*, was apparently worn out when they purchased the *Audrey B.*

Watson's wife was known only to de Poncins as Mrs. Watson or by her nick name "Tiny." The Robinsons related in their book that they had interviewed the Watson's daughter Muriel Breber. Presumably from this interview, they learned Mrs. Watson lived in a small house in Coppermine while raising their several children, running the trading business on the ship when her husband was trapping, and providing medical help to the community residents. Headlines were created in Winnipeg in 1934 when two of their sons were sent to St John's Anglican College for education. Muriel travelled with them on the *Audrey B.* in 1939. It is not known what happened to Watson and Purcell after their return to Vancouver in 1939. They indicated to reporters that they had thoughts of rejoining the military.

Storr was born in Yorkshire in 1903 and died in Aklavik in 1969. His Inuit wife Lucy trapped with him during the winters. He worked briefly in the mining exploration boom in the Coppermine area in 1929 and 1930 that came to an abrupt halt at the onset of the Great Depression. He remained in the Arctic after the *Audrey B.* returned south and his descendants still live there. One of his later jobs was running a small patrol schooner, the *Aklavik II*, on the Mackenzie River for the RCMP.

Former Hudson's Bay Company Manager Jack Wood (during an interview conducted by marine historian John MacFarlane in 1991) noted that the partners "...established a fur trading post at Stypleton Bay [now Stapylton Bay, Nunavut] and operated a trap line there as well as running the ship as a mobile trading post ..." and then goes on to relate that *Audrey B.* "... operating out of Tuktoyaktuk as a trader...proved unsuccessful."

The following photograph is of the partners, and others, in front of the Hudson's Bay post at Read Island about 1936. One of the men, George Porter (a fellow Canadian Centennial Medal winner to Scotty Gall), was the Canalaska Trading Company's manager at King William Land and sometimes visited their post on Read (also referred to as Reid) Island on their trading motor schooner the *Nigalik*.

Photo 25-1

The partners, and others, in front of the Hudson's Bay post at Read Island about 1936. Storr is second from the left, Purcell is standing in the doorway and Watson is in the coveralls second from the right. All the others are unidentified except George Porter who is on the extreme right.
Glenbows Archives photograph NA-1261-9

Although *Audrey B.*'s reported use as a mobile trading post may not have been successful, as suggested by Wood, her timely arrival and success as a replacement freighting vessel must have been a godsend, not only to the Hudson's Bay Company, but to the whole western Arctic. Very difficult ice conditions occurred in 1936 and 1937 and the Company experienced damage and losses to its fleet. The presence of the *Audrey B.* may have prevented the recurrence of hardship such as was endured in 1924 when the supply ship *Lady Kindersley* was lost in the ice near Point Barrow, Alaska. In that year there was such an extreme shortage of supplies and fuel that the post at Cambridge Bay had to be shut down.

Prior to 1934 the HBC supplied most of their Arctic posts from Vancouver by ocean-going vessels operating around Alaska. As previously mentioned in Chapter 21, their last major attempt using this route was a failed voyage by the chartered freighter *Anyox* in 1933. In 1934, with the extension of river navigation through the Mackenzie Delta and the establishment of the new port of Tuktoyaktuk east of the Delta, the Company switched its supply route for their western Arctic posts almost exclusively to the Mackenzie River route. To provide capacity for forwarding supplies eastward and to local posts from the new port, which the larger ocean-going vessels such as the *Lady Kindersley* (1919-1923), the *Baychimo* (1925-1931) and the chartered *Karise* (1932) had previously provided, the Company-needed vessels for local delivery.

In 1934 the HBC transferred its large motor schooner the *Fort James* from eastern Canada to the western Arctic. The *Fort James* sailed from St John's on 24 April 1934 and arrived at Tuktoyaktuk on 29 August, completing a 12,000-mile voyage. She then went on to deliver supplies to Cambridge Bay and returned to a winter berth at Bernard Harbour. Incredibly, the voyage reaching Cambridge Bay—combined with a 1928-1930 trip from St. John's, Newfoundland, to King William Island—was only 200 miles short of a complete circumnavigation of North America. The Company also acquired a smaller fish-packer type vessel, the *Margaret A.*, to assist in the deliveries.

In 1934 and 1935 the *Fort James,* supplemented by the *Margaret A.*, *Aklavik* and other Company vessels, was able to complete all deliveries, even with the loss of assistance from *Margaret A.* in 1935 when she was damaged in the spring breakup and had to be returned upriver to Fort Smith for repairs.

In the spring of 1936, it was discovered that the hull of *Fort James* had been severely damaged by ice pressure while at her winter berth in Tuktoyaktuk. Careening her for repairs took up much of the available navigation season. As a result, the Company found it necessary to engage the *Audrey B.* to forward supplies that had been accumulating at Tuktoyaktuk. During this season *Audrey B.* made one trip from Tuktoyaktuk to Cambridge Bay delivering Company supplies and trade goods before returning to her base at Coppermine.

After repairs, the *Fort James* made one trip to the east and returned to Read Island where she went into winter quarters. The reconditioned *Margaret A.* made one trip to the eastward but could only reach Inman River. Here she met with, and transferred her cargo to, the RCMP's *St. Roch* for forwarding to Coppermine. An article from the June 1944 issue of *The Beaver* "Over the Sea by Tractor" describes one of the consequences of the difficult 1936 delivery season and contains a photo (probably taken in 1938) of the *Audrey B.* leaving the Perry River Post.

In 1937 ice conditions at the start of the navigation season were even more difficult than in 1936. The situation became desperate for the Company when the *Fort James* was crushed in the ice flows and quickly sank in Dolphin and Union Strait on her way from winter quarters at Read Island to Tuktoyaktuk. Captain R. J. Summers and all of his crew were rescued by the *St. Roch*, fortuitously nearby, but several bales of fur and business records carried by the *Fort James* were lost. Manager of the Western Arctic District Dudley Copland was in Tuktoyaktuk when news of the loss reached him. He realized that there was only one sure way to have his freight delivered that summer. He quickly wired Arthur Watson at Coppermine to come to Tuktoyaktuk to discuss a freighting contract for the *Audrey B.*

Audrey B. arrived at Tuktoyaktuk on 7 August 1937, a few days after Copland's wire. It is worth quoting Copland's articulate words about the freighting contract and the character of the players that apparently saved the Company's "bacon" in 1937 and 1938.

> The first to come ashore was Art Watson. Art had trained his face to look neutral after the best part of a life dickering. It gave nothing away. But his first words went right to the heart of things, and bit deep into the tender quick of my fur trader's soul.
>
> 'Well Copland', he began, 'I guess we have you over a barrel?'
>
> This I must have acknowledged with a sickly grin, since our only other vessel, the *Margaret A*, was not fit for the kind of years we were having. It did not take long for the partners to convince me that only one hundred dollars per ton for all classes of cargo, and some slight concessions on fuel, was all that they wanted. They would take one hundred tons on each trip, and would make two

> trips each season if required and ice conditions would permit. Written contracts were not required and the owners started to load without further delay.

The *St. Roch*, despite sustaining damage early in the season, helped mitigate the 1937 transport problem by carrying 100 tons of supplies from Tuktoyaktuk to Coppermine before leaving the Arctic to head for Vancouver for repairs. *Audrey B.* made three eastward trips and managed to deliver over 300 tons before ending the season on 6 October 1937 at Coppermine, equalling or exceeding the *Fort James* 1935 record.

In a 1949 *Arctic Journal* article "The Voyage of the *Snowbird II*" about transporting fuel and supplies for Arctic operations, Flight Lieutenant Scott E. Alexander of the Royal Canadian Air Force had this to say about *Audrey B.*'s Arctic exploits, particularly those in 1937:

> *Audrey B.* not only arrived at her destination safely but broke all records for speedy trips along the Arctic coast. In 1937 she survived one of the worst ice years, while the Hudson's Bay Company's ship was crushed in the pack and lost in Dolphin and Union Strait, near Cape Bexley, and the R.C.M.P. vessel '*St Rock*' (sic) was so severely strained by ice pressure that she had to be taken to Vancouver for repairs.

Alexander was a very interesting and accomplished individual, a member of the Royal Canadian Mounted Police from 1932-1942, and a former crewmember of the *St. Roch*, he then served with the RCAF, finishing with the rank of Squadron Leader. Later, following his air force service, he became known as an Arctic expert, and served as a consultant in Arctic matters. He is credited as the inventor of a special ice-breaking bow, known as an Alexbow, and cited as a business partner with several other very successful men.

Audrey B.'s first 1937 Tuktoyaktuk departure is historically significant. She had been tasked to carry the supplies for the motor schooner *Aklavik* and the trade "outfit" for the King William Post for the voyage that would establish the first commercial use of the Northwest Passage. *Audrey B.* was able to complete the first leg of this historic journey through the difficult ice conditions to Cambridge Bay sufficiently early to allow the balance of the voyage to be completed by the *Aklavik* under Scotty Gall and his crew.

Dudley Copland, who was the sponsor of this enterprise, travelled with *Audrey B.* to Cambridge Bay. One of the two figures on the deck of *Audrey B.*, shown in the following photograph, is probably Copland and the other may be Inspector George Curleigh of the RCMP who travelled with the vessel to Cambridge Bay. The vessel shown immediately on her port bow is the *North Star* then owned by Jim Wolki, the son of Fritz Wolki. (She was subsequently purchased by Sven Johansson who renamed her *North Star of Herschel Island.*)

Photo 25-2

Audrey B. leaving Tuktoyaktuk, 1937.
NWT Archives photograph (Charles Rowan fonds/N-1991-068: 0267)

Audrey B.'s final year freighting for the Hudson's Bay Company was 1938. Before the start of the navigation season her rudder was damaged at Coppermine. To ensure she would be available for use, the Company arranged for the supply of a replacement rudder as well as replacement timing gears for one of her engines to be flown from Edmonton to Coppermine. This extraordinary action reflected the importance of the vessel to the Company's transportation needs at that time.

Audrey B. completed one eastward trip sharing the delivery of supplies in 1938 with the Company's new vessel, *Fort Ross* under Captain R. J. Summers, the replacement vessel for the *Fort James*. *Fort Ross* was a motor schooner constructed in Nova Scotia and arrived in the Arctic in late summer via the Panama Canal and the west coast, carrying a full load of supplies from Vancouver. That year the Company also acquired the motor schooner *Nigalik* when it took over (rival trading company) Canalaska Trading Company. The *Nigalik* spent the summer under overhaul at Tuktoyaktuk in preparation for her use the following summer as a back-up vessel for the *Fort Ross*.

In 1939 with further freighting prospects dim and a collapsing fur trade, the three partners decided to dissolve their interests. It was determined that Purcell and Watson would return the vessel to Vancouver (with Mrs. Watson and the Watson's daughter Muriel on board) while Storr would stay in the Artic with his family.

As the returning pair needed help to crew the vessel, it was fortunate that they were able to recruit de Poncins to work his passage to Vancouver. De Poncins had spent sixteen months living and travelling amongst the Inuit of the western and central Arctic which made him a valuable addition to the crew.

One of the draws of the voyage for de Poncins was the opportunity of rounding the northwest corner of the North American continent around Point Barrow and transiting the Bering Strait. His perception was that Point Barrow was the most northern point on continental North America. In truth, the Boothia Peninsula opposite the King William Island Post, where he spent the winter with Hudson's Bay Chief Trader William "Paddy" Gibson, holds this distinction.

In *The Ghost Voyage out of Eskimo Land*, de Poncins offers, besides the factual details of the trip, introspective musing about his life among the Inuit, arctic wildlife, former experiences, prominent Arctic personalities and his philosophising about human behaviour in remote locations. Regarding the remarkable, perhaps even foolhardy, 57-day journey from Coppermine to Vancouver, it was made against terrific difficulties and uncertainty which included: fumbling navigation, an inadequate-sized crew, the impediment and danger of drifting ice, crew fatigue and a need to navigate for days in fog in hazardous waters.

His anticipation of a triumphal Cape Horn-type rounding experience seems to have given way to one of frustration, brought on by fatigue and his sense of loneliness, and his inability to communicate, share fellowship, and his utter failure to comprehend his fellow travellers. The voyage was a mixed bag of luck and near-disaster.

The *Audrey B.* experienced a grounding, engine difficulties and failure, an on-board fire, and loss of an anchor and distance measuring log. In Dutch Harbour she took on a second "passenger," George Merodes, a Greek trapper and fisherman to assist in the leg of the journey across the Pacific. Instead of following close to the coast line as recommended by officials in Dutch Harbour, Purcell and Watson elected a course across the Gulf of Alaska directly to Canada's west coast across two huge atmospheric depressions. Debilitating and prolonged sea-sickness affected all on board except de Poncins and Watson's young daughter Muriel.

It was fortunate that de Poncins did not suffer from this malady. It was reported that in one instance he fought the wheel for sixteen hours without relief. The only navigational equipment on the ship were a pair of disagreeing compasses, a speed measuring log, a sounding line and some crude charts and some old sailing instructions.

Richard H. G. Bonnycastle, a well-known Hudson's Bay Company manager (and later founder of Harlequin Books) provides an independent view of the partners, de Poncins and their interactions in his book review published in the August 1955 issue of *The Beaver* magazine.

An interesting anecdote about the voyage was that the *Audrey B.*, apparently sighted nearing the west coast of Canada about 10 September 1939, was falsely identified as an enemy submarine. Her low profile and the heavy seas at the time undoubtedly contributed to this error. The sighting gave rise to an announcement by American president Franklin D. Roosevelt and interesting headlines appearing in newspapers such as the *Oakland Tribune* of 26 September 1939: "Phantom Sub of Alaska May be Old Rum Runner."

Photo 25-3

Return to civilization of the *Audrey B.* and a happy group back in Vancouver after a four-year trapping and trading expedition to the Arctic coast. From left: Mrs. Arthur Watson, her daughter Muriel; George Merodes, trapper and fisherman; William Purcell and Arthur Watson, partners in the expedition. Missing: de Poncins had left the vessel within minutes of arrival for a hotel with a hot bath.
Vancouver Sun, 25 September 1939

Following her return to Vancouver, *Audrey B.* was sold to Nelson Brothers Fisheries and after modifications, she was employed as a fish packer. The necessary repairs and modifications were apparently made at Burrard Shipyard & Engineering Works Ltd. in Vancouver. Work included enlarging her deck house, and the pilot house was moved to the second deck level. She was employed by Nelson Brothers both during and after World War II up to 1962, when she was sold to West Coast Salvage and Construction Company. A *Province* article of June 1962 reported that the *Audrey B.* was offered up as part payment by Nelson Brothers for the 130-foot coastal freighter *Chenega* which they were acquiring from West Coast Salvage. *Chenega* had formerly been operated by Union Steamships Ltd.

As related by Stephen Oura, a university student at the time (and friend of the author), he hitched a ride on her from Nelson Brothers' cannery at Port Edward near Prince Rupert, where he had a summer job, to his home in Steveston. His main recollection of that trip was a terrific dock-damaging impact, possibly at the old cannery site of Namu, and the ensuing abusive reprimand from the deckhand to the skipper about the incompetent landing. This may, in fact, have been one of *Audrey B.*'s last voyages as a fish packer in the early 1960s.

Nelson Brothers had been using the *Audrey B.* to transport nets for their gill-net fleet between its northern and southern operations. Replacement nets of varying colours and mesh sizes were required to meet specific conditions, and the smaller fishing vessels did not have the capacity to carry all of the net types required.

Photo 25-4

Herring fleet at Fish Dock in 1945; *Audrey B.* is the outermost vessel.
Prince Rupert City & Regional Archives & Museum of Northern B.C., Wrathall collection, JRW1506A

Photo 25-5

Audrey B. at a remote fishing site at a coastal inlet, date unknown.
UBC Open Collections, Fisherman Publishing Society Collection photograph B1532/458/1

In June 1963 *Audrey B.* was purchased by Harold Tarris, his wife Frances, and son Jeffery for use as a private yacht. She was renamed *Tarfran*; an amalgamation of Tarris and Frances. Another son, David Tarris, recollects that the vessel was towed to her new home at the Deep Cove Marina from the North Vancouver Osbourne Shipyard in June 1963. The vendor as shown on the Bill of Sale of 3 June 1963 was West Coast Salvage & Contracting Co. Ltd., Vancouver, BC.

The Tarris family (including children Jeffery, Lea, David, Donald and Pauline) lived on the *Tarfran* at the Deep Cove Marina in North Vancouver from 1963 until 1975. During this time, they made extensive renovations and improvements to make the vessel into a comfortable floating home. Harold and Frances became friends with the Robinsons (during their research about rum running boats) after visiting them in eastern Canada before the final printing in 1995 of the Robinsons' book *It Came By The Boatload.* The following statement appears in the book about the Tarris' transformations:

> Husband and wife were extraordinarily talented, and converted the vessel themselves into a palatial houseboat, which they tied up at Deep Cove, North Vancouver. We have seen photographs after the work was completed, which amply demonstrate how successful they were.

Daughter Pauline (Pilkington) lived on the vessel throughout her school years. Jeff was already a young working adult when he returned home in 1963 to find the family had moved from their house in North

Vancouver to live on the vessel. He indicated, although the old "punk – started" engines were still operable, the only two times he can recall the vessel actually under way was once to have her bottom cleaned and painted at the Osbourne Shipyard in North Vancouver, and once for a brief test run up Indian Arm. Each was fraught with mishap.

The first transit involved a passage under the Second Narrows railway lift bridge. With Keith Hutton (son of the marina owners Betty and Art George) at the helm assisted by Jeff and Harold (also known as "Terry") manipulating the engines, they followed a tug through the opening. They nearly came to grief because they had no radio and could not communicate with the bridge operator who had commenced lowering the span on them. Anxious moments, punctuated by loud bursts from their air horn, finally caught the operator's attention. Jeff did not participate in the second voyage but advises "Dad discovered *Audrey B.* to be less responsive in turning in one direction over the other." One can only imagine the incident that inspired such an observation.

At one time nine people made their home on *Tarfran.* In addition to the seven family members, a co-worker of his dad, Roy Wayne, and a good friend, Jay Mersereau, were welcomed to live on board *Tarfran.* The collective family remembrance of the *Tarfran* is that she was at Deep Cove until at least 1975. That summer, she was sold to a young couple who continued to live on her at the marina. They changed her name back to *Audrey B.*

Photo 25-6

Tarfran at Deep Cove Marina in mid-1970s, the former *Audrey B.* having been transformed into a "palatial" house boat.
Pauline Pilkington (nee Tarris) collection (with permission to the author)

Photo 25-7

Additional photographs of *Tarfran* during her ownership by the Tarris family.
Pauline Pilkington collection

Later, ownership passed to someone involved in the start up of a helicopter company who intended to refurbish her. At this point, *Audrey B.* had been stripped of her wheel, compass, anchor, and other items, but retained the spectacular heavy wood doors with brass trim, the brass scuttles, and other bright works. The new owner's time became too hectic with the start of his company and he ultimately disposed of the vessel.

Sadly, it is thought by the Tarris family, that *Audrey B.* fell into the hands of a group that started a meth lab. As a result of an accident, she suffered a devastating explosion, caught fire, and sank—ending up as a wreck in the Fraser River, lying along the shore at the east end of Tilbury Island, in the early 1980s.

Photo 25-8

Audrey B. hulk in the Fraser River north end of Tilbury Island, July 1983.
Pauline Pilkington collection (with permission to the author)

Curiously, the registration for *Audrey B.* was closed on 28 May 2010, thirty years after her complete destruction. Truly a sad end for such a hard-working miscast vessel, which first toiled as a rum runner, then served valiantly in the Arctic, and in her waning years provided housing for a family and their friends. For a small ship, her keel, indeed, plied the waves of three giant oceans.

26

An Unusual Tribute to the Fur Trade

Photo 26-1

The barge *L. A. Learmonth*, pushed by the tug *Irving Birch*, testing the inventive icebreaking Alexbow.
Lorenz Learmonth fonds, Nunavut Archives, N-1987-088-0811

In 2016 an episode of the "Polar Sea" (a television series that aired on a Vancouver television channel) showed a collection of yachts in 2013, barred in their pursuit of the Northwest Passage, at the western end of Bellot Strait. The 25-km-long passage was completely blocked at its western end by impenetrable ice. From its eastern end, the icebreaker Canadian Coast Guard Ship CCGS *Henry Larsen*, was smashing a lead through the ice for a Russian Arctic cruise ship and another vessel, at a ponderous 10 knots. Once her work with these vessels was complete, *Larsen* turned to reopen the closing ice and stood by until the yachts safely passed into open water. Without the assistance of the ice breaker, these smaller ships would not have been able to pass. Certainly, this proved the case when Captain Leopold McClintock, in

1858 at this very same location, repeatedly attempted to break through blocking flows in his under-powered ship *Fox* without success.

It is appropriate that the *Henry Larsen* was the assisting ship, named for the Master of the RCMP schooner *St. Roch,* the third vessel to navigate this strait, west to east, 1940-42. Just as fittingly, an icebreaker named *Scotty Gall* would have been appropriate, commemorating the first navigator to successfully transit this waterway. As previously related in earlier chapters, he accomplished this feat in 1937 in the small motor schooner *Aklavik*, similar in size to the yachts that were assisted in their passage by the *Henry Larsen.* The second vessel to navigate the strait was the Hudson's Bay Company motor boat *Seal* under Ernie Lyall in 1938.

Photo 26-2

Pack ice in Bellot Strait, 24 August 2010. It is always a matter of luck whether navigators are able to pass.
Photo UXW 0139.jpg by Ansgar Walk uploaded to Wikimedia Commons

It is surprising, given the fact that the fur trade was instrumental in establishing the string of settlements across the Northwest Passage, and strengthening Canada's sovereignty in the Arctic, that its navigators have not been better recognized by the naming of government vessels that now ply these waters.

Panarctic Oils, in 1968 and 1969, named steel barges constructed in support of their operations in the high Arctic in honour of three fur trade pioneers, all of whom were retired Hudson's Bay Company employees. Unfortunately, the life of these vessels was so short or their tasking so obscure that they are barely remembered in our maritime history.

Panarctic Oils was created by the Canadian Government, in partnership with a large number of private oil companies, to exploit the petroleum potential on Canada's Arctic islands—principally on Melville and Devon Islands—while at the same time establishing and maintaining sovereignty in the area. Their efforts were highly successful in identifying huge gas reserves and they were also successful in producing and transporting 2.8 million barrels of oil from the small Horn Brent oil field on Cameron Island, Nunavut, which was shipped to Montreal, Québec, between 1985 and 1996. While the operations were probably uneconomical, the company was successful in demonstrating the technical feasibility of Arctic petroleum production. The extraction was not without risk and danger. Two of their initial gas wells produced spectacular blowouts and fires that required experts to extinguish. Water pouring into a relief well and then spewing out the open main bore at their 1969 Drake Point discovery site resulted in an astonishing ice cone two hundred feet high.

Two of the barges, the *L. A. Learmonth* and the *Scotty Gall*, were named for retired Hudson's Bay Company (HBC) employees Lorenz Learmonth and Scotty Gall. They were constructed in 1968 by Lakehead Shipyards at Port Arthur (now Thunder Bay, Ontario) based on the designs of German and Milne Naval Architects of Montreal. The third, the *Johnny Norberg*, (sister vessel to the *Scotty Gall* and named in honour of Captain John Norberg), was constructed by St. John Shipyard in New Brunswick in 1969.

Photo 26-3

L. A. Learmonth sporting the ice-breaking Alexbow and (assumed to be) barge *Scotty Gall* with the tug *Irving Birch* in Arctic Convoy.
Courtesy of Dave Benedet

When Panarctic Oils was formed they purchased the rights for a special ice-breaking bow from its inventor Scott E. Alexander, a former crewman of the *St. Roch.* The device, known as an Alexbow, functioned much like a snow-plough, cutting the ice from below the surface and pushing it to the sides when advanced through the ice. The *L. A. Learmonth* was equipped with just such a prototype bow for testing in the Arctic. Unlike the other two vessels, which were 175-foot, eight-compartment tanker barges designed primarily for transportation and storage of Artic diesel fuel, the 190-foot *L. A. Learmonth* was a dry goods vessel with ten separate holds and covered hatches. A formal launching ceremony was held for the *L.A. Learmonth* at the shipyard on 5 July 1968. The vessel was sponsored and launched by Mrs. Alexander, the wife of the Alexbow inventor. Lorenz Learmonth also attended.

Details of the successful 1968 voyage north to the Panarctic Oils base at Rea Point on Melville Island are sketchy. The *L. A. Learmonth* and the *Scotty Gall* were towed north by the ice-strengthened tug *Irving Birch.* Commander Robbie Robertson, the well-known Arctic navigator and former captain of the RCN's wind-class ice breaker HMCS *Labrador*, "shipped on" (was aboard) the tug as navigation advisor. He was at the time a business partner of Scott E. Alexander, Naval Architect William German, and retired naval Captain Tom Pullen with the firm Northern Associates.

The tow left Dartmouth, Nova Scotia, after loading fuel oil into the *Scotty Gall* and arrived at Rea Point in the early fall 1968. They followed the northern "McClure" limb of the Northwest Passage through the Arctic islands. The *L. A. Learmonth* carried an 1,800-ton cargo of cement, drilling mud and drilling casings, while the *Scotty Gall* was loaded with 480,000 gallons of diesel. At Rea Point the *Learmonth*'s cargo was discharged and the *Scotty Gall* was grounded on the beach to serve as a fuel supply and reservoir for the drilling operations. It is not known how she was employed after that but the vessel remained on Transport Canada's records until 1997. After taking on water ballast the *L. A. Learmonth* and the tug returned to Resolute, near Cornwallis Island, Nunavut, where tests were made of the Alexbow. It was found to work quite well in continuous ice unbroken by ridges to a thickness of four feet.

An attempted repeat voyage in 1969—with the *Irving Birch* towing the *L. A. Learmonth* loaded with drilling supplies, and the new tanker barge, the *Johnny Norberg* loaded with diesel—proved to be a complete disaster. Both barges were lost and there was a resulting spill. The loss occurred in an ice flow only a few thousand yards from open water and just fifty nautical miles short of their destination at Rea Point. At this point while the vessels were in the ice, *Irving Birch* was pushing the *Learmonth* and towing the *Norberg*. (For the long voyage north, the barges were towed but in ice *Learmonth* was designed to be pushed as an ice breaker.)

They were following the CCGS *Labrador* (before 1958 HMCS *Labrador*) when the ice breaker suffered engine failure in a pressure ridge. In the crush of the flows, the tug had to detach from the barges. The *Learmonth* listed, her cargo shifted, and she sank immediately while the *Norberg* trailed behind, a punctured hull leaking her diesel cargo. Despite losing a large amount of fuel cargo, she remained afloat. The incident attracted considerable publicity as it was the year the mammoth Humble Oil tanker SS *Manhattan* was undertaking her pioneering voyage through the Northwest Passage as a test to demonstrate the feasibility of shipping Prudhoe Bay oil to the U.S. east coast.

Map 26-1

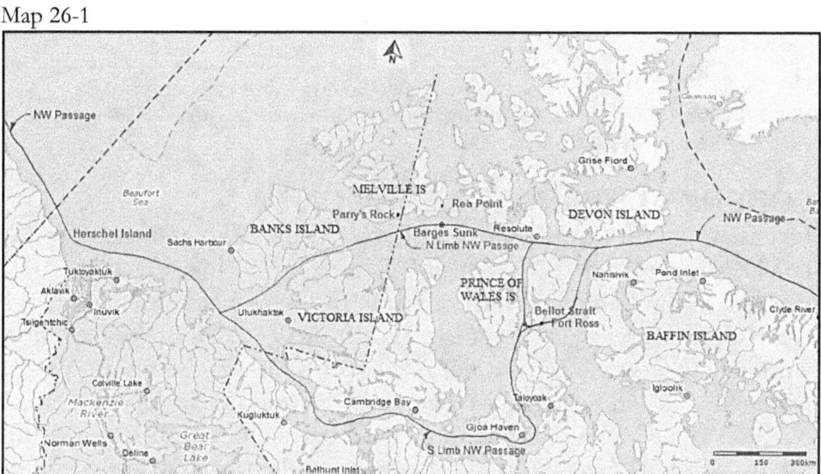

Location of the sunken barges; Atlas of Canada Toporama with mark-ups by author

The perceived hazard to navigation posed by the drifting hulk of the *Norberg* provided a convenient reason for the Canadian Government to dispatch Navy divers to "secure her to the bottom." (This sinkage presumably followed the removal of all remaining oil to prevent continued seepage and water contamination.) Lost on her maiden voyage in the year of construction, it is difficult to determine if the *Johnny Norberg* was ever registered in Canada.

While the service of the barges was brief, Panarctic Oils' naming of them to honour three former Hudson's Bay colleagues—Lorenz A. Learmonth, Scotty Gall and Johnny Norberg, and all intimately involved with the opening of the Arctic—was a commendable action.

It is a shame, therefore, after contributing such important service in the Arctic, that the vessels named for them ended so poorly.

Photo 26-4

Photograph taken at Cambridge Bay: L. A. Learmonth (with camera at centre), Mrs. Isobel Gall to the right in dark parka, and Scotty Gall at the extreme right. Vol 24 March 1945 issue of *The Beaver* (Canada's History www.canadashistory.ca, photo by Kaitok, an Inuit photographer)

LORENZ ALEXANDER LEARMONTH

Like many HBC apprentices, Lorenz Learmonth, and his brother David, were recruited in Scotland. Lorenz made his way to his first posting on the Labrador coast on the HBC supply ship *Pelican* in 1911. Apart from service in the First World War (1914-1919) his entire working career was spent in the Arctic fur trade for the Hudson's Bay Company. When he began service, the HBC did not have a post north of the Arctic Circle. He retired in 1957 when the construction of the DEW (Distant Early Warning) line was underway and the fur trade was ending. Dermot Campbell (Learmonth's nephew) described his uncle during a 2006 interview as:

> He was a quiet, self–reliant, dedicated individual. He loved the Arctic, and he was a man of his word. He told the company he would do something or if he told a friend or a relative, he would do something, it was done.

Lorenz Learmonth was tremendously talented and could handle sled dogs, survive long journeys through the wilderness, was fluent in Inuit dialects, and proficient in handling the business of the fur trade. He left a legacy of photographs and articles to various Canadian archives, many of which appeared in the HBC-sponsored history magazine, *The Beaver*. Learmonth was held in high regard by the crew of the *St. Roch* and referred to as "our friend" by her captain, Henry Larsen, a compliment bestowed of the highest order. Learmonth was intensely interested in Arctic history, the Inuit culture, anthropology, and archaeology. As a result of his residency on King William Island, and through his research, he became an important local expert on the lost Franklin expedition. He was elected as a Fellow of the Arctic Institute of North America when the honour was established in 1948.

Photo 26-5

Arctic fox pelts stored at HBC trading post at Fort Ross. A fashion craze for this fur precipitated development of trading posts adjacent to Inuit camps along the Northwest Passage.
Lorenz Learmonth fonds, Nunavut Archives, N-1987-088-0957

One of Learmonth's passions, after transferring from the eastern to the central Arctic, was the establishment of the final fur trading post at Fort Ross, located at the eastern end of Bellot Strait, thus linking fur trading posts and communities across the entire Arctic. The story of how he and his apprentice D. G. Sturrock made a remarkable whaleboat and canoe journey from King William Island up the western coast of the Boothia Peninsula—first by boat and then across its tip by land portaging their canoe and outboard motor for the final crossing of Bellot Strait—is told in greater detail in "Trading into the North West Passage" by Richard Finnie in the September 1937 edition of the *Beaver* magazine (referred to in Chapter 23). Despite the many hardships and dangers, he encountered—including suffering broken ribs from a fall off *Aklavik*'s rigging as he attempted to board the HBC-owned ship *Nascopie*—Learmonth stayed on for two years to manage the new post.

During a long retirement spent living in Georgetown, Ontario, Learmonth continued to pursue his love and interest of the Arctic. These are words he penned for his friend Richard Bonnycastle, former popular Hudson's Bay Company Arctic Manager and subsequent founder of Harlequin Books: "He was a clever man, a wise man, a reasonable man. He was a lovely man." It seems these words should apply to Learmonth as well. He died suddenly at Georgetown on 10 December 1985.

ERNEST JAMES "SCOTTY" GALL

Photo 26-6

Scotty Gall aboard the motor schooner *Aklavik*.
Jack Wood family fonds, Nunavut Archives, N-1986-041-0869

In addition to outstanding service to the HBC, Scotty Gall also served the north, firstly as an appointed official then later as an elected government representative of the Northwest Territories. He was particularly passionate in trying to provide job opportunities for northerners and to reduce living costs. As a mariner, his crowning achievement in 1937 was the first-ever navigation of Bellot Strait in the Northwest Passage as captain of the motor schooner *Aklavik*. This accomplishment was with well-known trader and trapper Patsy Klengenberg and his family, fellow HBC-employee John R. Ford, and Inuit pilot Tommy Norkow—one of many accolades in a long and full northern life.

When Scotty Gall arrived to work for the Hudson's Bay Company at Canada's mostly westerly outpost at Herschel Island in 1923, the HBC was struggling to dominate a new fur trade on the Arctic coast. The relatively new post, established in 1915, was the beachhead for trade and during Gall's working life he was to see the establishment of a string of fur trading posts and permanent settlements along the southern limb of the Northwest Passage. Canada relied—and continues to rely—on these settlements as proof of its sovereignty in the Arctic. Tuktoyaktuk (replacing Herschel Island in 1934), Kugluktuk (Coppermine), Cambridge Bay, Gjoa Haven, Taloyoak (Spence Bay, replacing Fort Ross), Arctic Bay, and Pond Inlet were all established by, or had strong connections to, the fur trade.

Scotty Gall led an adventurous life in the north and was a true pioneer for helping to establish the fur trade and improve conditions for those living there. As seen in the letter from Fur Trade Commissioner Ralph Parsons, Gall was highly thought-of and his work did not go completely unrecognized by his employer. He was awarded a cheque for an unknown amount and a "souvenir" consisting of the silver cigar box.

Hudson's Bay Company

INCORPORATED 2ND MAY 1670.

FUR TRADE COMMISSIONER'S OFFICE

ALL OFFICIAL CORRESPONDENCE TO BE ADDRESSED THE FUR TRADE COMMISSIONER HUDSON'S BAY COMPANY HUDSON'S BAY HOUSE WINNIPEG

WINNIPEG, MAN. June 26, 1938.

IN YOUR REPLY REFER TO NO.______

E.J. Gall, Esq.,
c/o Western Arctic District Office,
Hudson's Bay Company,
WINNIPEG.

Dear Mr. Gall:

I have had in mind for a considerable length of time sending you some recognition of our appreciation of the extraordinarily fine voyage with the "Aklavik" which you made last summer from King William Land to Fort Ross.

It is not often in the present day that such voyages are undertaken, and I think your effort deserves to rank with those of the great explorers.

Accordingly, I ask you to accept the enclosed cheque and the souvenir I am sending you, as an indication of the Company's pride in your accomplishment.

Yours sincerely,

Ralph Parsons
Fur Trade Commissioner.

The second letter of commendation received by Ernest James "Scotty" Gall from the Fur Trade Commissioner Ralph Parsons.
Jack Wood family fonds, Nunavut Archives, N-1988-041:2-5

JOHN NORBERG

John Norberg was a member of a remarkable and well-known northern family. His Swedish-born father Pete (whose exploits are described in previous chapters) was a true adventurer, while his Gwich'in mother Doris Kwatlatyi was an Arctic heroine. (The Gwich'in—People of the Caribou—are one of the most northerly indigenous peoples on the North American continent.) Pete and Doris were married in a triple marriage ceremony at Old Crow, Yukon in 1909. She met an untimely death in 1916; caught in a blizzard, she froze to death selflessly saving the nieces in her care by wrapping them in her clothing and protecting them with her body.

John's sister Agnes, who married American trader Fred L. ("Slim") Semmler (Chapter 17), is extremely well-recognized in the north. As previously mentioned, in 1967 she received the National Council of Jewish Women award as the "Woman of the Century in the North." She became the first woman Justice of the Peace and the first woman member of the government of the Northwest Territories.

Photo 26-7

Captain John Norberg on board the Hudson's Bay Company supply vessel *Nigalik* at Tuktoyaktuk.
NWT Archives, Terrace Hunt fonds, N-1979-062-0029

Motherless at an early age, John and Agnes spent much of their childhood in a residential school at Hay River. As teenagers, John and Agnes joined their father Pete on the Arctic coast in 1925 where he was engaged as a trapper and fur trader for the Hudson's Bay Company. Pete was one of the few Europeans who understood and communicated with the Inuit people of the central Arctic, who up to the early part of the twentieth century, had only limited contact with the outside world. Pete and his helper Henry Bjorn established the first trading post on King William Island in 1923.

John continued to work with his father until Pete disappeared on a winter journey from a camp near the headwaters of the Coppermine River to Fort Hearne in 1933. John, accompanied by RCMP Corporal Wall, searched extensively but Pete was never found. In 1936 John purchased the small trading motor schooner *Eagle* from William Storr, who became a partner with Arthur Watson and Slim Purchell in a venture to bring the rum runner *Audrey B.* to the Arctic to start a floating trading business (Chapter 25).

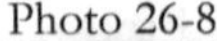
Photo 26-8

Captain John Norberg (left) with his schooner *Eagle* at Coppermine, 15 October 1943, HBCA/1987/E363/4.
Hudson Bay Archives, Archives of Manitoba, L. A. Learmonth fonds.

John married local Inuit Lena Kopiona in 1946 and they raised their family of five boys and four girls on Read (sometimes referred to as Reid) Island in the Coronation Gulf. In the navigation season John operated a freighting business with the *Eagle*. In 1956 he sold the vessel and moved the family to Tuktoyaktuk to take up employment with the Hudson's Bay Company.

It did not take the HBC long to recognize John's navigational abilities. These skills, like those of his father and Scotty Gall, had been learned largely from the school of hard knocks. He was quickly promoted and put in charge of the company's trading vessel *Nigalik*. Later he went to Vancouver to write (take) exams for both Mate and Master to qualify for assignment to larger company vessels such as the *Banksland, Nechilik* and *Fort Hearne*. For many years he served on these vessels across the central Arctic, delivering the vital goods and supplies needed to sustain communities that were initially reliant on the fur trade-established routes along the Northwest Passage.

John continued with the Hudson's Bay Company until 1956 when the Company sold its vessels and withdrew from the Arctic navigation freight business. He then worked for Northern Transportation Company Limited (NTCL) in various capacities, based at Tuktoyaktuk. After retirement from that company in 1978, John, like his sister, served the community as a Justice of the Peace. In 1968 he presented evidence to the Berger Commission on the Mackenzie Valley Pipeline Inquiry. A large part of his testimony brought attention to the hazards and risks posed by potential oil spills in Arctic waters. Unfortunately, a year later, the barge bearing his name was the cause of the first oil spill in the Arctic.

John Norberg passed away at Tuktoyaktuk in 1978. Many of his children and grandchildren continue to live in the north and contribute to its advancement. His son, Gordon, had a long and varied career as manager of marketing and traffic coordination for NTCL. His first granddaughter Edna Elias completed her term as fourth Commissioner of Nunavut in 2015.

One of the intriguing items in the Learmonth fonds (held at the Nunavut Archives) are two photographs of Parry's Rock. This isolated boulder on Melville Island was engraved by the crews of the Royal Navy ships HMS *Gripper* and *Helca* in 1813 denoting the remarkable penetration of these sailing ships from the east into the Northwest Passage decades before the Franklin expedition. It is not known if Learmonth took these photos or they were given to him, but as a keen student of Arctic history, he was certainly aware of their historical significance. This rock, serving as a classic highway marker of the Northwest Passage, also became a claim marker for Canadian sovereignty after being affixed with a plaque in 1909 by Captain Joseph-Elzéar Bernier. Bernier, a lesser-known legend of the Canadian Arctic, led many expeditions into the north on the Canadian Government steamship *Arctic* between 1904 and 1911.

Photo 26-9

Parry's Rock, an iconic road marker of the Northwest Passage, at Winter Harbour, Melville Island. Here, an unidentified traveler stops to have a look, as so many have done before.
Lorenz Learmonth fonds, Nunavut Archives, N-1987- 033-0404

Panarctic Oils, in recognition of Learmonth, Gall, and Norberg, remind us of those who served in the fur industry and contributed greatly to advance Canadian interests in Arctic regions. These men helped to establish the early trade that then led to the opening of other commercial ventures in the Arctic. It remains to be seen whether their pioneering efforts will continue to be built-on, to achieve significant economic benefits for the next generations, and whether or not increasingly accessible Arctic waters will mean more marine traffic, and as a result, an increase in challenges to Canadian sovereignty.

Appendix A: Vessels Designed or Built by George F. Askew

Year	Original and Subsequent Names	Reg. No.	Vessel Type	Notes
1908	*Ardrie, Snookey*		gaff-rigged sloop	Askew's yacht, built at Prince Rupert, raced at RVYC
1911	*Kit-ex-chen*		tunnel passenger boat	Built for "Wiggs" O'Neill at Cow Bay, Prince Rupert
1912	*Conveyor (II)*	130885	sternwheeler	Built for GTP Railway contractor, assembled at Tete Jaune Cache
1912	*Operator (II)*	130886	sternwheeler	Built for GTP Railway contractor, assembled at Tete Jaune Cache
1916	*D. A. Thomas*	138420	sternwheeler	Built for Peace River Development at Peace River
1916	*Lady Mackworth*	138621	tunnel boat, passenger boat/tug	Built for Peace River Development at Peace River
1919	*Canadusa*	150521	tunnel boat, passenger boat/tug	Built for Lamson and Hubbard, assembled at Fort McMurray
1920	*Distributor (III)*	150523	sternwheeler	Built for Lamson and Hubbard, assembled at Fort Smith
1921	*Weenusk*	138630	tunnel boat, passenger boat/tug	Built for HBC in Vancouver, launched at Peace River

1921	2 Launches and 2 Barges for Siberia		tunnel boat, passenger boat/tug	Built for HBC at Vancouver, transported on MV *Casco* to Kamchatka Peninsula
1921	*Fort Vermilion*	150524	75 ft. scow	Built for HBC, assembled at Peace River
1921	*Fort Chipewyan*	150525	75 ft. scow	Built for HBC, assembled at Fort Smith
1921	*Fort Resolution*	150526	75 ft. gasoline screw scow	Built for HBC, assembled at Fort Smith
1921	*Fort Wrigley*	150527	75 ft. tow barge	Built for HBC, assembled at Fort McMurray
1921	*Fort Norman*	150528	75 ft. scow	Built for HBC, assembled at Fort Smith
1922	*Athabasca River (II)*	150792	sternwheeler	Built for HBC, assembled at Fort McMurray
1923	*Liard River (II)*	150795	tunnel boat, passenger boat/tug	Built for HBC, assembled at Fort McMurray
1923	*Aklavik (IV)*	150796	Arctic trading schooner	Built for HBC, assembled at Fort McMurray
1923	*Fond du Lac*	150797	41 ft. gasoline screw boat	Built for HBC, assembled at Fort McMurray
1923	*Fort Nelson*	150798	81 ft. tow barge	Built for HBC, assembled at Fort McMurray
1924	*Doris*		32 ft. auxiliary sloop	Built in Vancouver for George Askew, RVYC
1925	*Gamine*		30 ft. sloop designed by Alden	Built for L. T. Alden, Vancouver, RVYC
1926	*Allan S. (I), New Westminster Wave, Chugaway II (I), Check Mate*	153381	25 ft. tug	Built for Nelson Spencer Ltd.
1926	*Stewart F.*	153385	25 ft. fishboat	Built for Norman B. Forbes
1927	*Barge 100*	152585	91 ft. barge	Built for HBC, assembled at Fort McMurray

1927	*Barge 300*	152866	132 ft., covered 300-ton freight/ passenger barge	Built for HBC, assembled at Fort McMurray
1927	*Argent*	153404	44 ft. seiner	Built for Brydon L. Tingley
1927	*Whitewings II (I), Westward Ho (I)*	154914	40 ft. yawl	Built in Vancouver for Walter Cline, RVYC
1928	*Leola V.*	154946	39 ft. power cruiser, designed by Thomas Halliday	Built in Vancouver for William Vivian, RVYC
1929	*Yukon Rose*	116630	61 ft. tunnel boat, passenger boat/tug	Built in Vancouver for Taylor Drury Stores Yukon, sailed to Skagway, shipped WP Railway to Whitehorse Railway
1929	*Cresset, Cresset II*	155106	40 ft. cutter	Built in Vancouver for Douglas P. and F. Wavell Urry, RVYC
1929	*Barge 201*	156562	105 ft. barge	Built for HBC, Vancouver
1930	*Buffalo Lake, Barge 87*	156567	91 ft. tunnel boat, passenger/freight boat	Built for HBC, assembled at Peace River
1930	*Nelmar (II)*	156621	40 ft. yawl	Built in Vancouver for Alex MacDonald, sister to *Hereanthere*, RVYC
1930	*Hereanthere*	156897	40 ft. yawl	Built in Vancouver for George Askew, sister to *Nelmar*, RVYC
1932	*Windor*		23 ft. Star-class racing sailboat	Built in Vancouver, tied for 3rd in Los Angeles Olympic Games
1930	*Akuvik, Herschel (I), Aklavik I* RCMP	RCMP 7501	Arctic motor schooner	Built for Inuit Customer by HBC, taken back, sold to RCMP
1934	*Sternwheeler, Silver Queen (III)*	170758	84 ft. motor sternwheeler, tug	Built for Northern Transportation Company, assembled at Fort McMurray

1934	N.T. *Barge Number 3*	170759	71 ft. barge	Built for Northern Transportation Company, assembled at Fort McMurray
1934	N.T. *Barge Number 4*	170760	71 ft. barge	Built for Northern Transportation Company, assembled at Waterways
1934	*Great Bear*	170938	91 ft. tunnel boat, passenger/freight boat/tug	Built for Northern Transportation Company, assembled at Fort Smith
1936			40 ft. tunnel boat/tug	Built for Lamb Lumber Company at Vancouver, for handling logs on Mohun Lake
1937	*Radium Barge Number 1*	170774	107 ft. barge	Built for Northern Transportation Company, assembled at Fort Smith
1937	*Radium Barge Number 2*	173373	122 ft. barge	Built for Northern Transportation Company, assembled at Fort McMurray
1937	*Radium Barge Number 3*	170775	89 ft. barge	Built for Northern Transportation Company, assembled at Fort McMurray
1937	*Radium Barge Number 4*	170776	89 ft. barge	Built for Northern Transportation Company, assembled at Fort McMurray
1937	*Radium Barge Number 5*	170777	74 ft. barge	Built for Northern Transportation Company, assembled at Fort McMurray
1937	*Radium Barge Number 6*	170778	74 ft. barge	Built for Northern Transportation Company, assembled at Fort Smith

1938	*Porphyry*	157180	62 ft. propeller motor tug	Built for Cominco, assembled at Fort McMurray
1938	C.M.S. *Barge 102*	171641	94 ft. barge	Built for Cominco, assembled at Fort McMurray
1938	*Barge 103*	173702	94 ft. barge	Built for Cominco, assembled at Fort McMurray
1938	*Barge 500*	No record found	160 ft. barge, emergency build, cost $35,330	Built by J. A. Davis of HBC, designed by G. F. Askew, built at Fort Smith
1939	*Leola Vivian (I)*	171806	56 ft. power cruiser	Built in Vancouver for Will Vivan
1941	One motor sternwheeler, 2 tunnel boats, and 12 scows (Vancouver Sun 5 March 1941)	No records found	Vessels for supplying Watson Lake airfield construction	Preassembled at Hudson Street Vancouver, assembled at Dease Lake
1942	*Alcan (I)*	195230	66 ft. motor sternwheel tug	Built for the US Army, assembled at Peace River
1942	*La Garde (I)*	174071	82 ft. tug, designed by Thomas Halliday	Built for Vantug with their crew, Askew and Sinclair supervised construction
1944	*George Askew*	175156	87 ft. motor sternwheeler	Built for Northern Transportation Company, assembled at Waterways and taken over Smith Portage

Notes:

1. In Canada only one vessel can be registered under a specific name at any time.
2. In vessel names, numbers without parenthesis are part of vessels names.
3. Numbers within parenthesis are not part of the vessels' names, they indicate the order of usage of the name based on the *Nauticapedia.ca* vessel data base.
4. Shipbuilding noted performed at Fort McMurray, was actually performed at a location nearby on the Clearwater River that became known as Waterways – for the purpose of this table the community names are synonymous.

Photo Appendix-A

Sloop *Ardrie*, later renamed *Snookey*, built in Prince Rupert 1908.
Askew family collection

Appendix B: Vancouver Loaded Fur Trade Cargos

Year	Ship	Length Feet	Home Port	Captain (1)	Farthest Cargo Discharge Point
1914	*Fort McPherson*	58	Vancouver	Bucholtz	Teller (2)
1914	*Ruby*	132	Seattle	Knaflick	Teller (3)
1915	*Fort McPherson*	58	Vancouver	Hendrickson	Herschel Island (2)
1915	*Ruby*	132	Seattle	Cottle	Herschel Island (3)
1917	*Herman*	131	S. Francisco	Pedersen	Herschel Island
1918	*Bender Brothers*	78	Seattle	Whitlam	Herschel Island
1919	*Bender Brothers*	78	Seattle	Whitlam	Herschel Island
1920	*Ruby*	132	Seattle	Whitlam	Baillie Island
1921	*Lady Kindersley*	187	Vancouver	Foellmer	Tree Island
1922	*Lady Kindersley*	187	Vancouver	Foellmer	Herschel Island
1923	*Lady Kindersley*	187	Vancouver	Foellmer	Tree Island
1924	*Lady Kindersley*	187	Vancouver	Foellmer	Ship & cargo lost
1925	*Baychimo*	230	London	Cornwell	Cambridge Bay
1926	*Baychimo*	230	London	Cornwell	Cambridge Bay
1926	*Baymaud*	107	Vancouver	Foellmer	Cambridge Bay
1927	*Baychimo*	230	London	Cornwell	Cambridge Bay
1927	*Baymaud*	107	Vancouver	Foellmer	Local use only (4)
1928	*Baychimo*	230	London	Cornwell	Flag Staff Island
1929	*Baychimo*	230	London	Cornwell	Cambridge Bay

1929	*Old Maid No. 2*	110	Vancouver	Gillen	Not known
1930	*Baychimo*	230	London	Cornwell	Cambridge Bay
1930	*Old Maid No. 2*	110	Vancouver	Coe	Not known
1931	*Baychimo*	230	London	Cornwell	Coppermine
1932	*Karise*	149	Copenhagen	Murray	Coppermine
1933	*Anyox*	193	Vancouver	Johnston	Vancouver (5)

American ship captains; others are Canadian or British

(1) Captain's full names: Otto Bucholtz, F. L. Coe, Sydney A. Cornwell, Stephen F. Cottle, Gustav ("Gus") Foellmer, W. H. Gillen, Heinrich ("Swogger") Hendrickson, B. D. Johnston, Louis Knaflick, John Murray, Christian Theodore Pedersen, S. T. L. Whitlam.
(2) Ship hauled out and wintered in Teller in 1914 before proceeding to Herschel Island in 1915.
(3) Cargo unloaded in Teller in 1914. Reloaded when *Ruby* returned from the south and completed the voyage in 1915.
(4) Ship wintered in the Arctic 1926, used locally in 1927 and tied up permanently in Cambridge Bay 1927.
(5) Ship damaged near Point Barrow and had to return to Vancouver with cargo.

Appendix C: Arctic Fur Trading Posts Established Before 1934

Map Appendix C

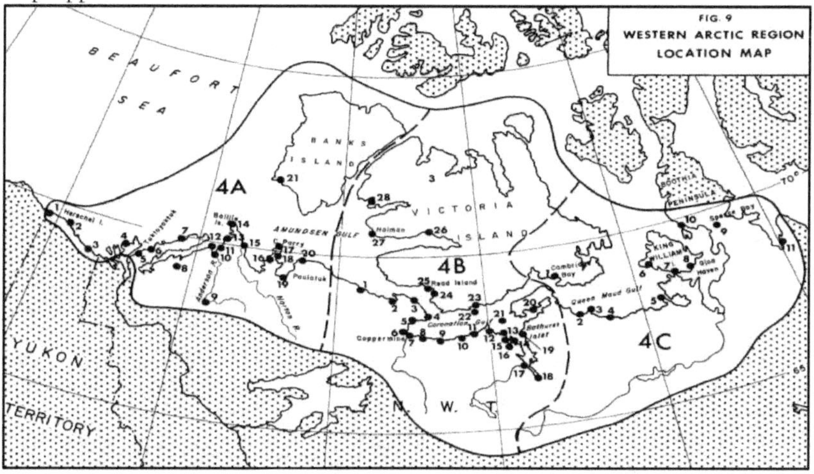

Arctic region
Source: *Fur Trade Posts of the NW Territories 1870-1970* by Peter J. Usher

Code	Post	Dates	Code	Post	Dates
4A1	Demarcation Point	1921-1924	4B11	Agiak, Gray's Bay	1917-1918
4A2	Herschel Island	1915-1938	4B14	Bathurst Inlet	1927-1930
4A3	Shingle Point	1920-1928	4B17	Burnside River	1930-1964
3B1	Aklavik	1912-settlement	4B18	Western River	1925-1927
4A5	Kittigazuit	1912-1934	4B20	Kent Peninsula	1920-1927
4A14	Baillie Island	1916-1939	4B22	Richardson Island	1933-1938
4A15	Horton River	1929-1931	4B24	Fort Harmon	1926-1928
4A18	Letty Harbour	1927-1936	4B25	Read Island	1931-1962
4A20	Pearce Point	1927-1934	4B26	Fort Brabant	1923-1928
4B1	Inman River	1926-1932	4B27	Fort Collinson	1928-1939
4B3	Bernard Harbour	1916-1932	4C1	Cambridge Bay	1923-settlement
4B4	Fort Hearne	1926-1929	4C2	Ellice River	1926-1927
4B7	Coppermine	1928-settlement	4C4	Perry River	1926-1927
4B9	Kugaryuak	1927-1930	4C7	Simpson Strait	1923-1927
4B10	Tree River	1918-1929	4C8	Gjoa Haven	1927-settlement

Source: *Fur Trade Posts of the NW Territories 1870-1970* by Peter J. Usher

Appendix D: 1928-1930 Voyage of the *Fort James*, and Conquest of the Northwest Passage, including Cecil Bradbury's Heroic Contribution

The best single account of the voyage of the *Fort James* is contained in a small out-of-print book by Cecil E. Bradbury: *Ten Years in the High Canadian Arctic – Being a personal account of his early life, more particularly his voyages as an employee of the Hudson's Bay Company between 1920 and 1930*, originally published in 1994 in Newfoundland. (Additional research, to supplement this invaluable document, includes a four-page letter written by Bradbury to Captain John A. Strand, Master of C.C.G.S. *Camsell* on 25 January 1967, and a copy of Wireless Operator Henry Lyall Ross Smyth's extensive diary, obtained from Archives Canada).

As set out in *Ten Years in the High Canadian Arctic*, the voyage had four objectives:

- To investigate the commercial possibilities of a water route between the eastern and western Arctic
- To survey a route to supply the Hudson's Bay Company western Arctic posts
- To study the hunting and trading potential in the vicinity of Cockburn Bay
- To rendezvous with the *Fort McPherson* (although this was achieved at Gjoa Haven in the summer of 1930, there seems to be clear expectation on the part of the crew that this was to be done at Cambridge Bay in the summer of 1929)

The motor vessel *Fort James* was a two-masted "banker" auxiliary schooner. Auxiliary schooner denotes that this type of fishing schooner, typically used on the Grand Banks of Newfoundland, was powered by both sail and engine. Her description as set-out in Bradbury's letter is as follows:

> The M.V. *Fort James* was built in Nova Scotia for Réveillon Freres in the early 20's. She was knock-about or banker design and was acquired by the Hudson's Bay Company in 1926. 100 feet overall, 96 tons, draft 12 feet, powered with 120 H.P. Fairbanks-Morse

diesel; full timbered, with 2 ½" oak planking, 2" greenhard sheathing, 3" B.C. Fir sealing and fitted with 12' ice beams

Departing St. John's Newfoundland on 28 July 1928, her 10-man crew, per HBC records, was comprised of the following individuals. (Full names have replaced initials, if they are known.)

Crew of Auxiliary Schooner *Fort James*

Name	Position
A. W. "Fred" Bush	Captain
Harvey Williams	Mate
A. Driscol	Chief Engineer
I. McConnell	Second Engineer
E. Morris	Steward & Cook
W. Stark	Seaman
E. Bonia	Seaman
A. Shane	Seaman
Cecil E. Bradbury	Trader
Henry Lyall Ross Smyth	W.O. (Wireless Operator)

In addition, Inuit families were also taken aboard: Mukie and Ungantcheak with their families at Pond Inlet, and Atagoottarluk and his wife at Leopold.

The partner in the epic meet-up of vessels was the motor schooner *Fort McPherson,* having sailed from Vancouver to Herschel Island in 1914, but was delayed in entering her final Arctic domain because of adverse ice conditions and had to winter in Teller, Alaska, until the summer of 1915. This humble hard-working vessel carried all conceivable manner of freight and passengers in the western Arctic including on voyages to Gjoa Haven beginning in 1925. She served exclusively in the Arctic until her loss in October 1930. In 2019, to recognize those many years of essential service, *Fort McPherson* received the Vancouver Maritime Museum Northwest Passage Hall of Fame award in the vessel category.

Photo Appendix D-1

Pat Weber and daughter Robin Weber accepting award from Duncan MacLeod, Curator Vancouver Maritime Museum, September 2019. Pat is daughter of well-respected HBC Arctic Post Manager Ray Ross and Robin is Archival/Library Technician at NWT Archives, Yellowknife, NWT.
Courtesy of Vancouver Maritime Museum

The crew and passenger of the *Fort McPherson*, as recorded in her log and other sources, in the eventual meeting of the vessels in 1930 is set out in the following table.

Crew of Motor Schooner *Fort McPherson*

Name	Position
David O. Morris	Captain
Mat Shand	Engineer
Corporal Alan Belcher, RCMP	Passenger

The *Fort James* reached Gjoa Haven on 14 September 1929, despite the difficulties encountered, using a damaged rudder during their transit from their winter quarters at Oscar Bay. Duplicating Amundsen's achievement (accomplished in a much smaller five-foot draft vessel) with a much larger ship and a 12-foot draft, was no mean feat.

Captain Bush, in command of the *Fort James*, reached Gjoa Haven but was not prepared to go further. His action meant the crew missed their opportunity to follow the schooner *Fort McPherson* back along the path to Cambridge Bay, which had left just seven hours before *Fort James'* arrival—a path that apparently remained open for several days. As a consequence, the crew and the HBC staff of the King William Island Post suffered through a winter of considerable discomfort at Gjoa Haven. Cecil Bradbury carried to his grave the disappointment of not reaching Cambridge Bay.

Photo Appendix D-2

Cecil Bradbury.
Cecily Hinton collection

The *Fort McPherson*, in the absence of seeing the *Fort James* at Gjoa Haven, and lacking radio communications for contact, took the winter stores for the *Fort James* back to Cambridge Bay, certain that the *Fort James* would head there also. Smaller amounts of supplies comprising part of the "trading outfit" left for the HBC post ran low after a few months, and Cecil Bradbury, with the assistance of a 13-year-old Inuit boy Arnetcheak (identified in wireless operator Henry Lyall Ross Smyth's diary), undertook a heroic dog sled journey to bring vital supplies from Cambridge Bay back to the crew—and the post—at Gjoa Haven, a return journey of around 500 miles.

They left on 18 January 1930, in the midst of cold and darkness, and in an area where compasses were not of much use for navigation because of proximity to the North Magnetic Pole, and arrived at Cambridge Bay on 12 February. After waiting for an ill-conceived air lift relief mission that never materialized, they started back with supplies on 10 March. At Perry River (see map) they were joined by HBC King William trader Jack Livingstone who assisted them with the strenuous task of hauling the supplies on to Gjoa Haven. They arrived back on 8 April 1930 with 2,500 lbs. of supplies. Between April and June, more supplies arrived, averting starvation, with Cecil Bradbury having taken the lead role, and with the assistance of his stalwart companions, brought the welcome first relief.

His daughter Cecily Hinton is right "to be in awe and admiration" of her father's selfless act:

> … when the supply ship didn't come and food ran low. Dad decided to go on dog team to get supplies but…the dogs all died on the way, and Dad had to pull the sled himself. The story ended well with supplies and no one was lost. He loved the north and nature, and had great respect and admiration for the Inuit and their culture and knowledge, as well as their sense of community.

Most of the crew, including Bradbury, had desired to achieve their Northwest Passage by pushing through to Cambridge Bay, even if it meant spending another winter in the Arctic. It was not in the cards, however, but it can be said that it was a successful undertaking as no lives were lost despite spending a perilous winter in an unforgiving environment. However, the additional winter in the Arctic had at least one benefit: As the *Fort McPherson* pulled alongside the *Fort James* on 6 August 1930, the final objective "To rendezvous with the *Fort McPherson*" was completed.

Measuring success after so many years is a tricky thing; the best we can do is to remember those involved and to celebrate their significant accomplishments. Cecil Bradbury is certainly deserving of remembrance for his life-saving actions at Gjoa Haven in addition to being part of the overall significant Arctic achievement of the passage of *Fort James* to Gjoa Haven and her often overlooked epic return to St. John's. That journey was the first transit west to east of any vessel along the Northwest Passage.

Map Appendix D

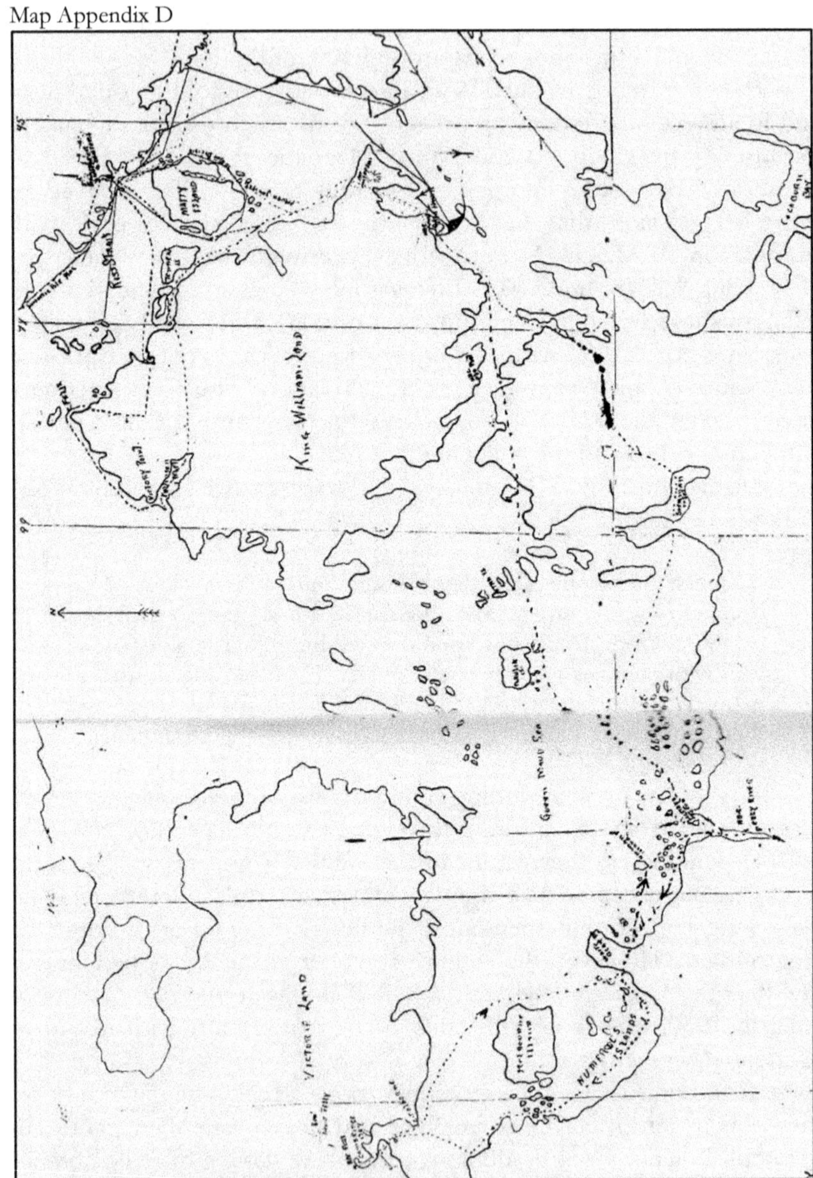

Cecil Bradbury's hand-drawn map of his travels,
from his book *Ten Years in the High Canadian Arctic.*
Courtesy of his daughter Cecily Hinton

Bibliography

Books

Amundsen, Roald. *The North West Passage Being the Record of a Voyage of Exploration of the Ship "Gjoa" with a Supplement by First Lieutenant Hansen Vice-Commander of the Expedition Vol. I & II.* New York: E.P. Dutton and Company, 1908.

Baird, Donal. *The Robbie Touch, Exploits of an Uncommon Sailor.* Canada: Baird Books, 1999.

Berton, Pierre. *Klondike, The Last Great Gold Rush, 1896-1897.* Toronto: McClelland and Stewart, 1958.

Berton, Pierre. *Prisoners of the North.* Canada: Doubleday, 2004.

Berton, Pierre. *The Arctic Grail, The Quest for the Northwest Passage and the North Pole 1818-1909.* Toronto: McClelland and Stewart, 1988.

Bradbury, Cecil E. *Ten Years in the High Canadian Arctic.* St. John's, Newfoundland: Creative Books, 1994.

Burwash, Major L.T. *Canada's Western Arctic Reports on Investigations in 1925-26, 1928-29, and 1930.* Ottawa: Department of the Interior Northwest Territories and Yukon Branch, 1931.

Cavell, Janice and Jeff Noakes. *Acts of Occupation, Canada and Arctic Sovereignty, 1918-1925.* Vancouver: UBC Press, 2010.

Coen, Ross. *Breaking Ice for Arctic Oil.* Fairbanks: University of Alaska Press, 2012.

Coffee, Phillip Michael. *El Sueño de Oro, The Dream of Gold.* Victoria: Trafford Publishing, 2007.

Copland, Dudley. *Coplalook: Chief Trader, Hudson's Bay Company, 1923-1939.* Winnipeg: J. Gordon Shillingford, 1998.

Dalton, Anthony. *"Baychimo": Arctic Ghost Ship.* Victoria: Heritage House, 2010.

—*The Fur Trade Fleet, Shipwrecks of the Hudson's Bay Company:* Victoria: Heritage House, 2011.

Department of Transport, Canada. *List of Vessels on the Registry Books of the Dominion of Canada*, Ottawa: Edward Cloutier, 1940.

De Poncins, Gontran. *Kabloona.* Garden City: Reyal & Company, 1941.

—*The Ghost Voyage out of Eskimo Land.* Garden City: Doubleday & Company, Inc., 1954.

Finnie, Richard. *Lure of the North.* Philadelphia: David McKay Company, 1940.

—*Canada Moves North*. Montana: Kessinger Legacy Reprints Publishing, 2009.

Fricker, Reginald Harold. *The Ramblings of a Matelot.* Ottawa: Royal Naval Telegraphists (1918) Association, 1971.

Gilbert, Walter E. (as told to Kathleen Shackelton). *Arctic Pilot.* United Kingdom: Thomas Nelson & Sons Ltd. 1941.

Godsell, Philip H. *Arctic Trader.* Toronto: The Macmillan Company, 1943.

—*They Got Their Man; on Patrol with the Northwest Mounted Police.* Toronto: The Ryerson Press, 1940.

—*Romance of the Alaska Highway*. Toronto: The Ryerson Press, 1944.

Gray, Doug. *R.M.S. "Nascopie" Ship of the North.* Ottawa: The Golden Dog Press, 1997.

Greene, Ruth. *Personality Ships of British Columbia.* Vancouver: Marine Tapestry, 1969.

Guay, David R. P. *Passenger and Merchant Ships of the Grand Trunk Pacific and Canadian Northern Railway*. Toronto: Dundurn, 2016.

Hacking, Norman. *Prince Ships of Northern BC: Ships of the Grand Trunk Pacific and Canadian National Railways.* Surrey: Heritage House Publishing Company Ltd., 1995.

Harvey, R.G. *Carving the Western Path By River, Rail, and Road Through Central and Northern B.C.* Surrey: Heritage House Publishing Company Ltd, 1999.

Hoare, Catherine A. *Adventures Unlimited.* NWT Archives: Unpublished manuscript, 1964.

Hudson, William E. *Icy Hell.* London: Constable & Company Ltd, 1937.

Hudson's Bay Company. *A Brief History*. London: Hudson's Bay House, E.C.2, 1934.

Jenness, Stuart E. *The Making of an Explorer: George Hubert Wilkins and the Canadian Arctic Expedition 1913-1916*. Montreal: McGill-Queen's University Press, 2004.

Klengenberg, Christian. *Klengenberg of the Arctic: An Autobiography*. London: Jonathan Cape, 1932.

Larsen, Henry P. *The Big Ship, an Autobiography (in Cooperation with Frank R. Sheer and Edvard Omholt-Jensen)*. Canada: McClelland & Stewart Ltd, 1967.

Lyall, Ernie. *Arctic Man*. Edmonton: Hurtig, 1979.

MacDonald, Bruce R. "*North Star of Herschel Island*". Manitoba: Friesen Press, 2012.

McClintock, Captain F.L. (with foreword by Shelagh D. Grant). *The Voyage of the "Fox" in the Arctic Seas, in Search of Franklin and his Companions*. Victoria: TouchWood, revised edition 2012.

Mills, Fraser. *Slow Boat on Rum Row.* Madeira Park: Harbour Publishing, 1992.

Mowatt, Farley. *Ordeal by Ice*. Toronto: McClelland and Stewart, 1989.

Newman, Peter C. *Merchant Princes.* Toronto: Penguin Books, 1992.

Nuligak. *I, Nuligak The Autobiography of a Canadian Eskimo.* New York: Simon & Schuster, 1971.

O'Neill, Wiggs. *Steamboat Days on the Skeena River British Columbia.* Kitimat: Northern Sentinel Press Limited, 1960.

Peake, Frank A. *The Bishop Who Ate His Boots.* Whitehorse: Yukon Church Heritage Society, second printing 2002.

Rasmussen, Knud. *Across Arctic America, Narrative of the Fifth Thule Expedition.* Fairbanks: University of Alaska Press, 1999.

Robertson, Heather. *A Gentleman Adventurer: The Arctic Diaries of Richard Bonnycastle.* Toronto: Lester & Orpen Dennys, 1984.

Robinson, Geoff and Dorothy. *It Came by the Boat Load.* Summerside: Self-published, 1984.

Sissons, Jack. *Judge of the Far North, The Memoirs of Jack Sissons.* Toronto: McClelland & Stewart, 1968.

Smyth, Henry Lyall Ross. *Diary concerning the Hudson's Bay Fort James Expedition to survey the Northwest Passage.* Library and Archives Canada, Reference MG30-B132 unpublished manuscript, 1928-1930.

—*Correspondence, essay and reports.* Library and Archives Canada, Reference MG30-B132 unpublished manuscript, 1928-1930 and 1973.

Stefansson, Vilhjalmur. *My Life with the Eskimo.* New York: The MacMillan Company, 1924.

—*The Friendly Arctic: The Story of Five Years in Polar Regions.* New York: The Macmillan Company, 1922.

Terpening, Rex. *Bent Props and Blow Pots, A Pioneer Remembers Northern Bush Flying.* Madeira Park: Harbour Publishing, 2015.

Tornfell, Evert E. and Michael Burwell. *Shipwrecks of the Alaska Shelf and Shore (1966).* Anchorage: US Department of the Interior, 1992.

Turner, Robert D. *The Klondike Gold Rush Steamers – A History of Yukon River Steam Navigation.* Winlaw: Sono Nis Press, 2015.

Usher, Peter J. *Fur Trade Posts of the North West Territories.* Ottawa: Information Canada, March 1971.

Van Wyck, Peter C. *The Highway of the Atom.* Montreal: McGill-Queen's University Press, 2010.

White, Patrick. *Mountie in Mukluks, the Arctic Adventures of Bill White.* Madeira Park: Harbour Publishing, 2004.
Windsor, Henry Haven (edited by). *The Wreck of the "Great Bear".* USA: Popular Mechanics Vol. 26, December 1916.

Archival Sources Consulted

Department of Marine and Fisheries, Canada. *Agreement of Articles and Accounts of Crews Re: "Audrey B."* Victoria: BC Archives.
Gall, Ernest J. *Personal diary written by Scotty Gall to Mr. V. W. West, District Accountant, HBC to account for his trip to Fairbanks and return.* Herschel Island: Unpublished material, February 1925.
HBC. *Master's Log of "Fort McPherson".* 30 June 1914 – 6 Oct. 1916. Archives of Manitoba, HBC Archives, Location Code RG3/27B/1
HBC. *Log of "Ruby"* and *Herschel Island Journal.* 13 July 1914-20 December 1917. Archives of Manitoba, HBC Archives, Location Code RG3/27B/2
HBC. Godsell, P.H. *Report on Western Arctic Division – Inspected July 6th – December 29th 1923.* Location Code H2-97-6-1 (A.102/1041)
HBC. *Master's Log of "Fort McPherson".* 9 July 1930-10 October 1930. Archives of Manitoba, HBC Archives, Location Code RG3/27C/16
HBC. *Tree River post journals.* 1926 -1928. Archives of Manitoba, HBC Archives, Location Codes: B.489/a/1and B.489/a/2.
HBC. *Kugaryuak and Tree River post journals.* 1928 -1929. Archives of Manitoba, HBC Archives, Location Codes: B.429/a/1.
HBC. *King William Island post journals.* 1928 – 1931. Archives of Manitoba, HBC Archives, Location Codes: B.427/a/3, B.427/a/4 and B.427/a/5.
Sessional Papers No. 28 of Dominion of Canada. *Reports of Royal Northwest Mounted Police 1913 – 1919* and *Royal Canadian Mounted Police 1920 - 1924.* Ottawa: 1914 – 1925.
Yukon Archives. *Employee Records for BYN Employee George F Askew.* Whitehorse: 1917.

Magazines / Journals

Arctic Journal
Harbour & Shipping
Macleans
Moccasin Telegraph
Pacific Motor Boat
Popular Mechanics
The Beaver

Newspapers

Alaska Daily Empire
Calgary Herald
Edmonton Journal
Greenville News (Greenville South Carolina)
Milwaukee Journal
Montreal Gazette
New York Times
Nome Nugget
Oakland Tribune
Prince Rupert Daily News
Regina Leader Post
San Francisco Call
San Francisco Examiner
Santa Ana Register
The Vancouver Daily Province
Vancouver Sun
Vancouver World
Victoria Daily Colonist
Victoria Times
Whitehorse Daily Star
Windsor Star
Winnipeg Free Press

Online Resources

Alaska Shipwrecks. *A Comprehensive Accounting of Alaka Shipwrecks and Loses of Life in Alaskan Waters.* USA (https://alaskashipwreck.com)

Arestad, Sverre. *Questing for Gold and Furs in Alaska.* Norwegian-American Studies 21 (1962): 54–94 (http://www.jstor.org)

Cameron, Iain. Blog Scotty Gall 1903-1996. (http://iain-cameron.blogspot.com/)

Colton, Tim. "Shipbuilding History" *Construction records of U.S. and Canadian shipbuilders and boatbuilders.* (http://www.shipbuildinghistory.com)

Department of Commerce Bureau of Navigation. *Annual List of Merchant Vessels of the United States with Official Numbers and Signal Letters and Lists of Vessels Belonging to the United States Government with distinguished listed signals.* USA, 1865 – 1979. (http://www.ibiblio.org)

Gray, David R. *Northern People, Northern Knowledge The Story of the Canadian Arctic Expedition 1913-1918.* Canadian Museum of History: Virtual Museum.ca (https://www.historymuseum.ca)

Johansson, Sven and John M. MacFarlane. *Captain Christian Theodore Pedersen and the Western Arctic Fur Trade* (www.nauticapedia.ca)

Kitikmeot Heritage Society. *Angulalik Inuinnaq Fur Trader.* (https://www.kitikmeotheritage.ca)

MacFarlane, John M. The Nauticapedia Project Searchable Vessels Database. (www.nauticapedia.ca)

Reidel, Doreen. *In Memory of Constable Ian MacDonald.* (www.rcmpveteransvancouver.com)

Royal Vancouver Yacht Club. *Annuals of the Royal Vancouver Yacht Club Part 1 (1903-1970).* (https://www.royalvan.com)

University of Calgary. *Daily journal/diary of Mrs. Frances Gladys O'Kelly, 1921*. Courtesy of Libraries and Cultural Digital Collections. (https://digitalcollections.ucalgary.ca)

University of Calgary. *Photograph album of Mrs. Frances Gladys O'Kelly, 1921*. Courtesy of Libraries and Cultural Resources Digital Collections. (https://digitalcollections.ucalgary.ca)

Index

About the Author

George Duddy is a retired Professional Engineer having worked 40+ years on hydro electric construction and construction planning with BC Hydro, and also as a consultant. George was born in Fort St. John where his father managed the Hudson's Bay Company store (his father joined the HBC as a fur trade apprentices in 1923). The family then moved to Vancouver Island in 1944. George's interest in maritime subjects was developed in his boyhood and youth while observing log transportation, naval exercises and incoming ships calling at the William Head Quarantine Station at Parry Bay near Esquimalt BC. Later he moved to White Rock (where he currently resides) and was active for many years with the Lower Mainland Yacht Co-op, serving as Commodore from 1989-1990. He actively enjoys historical research including corresponding with people around the world. His passion for the untold story, and his interest in the HBC fur trade and Arctic dealings, have led him to writing this, his first book.

www.ingramcontent.com/pod-product-compliance
Lightning Source LLC
LaVergne TN
LVHW020533100826
845148LV00010B/1441
9780788424007